Java™ Programming For Dummies®

COMPUTER
BOOK SERIES
FROM IDG

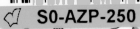

Cheat Sheet

Using Java Statements

To Use This Statement	Follow This Example (the elements that you must supply are shown in italics)
if	if (*expression*) {*contingent statements*}
if...else	if (*expression*) {*contingent statements*} else {*contingent statements*}

switch	switch (*expression*) {
	    case *val1*: *statements*; break;
	    case *val2*: *statements*; break;
	    ...
	    default: *statements*; break}

for	for (*initialization*; *expression*; *increment*) {*loop statements*}
while	while (*expression*) {*loop statements*}

Using Java GUI components

If You Want to Make	Follow This Example
button	Button *okButton* = new Button ("*OK*");
checkbox	Checkbox *espresso* = new Checkbox ("*Espresso*"); Checkbox *cappuccino* = new Checkbox ("*Cappuccino*"); add (*espresso*); add (*cappuccino*);
checkbox group (radio buttons)	CheckboxGroup *Coffee* = new CheckboxGroup() Checkbox *esp* = new Checkbox ("*Espresso*", *Coffee*, *true*); Checkbox *cap* = new Checkbox ("*Cappuccino*", *Coffee*, *false*); add (*esp*); add (*cap*);
choice (drop down list)	Choice *drinks* = new Choice(); *drinks*.addItem ("*Espresso*"); *drinks*.addItem ("*Cappuccino*");
list	List *coffee* = new List(); *coffee*.addItem ("*Espresso*"); *coffee*.addItem ("*Cappuccino*");
text field	TextField *textField* = new TextField("*TextField*"); add(*textField*);
text area (multi-line)	TextArea *textArea* = new TextArea(*5,10*); add(*textArea*);
label	Label *coffeeLabel* = new Label ("*Coffee, anyone?*");

. . .For Dummies: #1 Computer Book Series for Beginners

COMPUTER BOOK SERIES FROM IDG

Java™ Programming For Dummies®

Cheat Sheet

Responding to Java Events

To Handle This Event	Use handleEvent or This Special Purpose Method	Expect This Event
User moved mouse to object area	`public boolean mouseEnter`	`MOUSE_ENTER`
User moved mouse out of object area	`public boolean mouseExit`	`MOUSE_EXIT`
User pressed mouse button	`public boolean mouseDown`	`MOUSE_DOWN`
User released mouse button	`public boolean mouseUp`	`MOUSE_UP`
User moved mouse	`public boolean mouseMove`	`MOUSE_MOVE`
User dragged mouse	`public boolean mouseDrag`	`MOUSE_DRAG`
User pressed ASCII key	`public boolean keyDown`	`KEY_PRESS`
User released ASCII key	`public boolean keyUp`	`KEY_RELEASE`
User pressed function key	`public boolean keyDown`	`KEY_ACTION`
User released function key	`public boolean keyUp`	`KEY_ACTION_RELEASE`
User pressed Return key	`public boolean action`	`ACTION_EVENT`
User selected item		`LIST_SELECT`
User deselected item		`LIST_DESELECT`
User clicked button	`public boolean action`	`ACTION_EVENT`
User clicked checkbox	`public boolean action`	`ACTION_EVENT`
User selected item	`public boolean action`	`ACTION_EVENT`
User double-clicked item	`public boolean action`	`ACTION_EVENT`
Object got focus		`GOT_FOCUS`
Object lost focus		`LOST_FOCUS`

Using Java Classes

If You Want to Make	Follow This Example
package declaration	`package` *MyPackage*
class declaration	`public class` *MyClass* `extends` *MyParentClass* { *variable declarations constructors methods*}
constructor	*MyClass* (*type parameter1, type parameter2, and so on*) { *setup statements* ; }
method	`public` *returntype MyMethod* { *statements* ; }

IDG BOOKS WORLDWIDE

For more information
about IDG Books,
call 1-800-762-2974.

. . .For Dummies: #1 Computer Book Series for Beginners

JAVA™
PROGRAMMING
FOR
DUMMIES®

JAVA™ PROGRAMMING FOR DUMMIES®

by Donald J. Koosis and
David S. Koosis

Foreword by Kim Polese
Java Development Team

IDG BOOKS WORLDWIDE™

IDG Books Worldwide, Inc.
An International Data Group Company

Foster City, CA ♦ Chicago, IL ♦ Indianapolis, IN ♦ Braintree, MA ♦ Southlake, TX

Java™ Programming For Dummies®

Published by
IDG Books Worldwide, Inc.
An International Data Group Company
919 E. Hillsdale Blvd.
Suite 400
Foster City, CA 94404

Library of Congress Catalog Card No.: 96-76244

ISBN: 1-56884-995-8

Printed in the United States of America

10 9 8 7 6 5 4 3 2 1

1O/RX/QW/ZW/IN

Distributed in the United States by IDG Books Worldwide, Inc.

Distributed by Macmillan Canada for Canada; by Contemporanea de Ediciones for Venezuela; by Distribuidora Cuspide for Argentina; by CITEC for Brazil; by Ediciones ZETA S.C.R. Ltda. for Peru; by Editorial Limusa SA for Mexico; by Transworld Publishers Limited in the United Kingdom and Europe; by Academic Bookshop for Egypt; by Levant Distributors S.A.R.L. for Lebanon; by Al Jassim for Saudi Arabia; by Simron Pty. Ltd. for South Africa; by Pustak Mahal for India; by The Computer Bookshop for India; by Toppan Company Ltd. for Japan; by Addison Wesley Publishing Company for Korea; by Longman Singapore Publishers Ltd. for Singapore, Malaysia, Thailand, and Indonesia; by Unalis Corporation for Taiwan; by WS Computer Publishing Company, Inc. for the Philippines; by WoodsLane Pty. Ltd. for Australia; by WoodsLane Enterprises Ltd. for New Zealand. Authorized Sales Agent: Anthony Rudkin Associates for the Middle East and North Africa.

For information on where to purchase IDG Books Worldwide's books outside the U.S., contact IDG Books Worldwide's International Sales department at 415-655-3078 or fax 415-655-3281.

For information on foreign language translations, contact IDG Books Worldwide's Foreign & Subsidiary Rights department at 415-655-3018 or fax 415-655-3281.

For sales inquiries and special prices for bulk quantities, contact IDG Books Worldwide's Sales department at 415-655-3200 or write to the address above.

For information on using IDG Books Worldwide's books in the classroom, or for ordering examination copies, contact IDG Books Worldwide's Educational Sales department at 800-434-2086 or fax 817-251-8174.

For authorization to photocopy items for corporate, personal, or educational use, please contact Copyright Clearance Center, 222 Rosewood Drive, Danvers, MA 01923, or fax 508-750-4470.

About the Authors

Donald J. Koosis

Donald Koosis has developed materials to help people understand computers for more than 20 years. He has worked for IBM, Bell Labs, Xerox, and now owns his own company, Instructional Systems Co., Inc. He is the author of best-selling self-instructional books on Statistics and Electricity/Electronics. He can be reached at **donald@iscinc.com.**

David S. Koosis

David Koosis is a native citizen of cyberspace. He writes programs to help computers understand people, working in Java, Delphi, C++, and other unspeakable tongues. David has developed software for a variety of Fortune 500 companies and Wall St. firms. He co-developed the 1994 edition of PC Magazine's computer benchmarks and has contributed to several successful commercial software programs. He is head of software development for ISC Consultants, Inc., and can be reached at **dkoosis@iscinc.com.**

Welcome to the world of IDG Books Worldwide.

IDG Books Worldwide, Inc., is a subsidiary of International Data Group, the world's largest publisher of computer-related information and the leading global provider of information services on information technology. IDG was founded more than 25 years ago and now employs more than 7,700 people worldwide. IDG publishes more than 250 computer publications in 67 countries (see listing below). More than 70 million people read one or more IDG publications each month.

Launched in 1990, IDG Books Worldwide is today the #1 publisher of best-selling computer books in the United States. We are proud to have received 8 awards from the Computer Press Association in recognition of editorial excellence and three from Computer Currents' First Annual Readers' Choice Awards, and our best-selling ...*For Dummies*® series has more than 19 million copies in print with translations in 28 languages. IDG Books Worldwide, through a joint venture with IDG's Hi-Tech Beijing, became the first U.S. publisher to publish a computer book in the People's Republic of China. In record time, IDG Books Worldwide has become the first choice for millions of readers around the world who want to learn how to better manage their businesses.

Our mission is simple: Every one of our books is designed to bring extra value and skill-building instructions to the reader. Our books are written by experts who understand and care about our readers. The knowledge base of our editorial staff comes from years of experience in publishing, education, and journalism — experience which we use to produce books for the '90s. In short, we care about books, so we attract the best people. We devote special attention to details such as audience, interior design, use of icons, and illustrations. And because we use an efficient process of authoring, editing, and desktop publishing our books electronically, we can spend more time ensuring superior content and spend less time on the technicalities of making books.

You can count on our commitment to deliver high-quality books at competitive prices on topics you want to read about. At IDG Books Worldwide, we continue in the IDG tradition of delivering quality for more than 25 years. You'll find no better book on a subject than one from IDG Books Worldwide.

John Kilcullen
President and CEO
IDG Books Worldwide, Inc.

IDG Books Worldwide, Inc., is a subsidiary of International Data Group, the world's largest publisher of computer-related information and the leading global provider of information services on information technology. International Data Group publishes over 250 computer publications in 67 countries. Seventy million people read one or more International Data Group publications each month. International Data Group's publications include: **ARGENTINA:** Computerworld Argentina, GamePro, Infoworld, PC World Argentina; **AUSTRALIA:** Australian Macworld, Client/Server Journal, Computer Living, Computerworld, Digital News, Network World, PC World, Publishing Essentials, Reseller; **AUSTRIA:** Computerwelt, PC TEST; **BELARUS:** PC World Belarus; **BELGIUM:** Data News; **BRAZIL:** Annuário de Informática, Computerworld Brazil, Connections, Super Game Power, Macworld, PC World Brazil, Publish Brazil, SUPERGAME; **BULGARIA:** Computerworld Bulgaria, Networkworld/Bulgaria, PC & MacWorld Bulgaria; **CANADA:** CIO Canada, ComputerWorld Canada, InfoCanada, Network World Canada, Reseller World; **CHILE:** Computerworld Chile, GamePro, PC World Chile; **COLUMBIA:** Computerworld Colombia, GamePro, PC World Colombia; **COSTA RICA:** PC World Costa Rica/Nicaragua; **THE CZECH AND SLOVAK REPUBLICS:** Computerworld Czechoslovakia, Elektronika Czechoslovakia, PC World Czechoslovakia; **DENMARK:** Communications World, Computerworld Danmark, Macworld Danmark, PC World Danmark, PC World Danmark Supplements, TECH World; **DOMINICAN REPUBLIC:** PC World Republica Dominicana; **ECUADOR:** PC World Ecuador, GamePro; **EGYPT:** Computerworld Middle East, PC World Middle East; **EL SALVADOR:** PC World Centro America; **FINLAND:** MikroPC, Tietoverkko, Tietoviikko; **FRANCE:** Distributique, Golden, Info PC, Le Guide du Monde Informatique, Le Monde Informatique, Reseaux & Telecoms; **GERMANY:** Computer Business, Computerwoche, Computerwoche Extra, Computerwoche Focus, Electronic Entertainment, GamePro, I/M Information Management, Macwelt, PC Welt; **GREECE:** GamePro, Macworld & Publish; **GUATEMALA:** PC World Centro America; **HONDURAS:** PC World Centro America; **HONG KONG:** Computerworld Hong Kong, PCWorld Hong Kong, Publish in Asia; **HUNGARY:** ABCD CD-ROM, Computerworld Szamitastechnika, PC & Mac World Hungary, PC-X Magazine; **INDIA:** Computerworld India, PC World India, Publish in Asia; **INDONESIA:** InfoKomputer PC World, Komputek Computerworld, Publish in Asia; **IRELAND:** ComputerScope, PC Live!; **ISRAEL:** PC World 32 BIT, People & Computers; **ITALY:** Computerworld Italia, Computerworld Italia Special Editions, Lotus Italia, Macworld Italia, Networking Italia, PC Shopping, PC World Italia, PC World/Walt Disney; **JAPAN:** Macworld Japan, Nikkei Personal Computing, SunWorld Japan, Windows World Japan; **KENYA:** East African Computer News; **KOREA:** Hi-Tech Information/Computerworld, Macworld Korea, PC World Korea; **MACEDONIA:** PC World Macedonia; **MALAYSIA:** Computerworld Malaysia, PC World Malaysia, Publish in Asia; **MEXICO:** Computerworld Mexico, GamePro, Macworld, PC World Mexico; **MYANMAR:** PC World Myanmar; **NETHERLANDS:** Computable, Computer! Totaal, LAN Magazine, Macworld, Net Magazine; **NEW ZEALAND:** Computer Buyer, Computerworld New Zealand, MTB, Network World, PC World New Zealand; **NICARAGUA:** PC World Costa Rica/Nicaragua; **NIGERIA:** PC World Africa; **NORWAY:** Computerworld Norge, Computerworld Privat, CW Rapport Klient/Tjener, CW Rapport Nettverk & Telecom, CW Rapport Offentlig Sektor, IDG's KURSGUIDE, Macworld Norge, Multimedia World, PC World Ekspress, PC World Nettverk, PC World Norge, PC World's Produktguide, Windows World; **PAKISTAN:** Computerworld Pakistan, PC World Pakistan; **PANAMA:** GamePro, PC World Panama; **PARAGUAY:** PC World Paraguay; **P. R. OF CHINA:** China Computerworld, China Infoworld, Computer & Communication, Electronic Product World, Electronics Today, Game Camp, PC World China, Popular Computer Week, Software World, Telecom Product World; **PERU:** Computerworld Peru, GamePro, PC World Profesional Peru, PC World Peru; **POLAND:** Computerworld Poland, Computerworld Special Report, Macworld, Networld, PC World Komputer; **PHILIPPINES:** Computerworld Philippines, PC Digest, Publish in Asia; **PORTUGAL:** Cerebro/PC World, Correio Informático/Computerworld, Mac•In/PC•In Portugal; **PUERTO RICO:** PC World Puerto Rico; **ROMANIA:** Computerworld Romania, PC World Romania, Telecom Romania; **RUSSIA:** Computerworld Rossiya, Network World Russia, PC World Russia; **SINGAPORE:** Computerworld Singapore, PC World Singapore, Publish in Asia; **SLOVENIA:** MONITOR; **SOUTH AFRICA:** Computing S.A., Network World S.A., Software World; **SPAIN:** Computerworld España, COMUNICACIONES WORLD, Dealer World, Macworld España, PC World España; **SWEDEN:** CAP&Design, Computer Sweden, Corporate Computing, MacWorld, Maxi Data, MikroDatorn, Natverk & Kommunikation, PC/Aktiv, PC World, Windows World; **SWITZERLAND:** Computerworld Schweiz, Macworld Schweiz, PCtip; **TAIWAN:** Computerworld Taiwan, Macworld Taiwan, PC World Taiwan, Publish Taiwan, Windows World; **THAILAND:** Thai Computerworld, Publish in Asia; **TURKEY:** Computerworld Monitör, MACWORLD Turkiye, PC WORLD Turkiye; **UKRAINE:** Computerworld Kiev, Computers & Software Magazine, PC World Ukraine; **UNITED KINGDOM:** Acorn User, Amiga Action, Amiga Computing, Amiga, Appletalk, CD Powerplay, CD-ROM Now, Computing, Connexion, GamePro, Lotus Magazine, Macaction, Macworld, Open Computing, Parents and Computers, PC Home, PC Works, The WEB; **UNITED STATES:** Cable in the Classroom, CD Review, CIO Magazine, Computerworld, Computerworld Client/Server Journal, Digital Video Magazine, DOS World, Electronic, InfoWorld, I-Way, Macworld, Maximize, MULTIMEDIA WORLD, Network World, PC World, PUBLISH, SWATPro Magazine, Video Event, WebMaster; **URUGUAY:** PC World Uruguay; **VENEZUELA:** Computerworld Venezuela, GamePro, PC World Venezuela; and **VIETNAM:** PC World Vietnam.

10/17/95b

Dedication

To four generations of beautiful, bright, strong women:

Pauline

Irene

Rachel

Sarah

Authors' Acknowledgments

Our thanks to Kathy Cox, Leah Cameron, and Susan Christophersen for their intelligent and sensitive editorial guidance and assistance. They have been graceful partners under the pressures of a demanding schedule. And, similarly, thanks to our technical reviewer, Jack Stefani, for keeping us honest with attentive but constructive feedback.

Thanks to Diane Steele, Mary Bednarek, and Gareth Hancock for recognizing the need for a book like this one and allowing us to be its authors.

Besides being a pleasure to work with, our colleague Anatoly Goroshnik contributed three of the applets in Part III — Sprites, JavaBots, and Fractals. Rachel Vigier provided valuable assistance in obtaining permissions for the applets that appear on the CD that comes with this book. Generous programmers from all over the world — members of the Java Internet community — consented to share their work on the CD which comes with this book. We thank them and encourage you to follow their example.

Thanks also to Raymond Mungiu for reviewing the manuscript and to Aron Koosis for reminding us not to take ourselves too seriously.

Publisher's Acknowledgments

We're proud of this book; please send us your comments about it by using the Reader Response Card at the back of the book or by e-mailing us at feedback/dummies@idgbooks.com. Some of the people who helped bring this book to market include the following:

Acquisitions, Development, & Editorial

Project Editor: Kathleen M. Cox

Assistant Acquisitions Editor: Gareth Hancock

Product Development Manager: Mary Bednarek

Permissions Editor: Joyce Pepple

Copy Editors: Leah P. Cameron,
Susan M. Christophersen,
Tamara S. Castleman

Technical Reviewer: Jack Stefani

Disc Reviewers: Jim McCarter, Kevin Spencer

Editorial Managers: Mary C. Corder,
Kristin A. Cocks

Editorial Assistant: Chris H. Collins

Production

Associate Project Coordinator: Regina Snyder

Layout and Graphics: Brett Black,
J. Tyler Connor, Dominique DeFelice,
Maridee V. Ennis, Julie Jordan Forey,
Jane Martin, Anna Rohrer,
Tricia Reynolds, Angela F. Hunckler,
Brent Savage

Proofreaders: Betty Kish, Nancy L. Reinhardt,
Christine Meloy Beck, Michael Bolinger,
Nancy Price, Dwight Ramsey,
Robert Springer, Carrie Voorhis, Karen York

Indexer: Ty Koontz

General & Administrative

IDG Books Worldwide, Inc.: John Kilcullen, President & CEO; Steven Berkowitz,
COO & Publisher

Dummies, Inc.: Milissa Koloski, Executive Vice President & Publisher

Dummies Technology Press & Dummies Editorial: Diane Graves Steele, Associate Publisher;
Judith A. Taylor, Brand Manager; Myra Immell, Editorial Director

Dummies Trade Press: Kathleen A. Welton, Vice President & Publisher; Stacy S. Collins,
Brand Manager

IDG Books Production for Dummies Press: Beth Jenkins, Production Director; Cindy L. Phipps,
Supervisor of Project Coordination; Kathie S. Schnorr, Supervisor of Page Layout; Shelley Lea,
Supervisor of Graphics and Design

Dummies Packaging & Book Design: Erin McDermit, Packaging Coordinator; Kavish+Kavish,
Cover Design

◆

The publisher would like to give special thanks to Patrick J. McGovern,
without whom this book would not have been possible.

◆

Contents at a Glance

Cartoons at a Glance

By Rich Tennant • Fax: 508-546-7747 • E-mail: the5wave@tiac.net

page 283

page 315

page 167

page 7

page 293

page 67

Table of Contents

Foreword

● ●

*W*elcome to *Java Programming For Dummies!*

I'm glad you've picked up this book because it is a great introduction to Java. And if you read this book, you're no dummy — you're smart because you've chosen to become knowledgeable about one of the most important technological breakthroughs in the history of the computer industry.

Why so much fuss over a programming language? Well, Java is indeed a great programming language. It's powerful, simple, and elegantly designed. It has all the modern features you'd want in a programming language. It makes a splendid replacement for languages like C++. But it's much more than that. Java is the platform on which our new, networked world will soon run. Java will be everywhere — not only on your desktop computer, but in phones, building control systems, and yes, even toasters.

I first encountered Java three years ago. At that time, it was code-named *Oak* and was a still-secret engineering project at Sun Microsystems, Inc. I still remember vividly the feeling when I discovered what this small team of programmers had developed. I was amazed. I immediately felt a step closer to the future, and a world of new possibilities came into focus. I this new world, you'd never have to go to the store to buy software or ever install software again — because the programs would come to you from across the network and magically run, whenever you need them.

You could phone home on your cellular phone to turn on the heat in your house. An airplane mechanic could repair a plane by accessing terabytes of documentation at his fingertips on a PDA. Imagine running a sophisticated word processor that doesn't take up eight megabytes on your hard disk, but instead automatically loads features, such as a thesaurus, as needed from across the network. And wouldn't it be nice to buy a computer based on how powerful or easy it is to use — rather than the kind of programs it will run? Sounds like the stuff of science fiction. But these are all scenarios that Java makes possible — today.

Enthused, I joined the team as product manager and made it my mission to get this amazing technology out to the world, into the hands of developers who would create this exciting future. I changed the name to *Java* to reflect the dynamic nature of the language — and my conviction that Java was going to wake up the computer industry. And with the team, I set out to make Java ubiquitous. We created implementations of Java on the PC, the Macintosh, and Sun workstations.

We decided to give Java away for free, so that everyone could use it. We even gave the Java specification away — the cookbook that enables other people and companies to create their own implementations of Java without needing a license from Sun. This is what the word *open* really means. No one company can control Java and make it proprietary. Everyone is encouraged to participate and innovate. All interested parties can take Java and make a version of it that runs on their favorite computer.

When Mosaic came along, the team realized that this was the perfect way to introduce Java to the world. With Java, Web browsers come alive. Java applets run on any computer; they come to you from across the Web, install securely, run automatically, and then disappear when you no longer need them. You never have to think about what kind of operating system (or which version) your computer is running. Java empowers programmers and users by uniting the underlying systems, eliminating complexity, and making computers work for people, rather than the opposite.

To demonstrate the possibilities, we built the world's first interactive browser, HotJava, and released it with Java to the world in March 1995. Java caught on like wildfire, and today, a little over a year later, Java has become the programming language of choice for the Internet. Dozens of companies have adopted Java as a standard, thousands of developers are creating Java applications, leading universities are teaching Java in introductory programming courses, and a host of new Java-based devices will soon hit the market.

According to conventional wisdom, the best technologies often don't succeed, typically because of market factors that are unrelated to how good the technology is. The VHS-Beta war is a classic example of this scenario. When better technologies fail in the marketplace, companies sometimes win, but consumers always lose. Java is a shining contradiction to this scenario. Java is great technology — it deserves to succeed. And with Java, everyone wins. Java unites people and computers and moves us forward.

The philosophy behind Java is not about ownership or control, it's about freedom, creativity, and making people more important than computers. I know, this is lofty stuff. But it's all real. I'm tremendously excited about the future that Java enables, and I hope I've been able to convey my enthusiasm in these few words. I encourage you to read this book, start writing your own Java programs, and take a step toward into the future.

Kim Polese
June 1996

Introduction

* *

*W*elcome to *Java Programming For Dummies*! This book is the quickest way to start making your own Java applets to add to your World Wide Web pages or your corporate intranet. Java applets, short programs that add interactivity and computing power, can be distributed over the Internet or your intranet as part of a Web page and can run on any type of computer.

Other books about Java assume that you have a black belt in computer science and a burning desire to know the details of synchronizing threads, throwing exceptions, and other Java beasties.

This book assumes you want to make applets.

Who Are You?

Because you're holding this book in your hands, we want to make a few more assumptions about you:

- ✔ You have access to a computer that can run Java. (Most common types of personal computers and workstations that connect to the Internet qualify. See Appendix A if you're not sure.)
- ✔ You have surfed the World Wide Web.
- ✔ You know a bit of HTML and may have your own Web page.
- ✔ You've heard all the ruckus about Java and want to see what it's about.
- ✔ You may have written some macros or even programs in Visual Basic, C++, or Pascal.
- ✔ You do not invent your own computer languages as a form of relaxation.

About This Book

This book is intended to quickly get you writing your own Java applets. We don't intend for this book to turn you into an object-oriented programming guru, but we do want to give you the confidence to try your hand at putting interesting, fun, and useful Java applets on your Web pages.

We give you a firm foundation in the basic tools of a Java programmer without trying to explain every nook and cranny of the language. Sample topics you find in this book include the following:

Object-Oriented Programming: The Basic Elements

Inside the Programmer's Mind

The Java Interpreter

Writing the Code for Your Applet

Rules of Punctuation and Grammar for Class and Method Definitions

How This Book Is Organized

Part I: Hello, Java

This part is an overview of Java, the Internet, and the whole kettle of fish. We explain the significance of Java and its place in cyberspace as succinctly as we can. We talk about the unique features of Java, applications of Java on the World Wide Web, and the importance of having a Java-enabled Web browser (that's how you look at the wonderful applets you create).

Next, we introduce you to a simple Java applet and the thought processes (the dreaded mind of a programmer) that bring it about. Of course, we must include a chapter on HTML, HyperText Markup Language, so that you know how to include your Java applets on your Web pages. Finally, we give you an introduction to the terms and concepts relating to the components of object-oriented programming (and, you know, Java is an object-oriented programming language).

Part II: Javanese

In Part II, we talk about Java language basics. We start with *yet another* "Hello, World" program (with a New York twist) and explain how to embed applets in your Web pages. You discover the object of *objects* and *object-oriented programming*. You try out using some Java building blocks like *if, for,* and *while*. And you master *classes*.

Part III: Caffeinated Pages

This part is our cook book of Java applet examples:

- **Calendar:** A calendar class for selecting dates
- **Ticker Tape:** A scrolling ticker tape
- **Sprite:** A simple sprite class for making stuff fly around the screen
- **JavaBots:** An animated game written in Java
- **Quizem:** An interactive quiz engine
- **Shopping Cart:** A simple database applet which uses CGI (that is, Common Gateway Interface)
- **Fractal:** Where mathematics meets art

Along the way, we show you a bit about animation, databases, and other useful programming tools.

Part IV: Only Java

Part IV gives you the word about the other kind of Java programs, the ones that don't run in a Web browser: Java applications. And this part's solitary chapter looks at the current and future status of Java as a programming language.

Part V: The Part of Tens

This part, familiar to . . .*For Dummies* readers, provides a home for several of the goodies we couldn't bear to give up telling you about, but had trouble finding a home for. We include *Ten Common Mistakes,* and *Ten Facts about the Other Java.* (Yes, the island!)

Appendixes: Setting Up Java

The Appendixes contain the nuts and bolts of setting up Java to run on your system. First we tell you all the systems that run Java today and where to locate the most current software and documentation. Then we walk you through the process of installing, setting up your Java workspace, and testing the Java Developer's Kit on your specific system.

If you can't (or don't want to) use the Java Developer's Kit from the CD, we also tell you how to download the version that's appropriate for you from the Internet.

About the CD

The CD at the back of this book includes all the software you need to start writing Java applets, as well as some extra goodies:

- ✔ The Java Developer's Kit from Sun Microsystems Inc., for Windows 95, Windows NT, Macintosh System 7.5, and Solaris.
- ✔ Some nifty applets from the international online Java community including graphics effects, text effects, games, and more!
- ✔ The applets from Part III of this book.

See Appendix E for more about the CD.

Icons Used in This Book

When you see this icon, you know that the paragraph contains some technical details that may not be essential to your understanding or using Java, but they're interesting to know! (And if you read all the text next to these icons, you may find yourself developing a liking for pocket protectors.)

With this icon, we flag useful information, shortcuts, or any other hints we can think of to help you in your Java programming adventure.

Remember the text that's associated with this icon — the information may come in handy some day.

This icon is self-explanatory: Beware!

We use this icon to draw your attention to extra-special Java features or unique elements.

Use the text next to these icons to pattern your thinking; now all that unreadable code suddenly makes sense!

This icon marks the terms that all good little programmers know.

What Now?

Now it's up to you. Read this book and meet us in cyberspace! You'll find us at the *Java Programming For Dummies* Resource page `http://www.iscinc.com`.

Part I
Hello, Java

The 5th Wave — By Rich Tennant

"We're looking for applications that work well on a particularly open and distributed network."

In this part . . .

Because we believe in looking before we leap, we want to give you the vision to do the same. That's why Part I includes an introduction to the surroundings and characteristics of the Java programming language. We identify Java's place as a revolutionary addition of rapid animation and interactivity to the World Wide Web. Then we show you how to create your first simple Java applet to incorporate into your Web pages.

Web pages are designed using a language called *HyperText Markup Language* (HTML). We tell you the elements of HTML that you need to understand to include Java applets in your Web pages. We conclude Part I with an introduction to the basic elements of object-oriented programming (Java is an object-oriented programming language) where you discover the classes, objects, methods, and other structures used to create programs in Java.

And then you're ready to leap!

Chapter 1

Java and the World Wide Web

. . . .

In This Chapter

▶ Understanding the Internet and the World Wide Web

▶ Understanding intranets

▶ Writing portable programs

▶ Letting graphics create themselves

▶ Keeping the user's system safe

▶ Making intelligent Web pages

▶ Appreciating open systems

. . . .

*1*n the beginning, the Internet was quite literally for rocket scientists. The Net began as a system of interconnected computers used by government and academic researchers. By adhering to some standard ways of transferring data between varied computer systems, these researchers were able to trade raw data and to share computing resources.

When connected systems follow mutually-agreed standards, the users know how to share data and computing resources among the systems. Consider the following scenario as an example of the sharing made possible by Internet standards.

> A scientist at Upstate University connects through his university computing center to a statistical analysis program that is installed on a computer at the NASA data center. After analyzing his data, the scientist sends the results to the computer account of a colleague at Downstate University.

> The Downstate colleague, in turn, can access the raw data at the Upstate computing center and perform her own analysis with a program that she developed on the Downstate computer. Or she can use the NASA program.

Because they're connected through the Internet, the three computers (at Upstate, NASA, and Downstate) work together. The Internet now connects most of the large public computing facilities in the world.

The Internet: A Reality and an Idea

The Internet is both a physical reality and an idea.

The physical reality is that most large public computing centers in the world, such as university and government computing centers, are linked by a cross-connected web of data communications lines (see Figure 1-1). Although each center may be directly connected only to a few other centers, the interconnections enable any center to connect *indirectly* with any other center.

Figure 1-1:
The physical reality — most large computing centers in the world are connected.

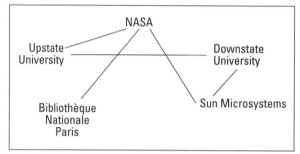

The idea is that after a number of computers are connected, passing information from any one computer to any other computer is easy, provided that users can agree on a single standard way to communicate. In the Internet community, as illustrated in Figure 1-2, all the participants have agreed to accept and forward messages by using mutually-agreed technical specifications and ways of addressing the messages. Believe it or not, Internet technical standards are set by a non-governmental committee of volunteers!

Figure 1-2:
The idea — users can pass information from any place to any other place.

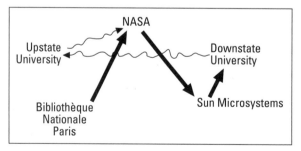

At first, if you wanted an Internet address, you had to claim some sort of connection with the government and the academic research community. But the attractions of the Internet were irresistible. College students discovered that being able to send e-mail to friends on other campuses was very convenient. Professors discovered that they could publish a research proposal or a simple request for information to the Internet community and receive valuable help from unexpected sources. As people moved on to different places and other jobs, they found ways to maintain their Internet accounts.

Eventually, the Internet was opened to the public. Now, millions of individuals in the general public have Internet accounts. The communications links of the Internet have extended and merged with telephone communications so that connecting any personal computer to the Internet is a simple matter.

The World Wide Web: Narrowing the Search

In the beginning, navigating the Internet was hard. You needed to memorize and type obscure commands and long, complicated addresses. Locating the person or information you were looking for was a matter of skill, persistence, and luck.

But bright, lazy people are always looking for an easier way to do things. As a result, they developed many tools and ideas to make communicating over the Internet easier. One of the most exciting developments is the idea called the World Wide Web (WWW).

The World Wide Web was invented by a research group at the European Center for Nuclear Research (CERN). The group set out to automate the process of following cross-references between documents posted on the Internet.

They noticed that often a technical paper posted to the Internet at one location would refer to another paper or data posted elsewhere. To follow the cross-reference required locating a new Internet address and then completing a series of steps to access the data. The CERN researchers proposed a standard way to include, within a document, the necessary Internet addresses for its cross-references.

This method for including cross-references is called *HyperText Markup Language* (HTML), and the universe of interconnected documents on Internet computers throughout the world is called the *World Wide Web*. Programs called *Web browsers* enable users to display HTML documents on the screen of a personal computer and to move between interconnected documents almost as easily as turning the pages of a book. Figure 1-3 shows an example of a Web document viewed with a Web browser.

Like the Internet, the World Wide Web was too good to leave to the academics. Computer users in general discovered the WWW and turned it into a broad communications medium.

Figure 1-3:
Web
browsers
make it
simple to
find
anything on
the World
Wide Web.

Intranets: Internal Corporate Web Sites

The computer network of a large corporation is often similar to the Internet in many ways:

- ✔ A network can contain many different types of computers in different locations.

- ✔ A network provides a web of data connections between computers.

- ✔ Network users need to share data and computing resources.

Many technologies compete to meet the networking needs of large organizations. But an increasing number of corporate networks are making use of the technology of the Internet and the World Wide Web.

Corporations are using Internet technologies to provide for communications between computers in different locations, dedicated to different primary uses. In the same way that a scientist can access NASA's data on the orbit of a planet, a branch manager in Singapore can study the results of an advertising campaign in Costa Rica. A salesperson with a laptop computer can check corporate data on inventories and prices.

Just like their academic sisters and brothers, corporate employees now forward internal memos with Internet e-mail tools and publish documentation in HTML to be read with a Web browser. When Internet technology is applied within a private organization's network, we refer to the resulting network as an *intranet*.

Java: The Magical Flying Program

At last we come to *Java*. Java does for programs what HTML and the World Wide Web do for documents. Java allows the creation of applets — small programs that attach to Web pages and move from computer to computer across the Internet. And these applets operate without concern for the logistics of installing software, without concern for security, and without concern for the type of computer hardware in use.

May I borrow that program?

To understand the role of Java, you must think for a moment about what happens when you want to borrow a program that someone else has written to run on your computer. If you are a serious personal computer user, you have probably shared an experience like this:

- ✔ Your friend makes a copy of the program on a diskette (or perhaps you use a modem to connect to her computer and download the program).

- ✔ If you are fortunate, your friend has the same type of computer you do. Otherwise, the program won't run on your computer.

- ✔ You scan the diskette for viruses to make sure that the code on the diskette won't do something nasty to your computer.

- ✔ You copy the program to your hard drive.

- ✔ You key in additional information needed to set up your system properly — a directory path, changes to operating system settings, and so on.

- ✔ If your friend completes a new, improved version the next day, you start the same process all over again.

Now that both you and your friend are programming in Java, you can bypass these problems when you want to borrow a program. Consider the following alternative experience:

- ✔ A program written in Java, as a Java *applet,* can be posted on a WWW page. If you want to use the Java applet your friend has written, you need only connect to her WWW page. The program automatically transfers itself to your computer over the Internet connection.

✔ A program written in Java runs on any type of computer that has a Java-enabled Web browser. The fact that your friend has a UNIX workstation and you have a PC doesn't matter.

✔ You don't need to copy the program or make setup adjustments to your computer — the program is designed to run on your computer with no installation or adjustments.

✔ You don't need to scan for a virus; the Java language locks the borrowed program out of all the areas of your computer where a virus might do harm.

✔ If your friend develops a new, improved version of the program, you automatically receive the update when you next connect to her WWW page.

Java effortlessly delivers the program over the Internet. Whether the program resides in your machine or your friend's machine makes no difference to you as a user.

Remember, it's portable

As you probably know, you can find programs specifically for Windows 95 and Windows NT, for Macintosh, for Solaris, for UNIX, and more. When a program is written in Java, however, you need only one version of the program — the Java version. The exact same program runs on all these operating systems and hardware platforms.

When you write programs in Java, you do not need to concern yourself about porting to different systems.

No more naptime

Creating a high-quality picture on the computer screen takes a lot of data. That is why you may notice that your Web browser becomes very sluggish when displaying Web pages with detailed graphics. The browser is waiting for the data to come in over the phone line. And you're waiting with it . . . waiting and waiting . . . snooze time!

If you want to display graphs of stock market data that are updated as prices change, you need something faster. And Java programs can be real eye-openers (see Figure 1-4). With Java, you don't have to transfer all the graphic data in the picture. Instead, you can send just the changing stock prices. A Java program can then use the power of the user's computer to draw a fresh copy of the graph.

Similarly, an applet can download a CAD file—a special file used by Computer Aided Design programs—which describes the Empire State Building,

Figure 1-4:
Naptime's
over.

for example. From that relatively small CAD file, the applet can generate infinite views of the building from different angles and varying degrees of magnification.

When it can be applied, this technique of using the computer to generate images (instead of using the phone line to transmit images) eliminates waiting time.

This *blueprint* approach can also save time when you transfer other kinds of data across the WWW. If you want to publish a table of computed data — for example, a table of squares and square roots — you could put the numbers into an HTML document, or you could put the formula for computing those numbers into a Java program. The Java program requires much less data communication time than the HTML document.

May this computer be safe from . . .

You have surely heard about viruses and hackers — that is, the programs and people that intentionally interfere with the normal operation of your computer. Whenever you connect one computer to another, you must be concerned about the possibility of an intruder.

The Java programming language is designed to work in a world of interconnected computers; therefore, the designers of Java built strong security features into the language. The following list outlines some of these features:

- **Run-time examination:** When your computer runs a Java program, the entire program is examined line by line to make sure that it contains only valid Java instructions that are prohibited from interfering with other programs or with the basic setup of your computer.

- **Restricted interactivity:** The Java language has built-in restrictions on establishing connections to other computers. Unless the user gives specific permission, a Java applet can only connect to the Internet location the applet came from.

> ✔ **Restricted access rights:** The Java language has built-in restrictions on the ability of the program to read and write data. The program can access only the parts of your computer where it has received advance permission to be.

Web page intelligence

The WWW is an easy and elegant way to provide access to information — technical references, product information, and marketing data. Java provides a way to add computer support in interacting with the data. A Java applet on a page of product information can allow anyone who browses the page to calculate the cost of any given combination of products or options. A Java applet can enable an employee to calculate his pension benefits. A Java applet can administer a quiz on the contents of a technical reference.

Java: An Open System

Many of the technical standards for computing hardware and software are *proprietary* — they are owned and well-protected by the companies who developed them. Individual companies have invested in perfecting a particular way of accomplishing a desired result. Understandably, they prefer not to share all the details with their competitors. So they use patents, copyrights, and secrecy to maintain a competitive advantage. These may be called *closed* systems.

On the other hand, some information must be shared if systems developed by different teams are to work together.

Technical specifications for the Internet and the World Wide Web are developed and maintained by committees representing many interested parties. The specifications are published to the world at large. Any hardware or software product that matches the published specifications works with the Internet and WWW. Such an arrangement is referred to as an *open system*.

With open systems, the published specifications establish a shared definition of how components of hardware and software from different sources must work together. You can assemble different components from different sources with the expectation that the combined system will work.

The Java language is an open system specification. Sun Microsystems, which developed the Java language, has published detailed specifications for Java. All products that adhere to the published specifications can work together. And in fact, a number of companies have developed Java software tools already.

As you read on, you, too, can join the community of Java developers.

Chapter 2

Writing a Simple Program: Yet Another HelloWorld

● ●

In This Chapter

▶ Reading the code of a simple Java applet

▶ Reading the mind of a simple Java programmer

▶ Tracing the steps from Java source code to the on-screen display

▶ Reading the mind of the computer

● ●

*W*riting a program that prints `Hello, World` on the screen is the traditional way to start using every programming language. Why should we be different? As you may discover, laziness is also an honored tradition in programming. And so we, too, begin with yet another "Hello, World" program.

If you already know a programming language such as Basic, Pascal, or C, then you've probably encountered the "Hello, World" tradition. If not, your initiation to the strange customs of programmers begins here.

Please give heed to these esteemed words to program by:

> "We will encourage you to develop the three great virtues of a programmer: laziness, impatience, and hubris."
> – Larry Wall, *Programming Perl,* Published by O'Reilly, 1991.

Some News about Java Programs

Before we plunge into the "Hello, World" program, we have some news for you.

When you write a Java applet, you manipulate words, numbers, and pictures that appear on the screen of your computer. You expect your Java applet to have a *graphical user interface (GUI)*. That is, you expect your applet to display windows and buttons and menus on your computer screen. You expect your users to point and click with a mouse or similar device to control the computer's actions. You expect information to display on the computer screen in a variety of colors, with different styles and sizes of type. The GUI enables you to do all these things in order to make your program easier for people to use.

The bad news

The bad news is that providing your program with a GUI is not easy. Deep down inside, what your computer does is staggeringly complicated. For example, just to maintain the display screen, your computer must keep track of the color and brightness of hundreds of thousands of individual points of light. A disk drive, mouse, and keyboard each bring with them similar degrees of complexity. The computer requires explicit instructions for what to do with each point of light on the screen, each keypress or mouse motion, and so on.

The good news

The good news is that you are not the first to want the features offered by a GUI. Program code already exists to implement all the commonly used features and behaviors you want — standard graphical user interface features — as well as many others. You can program almost anything you want without getting involved in the tacky details. Instead, you need only string together prewritten code to accomplish your goal.

However, the further news (good or bad, depending on how you choose to take it) is that you *do* need to learn how to select, assemble, and modify the prewritten code components. This book helps get you started.

A GUI that doesn't stick to one platform only

One of the important benefits of Java is that it provides a graphical user interface (GUI, pronounced "gooey") that runs on a variety of computer hardware. The GUI makes computer screens more attractive and user friendly. But the interface also creates more complexity that can prevent programs from moving easily from one platform to another.

The first GUI was developed by Xerox's PARC research center in the early '70s. This interface ran only on an $18,000 personal workstation called the *Star*. The Apple Macintosh operating system and, later, Microsoft Windows made GUIs familiar to most personal computer users. Other software provides GUIs for UNIX-based systems.

But a program written for any one of these systems cannot run on the others without special adaptation. A program written in Java can run on any Java-enabled system with no adaptation whatsoever, permitting programs to be more widely distributed and more easily used.

A typical Java applet

A Java *applet* is a miniprogram written in Java and attached to a Web page. It enhances the Web page's display or enables the user to complete some specific task. A typical Java applet consists of a number of lines that identify the prewritten code components that you want to use, followed by some lines that modify them, if necessary, and fit them together. The thought process of a Java applet programmer is somewhat like that of a cabinet maker who lays out her tools and materials, cuts parts to size, and then assembles the finished product.

As a result, Java code does not read like a bedtime story. Instead, the code reads like the assembly instructions for that bargain lawn furniture you bought at the discount warehouse. The first time you read the code of a Java applet, you may find it alarmingly inscrutable. Courage! With a little patience and persistence, you can figure out not only how to read Java, but even how to write it.

By the way, most of what we're going to tell you about applets applies equally well to Java applications. A Java *application* is a stand-alone program that you can run without using a Web browser. For more about Java applications, see Chapter 18.

"Hello, World" with Attitude

With no further ado, we give you our version of the text of "Hello, World" for Java, `HelloWorld`:

```
import java.applet.*;
import java.awt.*;
/**
 * HelloWorld
 * @version 0.1
 * @author dkoosis@iscinc.com
 */
public class HelloWorld extends Applet {
Label helloLabel = new Label("Yo, you lookin' at me?");
public void init() {
    setBackground(Color.yellow);
    add(helloLabel);
    }
}
```

When you install this applet on a WWW page and look at the page with a browser able to receive Java programs, a yellow square labeled with our greeting (Yo, you lookin' at me?) appears (see Figure 2-1).

Figure 2-1:
Hello,
World.

```
  Applet Viewer: HelloWorld.class
Applet
                Yo, you lookin' at me?


applet started
```

We are now going to walk you through everything that happens in the mind of the programmer on the way to making the little yellow square appear.

Inside the Programmer's Mind

The following stream-of-consciousness narration tells you what was going on in the programmer's head as he wrote this code:

The standard prewritten code for an applet is in a group of files whose names begin with `java.applet`. I had better tell the computer where to find that code so that I'm not expected to write it all. Also, I know that I want to use at least some of the GUI features like panels, labels, and buttons. Code for those features is in the *Abstract Windowing Toolkit* file — `java.awt`.

You are probably familiar with the use of a *wildcard* character, `*` (the asterisk), which stands for any file. For example, in the following line of code, `java.applet.*` means "any file whose name begins with *java.applet*."

```
import java.applet.*;
import java.awt.*;
```

I absolutely must document my code so that the next person who reads it can quickly comprehend what it does. I'll use a *doc* comment, beginning with two asterisks after the slash (`/**`), and the special `@version` and `@author` tags so that I can have the added benefit of using the Javadoc utility program to automatically generate additional documentation from my source code.

Information in a Java code file that is directed to human readers (the *documentation*), instead of to the computer, is set off as a *comment* by enclosing it between the characters `/*` (or `/**`) and `*/`. In this book, we also put comments in italics.

```
/**
 * HelloWorld
 * @version 0.1
 * @author dkoosis@iscinc.com
```

```
*/
```

I am writing a Java applet. Fortunately, I can rely on prewritten code that defines the behavior of an applet. I'll just extend the standard applet code to add the special properties and behaviors that I want. The changes fall in between the braces.

Everything that falls between the first left brace { and the last right brace } is part of the definition of the HelloWorld applet.

```
public class HelloWorld extends Applet {
...
}
```

I'm going to want to stick some text on-screen. For that, I'll use prewritten code called a *Label*; I'll call my label helloLabel. And I know exactly what I want for the contents of the label, so I'll put that special property information between the parentheses.

A label is one of those prewritten GUI features whose code is contained in the *Abstract Windowing Toolkit (AWT)*. To use a label here, the programmer gives the label a name and sets up its properties.

```
Label helloLabel = new Label("Yo, you lookin' at me?");
```

Now I'm finished laying out the parts. What do I want the applet to do? And when?

I want the applet to do its stuff right away — when the applet is downloaded from the Web server. The *init method* is what defines the actions the applet takes when initialized, so I can include the actions in the applet's init method. I can set the background color of the applet to be yellow. Then I can add helloLabel to the applet's space on the screen.

You describe everything you want to have happen when an application is *initialized* — downloaded from the Web server — in the init method.

```
public void init() {
setBackground(Color.yellow);
add(helloLabel);
}
```

Watch your capitalization; Java does!

Capitalization makes a difference. When you write Java code, you must pay close attention to how you capitalize words. As far as the computer is concerned, `HelloLabel` and `helloLabel` are two completely different names.

On the other hand, any amount of blank space is considered just "some white space." You can use indentation and extra space to make your code easier to read, or you can use just the bare minimum of space between words. The computer won't care.

For more about matters of code-writing style, see Chapter 20.

From the Programmer's Mind to the Computer's Chips

In its heart of hearts, the computer speaks electronic ones and zeros. When we write code in a programming language, the code must be translated into the ones and zeros of true computer language before it can be used to run the computer. Fortunately, the computer, guided by other programs, can do this translation for us.

Several variations exist for how this translation process may be organized. Figure 2-2 shows how the process happens with Java.

Compiling

The programmer writes in Java, the programming language. Despite how the lines of code may appear to you at the moment, Java is a language intended to be understood by human beings. This human language form of the program is called *Java source code*. Java source code is saved on the developer's computer in files with the extension `.java`. For example, in the section "Inside the Programmer's Mind," you read the contents of the file named `HelloWorld.java`.

When the Java source code is finished, the programmer turns it over to a computer program named *javac*, the Java compiler. The compiler sorts and organizes the program into a form that can make efficient use of computer resources. The compiler also translates the program into a language of ones and zeros that is suited for computer use. This new version of the program is called *bytecode*. The bytecode for Java applets is saved in files with the extension `.class`. For example, `HelloWorld.class`.

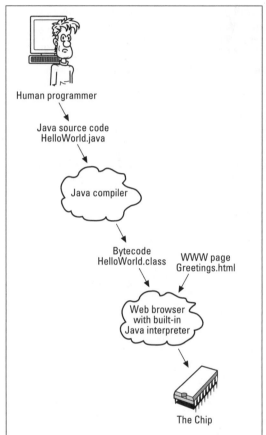

Figure 2-2:
From
programmer
to chip.

Putting an applet on the page

A Java applet is designed to be incorporated as part of a World Wide Web document. In the same way that a Web page can contain a graphic image or a sound clip, the page can contain a Java applet.

HTML — the language of Web pages — stands for HyperText Markup Language. HTML deserves the *markup* part of its name because it enables you to mark up text to indicate how you want the text to appear on a computer screen. HTML is a *hypertext* markup language because it also enables you to connect the on-screen text to text, images, and other objects (such as Java applets) that may reside anywhere on the Internet. If you don't already know about HTML, you find a very brief introduction to it in Chapter 3.

An HTML *tag* gives the name of the file that contains the bytecode for the applet:

```
<APPLET CODE="HelloWorld.class" WIDTH=300 HEIGHT=50 >
</APPLET>
```

The best way to test your applet is to write a simple Web document with the appropriate <APPLET> tag in it. You can then view the HTML file with your Web browser and see the applet in action. For example, you might write the following HTML file as a test page for HelloWorld:

```
<HTML>
<HEAD>
<TITLE>Test page for HelloWorld</TITLE>
</HEAD>
<BODY>
<HR>
This line comes before the applet.<P>
<APPLET CODE = "HelloWorld.class" WIDTH=300 HEIGHT=50>
</APPLET>
<P>
This line comes after the applet.
</BODY>
</HTML>
```

You need to save this file with the extension .html. For example, HelloTest.html.

To see the applet in action, make sure that HelloTest.html and HelloWorld.class are in the same directory. Use your Java-enabled Web browser to view HelloTest.html. You should see something like Figure 2-3.

Where's the class code? If you don't tell it otherwise, your browser looks for Java class code in the same place as the HTML page that refers to the code. In Chapter 3, we show you how to tell the browser where else to look.

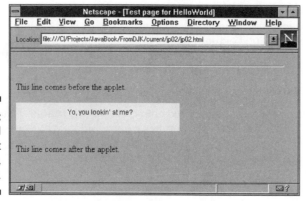

Figure 2-3: helloWorld in its test page, HelloTest.

The virtual chip

When you view `HelloTest.html` with your Java-enabled Web browser, the browser recognizes the Java applet tag and calls on the Java *interpreter* program, which is built into the code of the Web browser.

Every family of computer chips and every operating system is designed to use its own unique code of ones and zeros for basic operations. A PC containing an Intel 80486 chip uses different codes than a Macintosh containing a Motorola 68040 chip, which uses different codes than a Sun workstation containing a Sun SPARC chip.

Doesn't the Java virtual machine REALLY slow things down?

The Java virtual machine is much slower that an actual computer chip. If a Java program were fully translated into the native codes of an actual computer chip, it would run faster.

For most Web applications, where transactions happen over a relatively slow Internet connection, Java bytecodes run fast enough that performance is not an issue. Still, users care about speed, so tools are becoming available to do the final step of converting from bytecode to an actual chip's machine code on the fly. You can expect most Web browsers to do this *just-in-time* compiling from bytecode to machine code within the coming year.

For the true speed demon, Sun Microsystems, Inc., and others have announced their intentions to manufacture a computer chip that uses Java bytecode as its internal machine code. Of course, a computer built with an actual Java chip will be able to run Java bytecode programs with no need for a Java virtual chip.

The Java bytecode in a `.class` file is the unique code understood by a special chip called the *Java virtual machine*. Unlike the '486 or SPARC chip, if you open your computer, you don't actually see a chip for the Java virtual machine. The Java virtual machine is computer software that simulates a chip. At the time that you run a Java applet, the Java interpreter runs the bytecode on the Java virtual machine.

The advantage of a software-simulated chip is that it is portable. That is, Java programs can run on any kind of computer where someone has taken the time to make the simulated chip work. The disadvantage of a simulated chip is that it runs much slower than an actual computer chip like the '486 or SPARC.

Remember:

- ✔ When you write a Java program, you write in Java source code.
- ✔ You then use the compiler program to create a file of Java bytecode.
- ✔ When you run a Java program, you instruct the computer to run your Java bytecode file.
- ✔ The computer uses the Java interpreter program to run the Java bytecode on the Java virtual machine — a software-simulated chip.

Inside the Computer's Chips

As you probably know, your computer stores information and programs in the form of millions of ones and zeros. These ones and zeros are recorded in memory chips by turning millions of electronic switches on and off inside the computer.

You don't need to know the details of how a statement like

```
setBackground(Color.yellow);
```

is translated into ones and zeros, or how the ones and zeros result in making a part of the computer screen yellow. But having a general picture of what goes on when you compile and run a Java applet is helpful.

When you run the `HelloWorld` applet, your computer works with the following chunks of memory that you have set up in your program:

- ✔ An applet scratch pad called `HelloWorld`
- ✔ A copy of the label blueprint
- ✔ A label scratch pad called `helloLabel`

Scratch pads

The computer sets aside an area of memory for each object you are working with — in the case of HelloWorld, the applet and label objects. The computer keeps track of the properties and behavior of each object in the assigned area of memory for as long as the program uses the object. When the program is finished with an object, the computer releases the memory so that the memory is free to be used for something else. You might think of this memory as a temporary *scratch pad* that keeps track of an object as long as that object is in use and then is discarded when the object is no longer in use.

For example, the HelloWorld scratch pad includes a note to the effect that background color is yellow. And the helloLabel scratch pad contains a note of the text that appears on the label. Of course, how much memory must be set aside and how that memory should be organized depend on the specific object. In our example, the scratch pad for helloLabel needs space to keep track of the words that are the content of the label.

Blueprints

In the case of our simple HelloWorld applet, we know in advance that we have only one panel and one label. But complete advance knowledge is not always possible for more complex programs. For example, in a slightly more complex version of "Hello, World," the number of labels might depend on how the user responds to the program — the user input (see Figure 2-4).

To deal with this situation, the computer running Java applets maintains additional scratch pads that contain *blueprints* for setting up the kinds of objects we use in our program (we talk about objects in Chapter 4). In this way, if the computer needs to set up another label, it can refer to the label blueprint to find out how much space to allow, how to organize that space, and what standard information to include.

What is a text editor?

A *text editor* is a program that lets you type information, edit it, and save it without special format information such as fonts. Most programming language software includes a *programming editor* that is designed to make the painful process of programming and debugging a bit easier. For example, programming editors recognize the key words of the programming language and highlight them in a distinctive color.

When you compile code and receive an error message, the programming editor automatically positions you to edit the line where the compiler detected an error.

Borland Latté and Symantec Café for PCs or Symantec Caffeine for Macintosh are examples of programming environments that include a programming editor.

Figure 2-4:
An applet
where the
number of
labels
depends on
user input.

Write, compile, run, revise, compile, run, . . .

Unlike some programming languages (for example, some versions of Basic), Java does not provide instant gratification. You must go through a series of steps to create and run the `HelloWorld` program.

Writing the code for your applet

You begin the process of writing the `HelloWorld` program by creating a file that contains the text of the program. Use a *text editor* to enter the text of `HelloWorld` and save the file as `HelloWorld.java`. The `HelloWorld.java` file is the program's *source code* file.

Compiling your applet

You must run the Java compiler. The input to the compiler is your Java source code file, `HelloWorld.java`, which you have written with your text or programming editor. The output of the compiler is a file named `HelloWorld.class`. This compiler output file is the Java bytecode file.

If you are using development tools such as Symantec Café or Borland Latté, a keystroke or click on a button tells the computer to compile the file you are working on. If you do not use a development toolkit, you can find a description of how to run the compiler for the system you use in the "Installing and Configuring" appendixes near the back of this book.

You may get error messages when you run the compiler; to be honest, you *will* eventually get error messages when you run the compiler. People make mistakes, and sooner or later, you'll make some, too. We discuss error messages further in a later section of the chapter. If you are fortunate enough not to get error messages when you compile `HelloWorld.java`, that is only because `HelloWorld` is an extremely simple program.

Installing your applet in a Web page

Java applets are designed to live on a WWW page. Therefore, in order to see the applet run, you must write it into a Web page. Use a text editor to enter the text of `HelloTest` (see the sample `HelloTest` Web page text in the "Putting an applet on the page" section of this chapter) and save the file as `HelloTest.html`. Make sure that `HelloWorld.class` and `HelloTest.html` are in the same directory.

Testing your applet

Use your Web browser to view `HelloTest.html`. For example, if you are using Netscape 2.0, you may choose File⇨Open File and then use the dialog box to open `HelloTest.html`. If all goes well, you see the `HelloWorld` applet on its Web page, as shown in Figure 2-5.

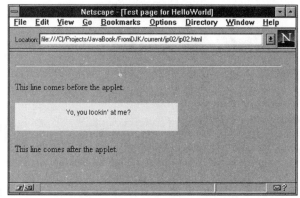

Figure 2-5:
Hello,
World.

If you get error messages

Error messages are displayed on the command line screen and look something like this:

```
C:\JAVA\book>javac HelloWorld.java
HelloWorld.java:20: '}' expected.
 }
   ^
```

For a simple applet like HelloWorld the only likely source of error is a mistake in typing. Every { must have a matching } later in the code. Every (must have a matching). The semicolon (;) that appears at the end of most lines is vital. If the semicolon is missing, you receive an error message. Figure 2-6 shows an example of the kind of error message that you may receive if you leave out a semicolon.

Figure 2-6:
An error
message
from the
Java
compiler.

```
                    Command Prompt

C:\java\source>javac hello.java
    compiling: hello.java
hello.java(15): ';' expected.
        resize(150,25)
                      ^
1 error

C:\java\source>_
```

As you can see from the sample error messages, the Java compiler is fairly helpful in pointing out obvious mistakes. Edit your Java source code file to correct the error and run the compiler again.

Creating HelloWorld: Just do it!

If you haven't already tried to enter and compile HelloWorld, we suggest that you stop reading and do some programming now.

Practice the physical steps of entering code, compiling, correcting, and testing so that the process becomes automatic. After you develop fluency in these steps, you won't even notice the mechanics of the process, and you can focus on the Java language and its capabilities.

You get used to this, honest

If this `HelloWorld` applet is your first exposure to programming, all of this process and jargon may seem hopelessly complicated. Please don't give up just yet.

The cycle of writing source code, compiling it into bytecode, and then running the bytecode from a Web page is the same for all applets. After a few repetitions, you may find the cycle natural and effortless.

Similarly, feeling a bit confused and frustrated by the strange appearance of Java source code is perfectly normal. You *will* get used to it quite quickly if you persevere.

Remember that you always have models to copy and modify. Professional programmers rarely start from scratch. Instead, professionals develop personal libraries of code snippets and examples. They refer to model programs and examples that are provided by software publishers. They save their own work and they trade tips and tricks with other programmers through Internet discussion groups. See Chapter 20 in Part V for some Internet sources of sample code.

Chapter 3

Jumping to Java from HTML

●　●

In This Chapter

▶ Using HTML to control the appearance of text

▶ Using HTML to create links to other documents

▶ Inserting graphic images with HTML

▶ Making a link with a graphic image

▶ Inserting a Java applet with HTML

▶ Using sound, movies, and forms

●　●

*Y*ou must use HTML to create World Wide Web pages, and Java applets reside in Web pages. Therefore, in order to place your applet on a Web page and test it out, you need to know some HTML.

Similarly, you need to know at least a bit of HTML to read and use this book. On the other hand, this book is not about HTML. (If you don't believe me, check the title page.) So if you're not already fluent in HTML, you may want to consult a very fine book, *HTML For Dummies,* 2nd Edition, authored by Ed Tittel and Steve James and published by IDG Books Worldwide, Inc., when you are ready to begin serious Web page design.

What you find in this chapter is just enough HTML overview and quick reference information to enable you to install and test Java applets.

HTML — the VAV (Very Abbreviated Version)

HTML stands for HyperText Markup Language. It is called a *Markup* Language because it enables you to mark up text to indicate how you want the text to display on a computer screen. HTML is a *HyperText* markup language because it also enables you to connect the on-screen text to text, images, and other objects (such as Java applets) that may reside anywhere on the Internet.

Text markup

The markup features of HTML enable you to indicate how Web browsers display your document on-screen. You mark up your text with special tags that control (turn on and turn off) format attributes and identify different parts of the document (see Figure 3-1).

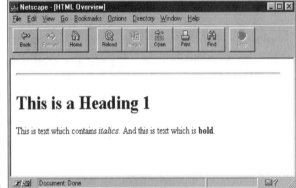

Figure 3-1:
HTML tags
control
format
attributes.

For example, if you want a display like the one shown in Figure 3-1 on-screen, you must create the following HTML text:

```
<HTML>
<HEAD>
<TITLE>HTML Overview</TITLE>
</HEAD>
<BODY>
<HR>
<H1>This is a Heading 1</H1><P>
This is text which contains <I>italics</I>. And this is text
which is <B>bold</B>.
</BODY>
</HTML>
```

The markup *tags* are the codes that appear inside angle brackets like `<THIS>`. Note that the tags themselves don't appear on screen; that is, the Web browser doesn't display the tags. Instead, the tags control the appearance of the rest of the text (your actual *content*).

For each characteristic of the text, HTML has an *on* tag and a corresponding *off* tag, which is indicated by `/`. For example, in this text:

✔ <I> turns on italics and </I> turns off italics

✔ <B> turns on bold text and </B> turns off bold text

✔ <H1> turns on the attributes your browser has set for a level 1 heading and </H1> turns off the level 1 heading attributes

HTML has other tags for other attributes. With these tags and attributes, you can control not only the appearance of text, but also its placement. For example, you can use tags to center a block of text, to organize text into a numbered list, or to place text into the columns and rows of a table.

You may notice that the use of tags in HTML is very similar to the system of formatting codes used in many word processing programs. For example, if you are familiar with the *Reveal Codes* feature of WordPerfect, you notice that the idea behind HTML is very similar — tags that identify the formats being applied.

Because HTML is designed to work on a variety of systems with different graphic capabilities and different display resources, many display details are left up to the individual Web browser. For example, HTML provides for six levels of headings, with the <H1> tag being the most emphasized, and the <H6> tag being the least emphasized. But the exact style of type used to provide the emphasis depends on the browser.

Figure 3-2 is an example of the same HTML text as shown in Figure 3-1, but displayed on a different system with a different browser. As you can see, the browser tries to accomplish the level of emphasis that the HTML author wants with the resources available on the system that the reader is using.

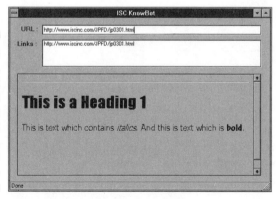

Figure 3-2:
An HTML document may look different on a different system, such as a Macintosh.

Functional markup

Besides directly controlling the appearance of text on the reader's screen, HTML tags may identify certain parts of the document by function. For example, in the HTML text of our example, the title is set off with <TITLE> and </TITLE> tags:

```
<TITLE>HTML Overview</TITLE>
```

The title of the document appears in the title bar of the browser, rather than as part of the body of the document. The body of the document must be separately identified by `<BODY>` and `</BODY>` tags. Similar tags exist for other logical elements of the document (such as author).

Links to other documents and files

What makes the World Wide Web exciting is the fact that documents and information from various sources can be linked together. One document may refer to another document that is maintained in a different location. And the user can jump from document to document by following the trail of references, with no need to deal with the mechanics of locating the host computer or establishing a connection and requesting the document.

For example, Figure 3-3 shows an HTML document with a hypertext link to the ISC home page (the authors' business, what a coincidence!).

Figure 3-3:
A hypertext
link.

A mouse-click on the highlighted words (in Figure 3-3, the words are underlined) causes your browser to locate the server for the ISC home page and display the page.

The HTML code that accomplishes this link is an *anchor* tag (`<A>` and `</A>`) that contains the WWW address of the ISC home page:

```
<HTML>
<HEAD>
<TITLE>HTML Links</TITLE>
</HEAD>
<BODY>
<HR>
<H1>Hypertext Links</H1>
```

```
<P>This is a link to the <A HREF="http://www.iscinc.com">
<B>ISC home page</B></A>.
</P>
</BODY>
</HTML>
```

This linking tag is a bit more complicated than text formatting tags, because you find two elements within the brackets of the initial tag. The first element is the name of the tag — <A>.

The second element in the tag is the *URL* (Uniform Resource Locator), or WWW address, of the linked document identified by HREF=. In this case, HREF="http://www.iscinc.com" means that the linked document is at the WWW address http://www.iscinc.com.

None of the information inside the brackets of the *begin anchor* tag (<A>) appears on screen. However, the begin tag is followed by text that does appear on screen, followed by the end anchor tag, </A>. Table 3-1 summarizes the HTML creation of the hyperlink.

Table 3-1	An HTML Hypertext Link	
Link Element	**The HTML Name**	**What It Does**
<A HREF="http://www.iscinc.com">	Begin Anchor Tag	Names the linked reference; note that the URL must be enclosed in quotation marks.
<B>ISC home page</B>	Anchor Text	Identifies the text that appears highlighted (in bold) on the browser screen.
</A>	End Anchor Tag	Closes the link.

Including Images in Your Web Pages

As we've discussed, Internet pages consist entirely of text. As a result, browsing the World Wide Web with a computer whose only input/output device is a teletype machine would be technically possible, although not much fun.

But most Internet users now have computers that can display high quality graphic images, and many World Wide Web pages contain pictures. The graphic images are optional. They're maintained as separate files and incorporated into WWW pages by means of an HTML tag in much the same way as a hypertext link to another HTML document.

URLs

Web pages are not the only type of resource on the Internet. In addition to Web pages, for example, you find news groups that post information on a topic of shared interest and file archives where material such as software upgrades and documentation are available for downloading.

A URL may point to any type of Internet resource. The first part of a URL is called the *protocol*, and it identifies the type of resource. HTTP, for example, specifies the *HyperText Transfer Protocol*, the protocol for Web pages. A URL might point to some other type of resource such as an e-mail address, a file archive, a file on your local hard disk, or a news group. Depending on the protocol, your Web browser attempts to take some appropriate action. If the URL is an e-mail address, for example, Netscape pops up a window in which you can enter an e-mail message to be sent to the specified e-mail address.

Some valid protocols are the following:

HTTP	for a web page
NEWS	for a news group
FTP	for a file archive
MAILTO	for an e-mail address

The <IMG> *tag*

You can insert graphics into a World Wide Web page by using the HTML <IMG> tag. HTML enables a document to incorporate a graphic image that exists in a separate computer file or even a different part of the world.

Sorry for the jargon. *Graphic image* sounds so much more sophisticated than *picture.* And besides, the term *graphic image* makes the point that sometimes the image is an artist's rendering of text. For example, in Figure 3-4, the picture of the White House on this WWW page is a graphic image, but the greeting *Good Afternoon,* rendered in fancy script, also happens to be a graphic image.

As we mentioned, the tag you use to incorporate pictures into a WWW page is the <IMG> tag. For example, the picture of the White House in Figure 3-4 comes from the following HTML code:

```
<IMG SRC="/WH/images/bevel.jpg" BORDER=0  HSPACE=10 VSPACE=3
ALIGN=middle ALT="[White House image]">
```

In the case of the <IMG> tag, everything is packed into one tag; you don't need a separate end tag. Table 3-2 outlines the example <IMG> tag elements and their purposes.

Figure 3-4:
Web pages
can have
pictures as
well as
words.

Table 3-2	The ⟨IMG⟩ Tag Elements
Tag Element	**What It Does**
SRC="/WH/images/bevel.jpg"	Gives the location of the file that contains the graphic image. (If the image is not on the same server as the Web page, a complete URL is required.)
BORDER=0	Gives the style of border to put around the picture; 0 means no border.
HSPACE=10 VSPACE=3	Gives the amount of horizontal and vertical blank space to leave around the edges of the picture.
ALIGN=middle	Tells how to align the picture in relation to the text.
ALT="[White House image]"	Gives the text to display in case a particular browser cannot handle graphics.

Whenever you use the <IMG> tag to insert a picture into your WWW page, you must use the IMG keyword and the SRC= attribute to tell the browser where the picture is located. You may add a number of optional expressions to the tag to control how the picture is displayed (see Figure 3-5). Table 3-3 shows the optional expressions, called *attributes,* that you can use with the <IMG> tag.

Table 3-3	Optional Expressions (Attributes) for the <IMG> Tag
Optional Expression	*What It Does*
ALT=". . ."	The text between the quotation marks is what appears if the browser viewing the page is not able to display graphics.
ALIGN= . . .	Controls how the picture lines up with the text. (See Figure 3-5.)
HEIGHT= . . .	Controls the vertical dimension of the picture.
WIDTH= . . .	Controls the horizontal dimension of the picture.
BORDER= . . .	Controls the appearance of a border around the picture.
HSPACE= . . .	Adds extra space to the right or left of the picture, between the picture and the adjoining text.
VSPACE= . . .	Adds extra space above and below the picture, between the picture and the adjoining text.

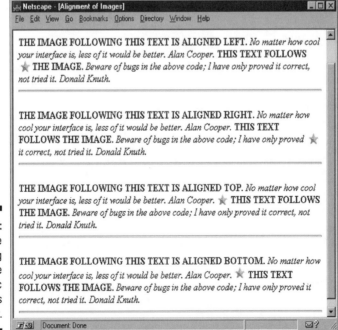

Figure 3-5: How the image tag affects the way graphic images appear.

Making a graphic link

An image can be used as a hypertext link. For example, clicking on the "What's New" icon shown back in Figure 3-4 displays a new page of data. The HTML markup that accomplishes this link includes a begin anchor tag, followed by an image tag in place of text, and then the end anchor tag.

```
<A HREF="/wh/new/html/new.html">
<IMG BORDER=0 SRC="/wh/images/calendar.jpg" ALT="[What's New
icon]">
</A>
```

At Last, Including Applets in Your Web Pages

You can incorporate applets into Web pages in much the same way as you do graphic images. And the HTML for incorporating an applet is very similar to the HTML for the <IMG> tag. Figure 3-6 shows several Hello applets on a Web page.

The <APPLET> tag

The tag used to incorporate applets into a Web page is the <APPLET> tag. For example, the applets in Figure 3-6 are placed on the screen by the following HTML tags:

```
<APPLET CODE="HelloAgainWorld.class"  WIDTH=100 HEIGHT=100
ALIGN=left>
<PARAM NAME=info VALUE="Hello.">
</APPLET>
```

```
<APPLET CODE=" HelloAgainWorld.class"  WIDTH=100 HEIGHT=100
ALIGN=right>
<PARAM NAME=info VALUE="Hi!">
</APPLET>
```

```
<APPLET CODE=" HelloAgainWorld.class"  WIDTH=100 HEIGHT=100
ALIGN=top>
<PARAM NAME=info value="How are ya?">
</APPLET>
```

```
<APPLET CODE=" HelloAgainWorld.class"  WIDTH=100 HEIGHT=100
ALIGN=bottom>
<PARAM NAME=info VALUE="Greetings!">
</APPLET>
```

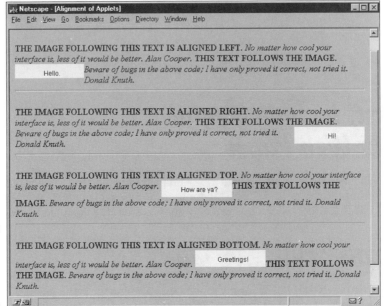

Figure 3-6:
Java applets
on a
Web page.

When you use the `<APPLET>` tag to insert an applet into your WWW page, you use the keyword `APPLET` and the `CODE=` attribute to tell the browser where the Java bytecode for the applet is located. Then, you may add optional expressions to the tag to control how the applet is displayed in the same way that you control how a picture is displayed. Table 3-4 describes the attributes that you can use with the `<APPLET>` tag.

Table 3-4	Attributes for the `<APPLET>` Tag
Attribute	**What It Does**
`ALT="..."`	The text between the quotation marks is what appears if the browser viewing the page is not able to run Java applets.
`ALIGN= ...`	Controls how the applet lines up with the text. `ALIGN` works the same way as for graphic images. (Refer to Figure 3-5.)

Attribute	What It Does
HEIGHT= . . .	Controls the vertical dimension of the applet's screen space.
WIDTH= . . .	Controls the horizontal dimension of the applet's screen space.
BORDER= . . .	Controls the appearance of a border around the applet.
HSPACE= . . .	Adds extra space to the right or left of the applet space, between the applet space and the adjoining text.
VSPACE= . . .	Adds extra space above and below the applet space, between the applet space and the adjoining text.

The WWW page can send information to the applet when it starts the applet. This information is sent by means of parameter tags (<PARAM>). A <PARAM> tag gives the name of the particular bit of information and its value. In the very next section, we show you how to write applets that use parameter input.

After any parameter tags, the final item required to run an applet is the applet end tag </APPLET>. Table 3-5 summarizes the <APPLET> tag elements and their purposes.

Table 3-5	The <APPLET> Tag Elements	
Tag Element	**The HTML Name**	**What It Does**
<APPLET CODE= "HelloW3.class" WIDTH=100 HEIGHT=100 ALIGN=top>	Begin Applet Tag	Identifies the linked applet; note that the URL of the applet code must be enclosed in quotation marks.
<PARAM NAME=info VALUE="Hello">	Parameters	Optional inputs for sending information to the applet.
</APPLET>	End Applet Tag	Closes out the tag; it is required even when you have no parameters.

Passing parameters: a brief detour back to Java

When you want to use an HTML tag to give an applet some information, such as the contents of a label, you must also tell the applet how to find and use this information. Passing information to a Java applet involves three general steps (which we explain further with the example that follows):

1. **Set up a spot to keep track of the information and give the information a name.**

2. **Tell the applet to get the parameter and put the information in the spot you have prepared.**

3. **Use the passed information in place of something you would otherwise type in when you the write the applet.**

The following example and explanation tell you more about getting information to an applet:

```
import java.applet.*;
import java.awt.*;
import java.lang.*;
/**
*   HelloAgainWorld.class
* @version 0.1
* @author dkoosis@iscinc.com
*/

public class HelloAgainWorld extends Applet {

    Label helloLabel = new Label();
    String infoString = null;

    public void init() {
        infoString = getParameter("info");
        helloLabel.setText(InfoString);
        add(helloLabel);
    }
}
```

The line that follows sets up a place in the computer's memory to keep the parameter. It also provides a name (infoString) so that we can refer to this information later.

```
String infoString = null;
```

The next line gets the parameter from the HTML page and puts the information into the place prepared for it (in the computer's memory).

```
infoString = getParameter("info");
```

This last line uses the passed information. When we wrote this line of code, instead of typing the text that is to appear on the label, we typed the *name* given to this text — infoString.

```
helloLabel.setText(infoString);
```

A *string* is a series of characters that the computer treats as text. You can tell the computer that you want something to be treated as a string by enclosing the text in quotation marks:

"This is a string of number characters: 1, 2, 3, 4, 5."

We tell you more about Java strings in Chapter 10.

Movies and Talking Pages

A Web page can call up graphics stored in separate files by using a tag that gives the Uniform Resource Locator (URL) of the graphics file. Similarly, a Web page can include Java applets by giving the URL of the Java bytecode. In much the same way, other HTML tags enable you to call up video, sound, and other types of data. Sometimes using these HTML features is a good alternative to writing Java applets if you don't really need the full power of Java. We recommend that you make yourself familiar with the features available. *HTML For Dummies,* 2nd Edition, which we mention at the beginning of the chapter, is a good resource.

Talking Back to the Internet

Using the HTML that we've shown you to this point enables users to read pages stored on a Web server. If they want to use an Internet *search engine,* sign someone's Internet *guest book,* or place a credit card order, users must not only read data from the server, but also send data to the server.

Today, the standard way to send information to a Web server is by using HTML forms and *CGI* (the Common Gateway Interface). You make Web forms by using standard HTML tags that provide common data entry features: text entry fields, check boxes, and selectable lists. When the users finish entering data, they can click on a button that (depending on the application) typically says something like *Submit* or *Search* or *Place Order.* When users press the appropriate button, the data entered on the form is sent to a software program on the server. The program on the server can save the entered data to a database, run a search program and display results, or do anything else a programmer can dream up.

Communication with the server through CGI enables the users to request a
database search or to place an order with a vendor. See Figure 3-7 for an
example of a search request screen.

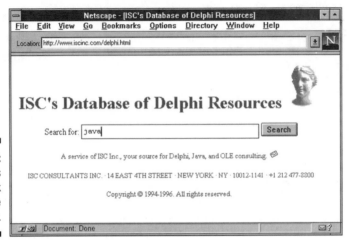

Java applets provide more powerful and flexible tools for creating user interfaces than are provided by CGI, but not all Web browsers are able to run Java
applets at this time. You should be aware of the capabilities of CGI if you are
concerned with receiving and responding to user input. In Chapters 15 and 16,
we show you how to use Java-powered communications with the server.

Chapter 4

The Object All Sublime: Object-Oriented Programming

. . . .

In This Chapter

▶ Using the library code for a class

▶ Creating a class of your own

▶ Telling the difference between a class and an object

▶ Creating an object

▶ Using inheritance to create a class

▶ Using polymorphism

▶ Using encapsulation

. . . .

*T*o begin writing more useful code and to understand the code you write, you must know a few technical terms and understand a few basic ideas about object-oriented programming.

A Primer on Object-Oriented Programming

If you have written some word processing or spreadsheet macros or done a little programming in the Basic programming language, you may already have noticed that Java code looks quite different from macros or Basic. Many fundamentals that you know still apply, but the feel and thought processes of Java are very different from these *procedural* languages, in which the code is organized as a step-by-step description of what happens next.

In an object-oriented programming (OOP) language such as Java, the program code is organized in terms of *objects*. A *class* describes a category of objects with particular properties and behaviors. Java programmers can use classes as they are, or can extend and modify classes through a process called *inheritance*. We discuss these concepts in more detail throughout this chapter. Object-oriented programming makes possible more flexible and more powerful code development.

A *class* is a description of some data and the procedures used to work with that data. All the standard *GUI* (graphical user interface) features — `Button`, `CheckboxGroup`, `Menu`, `Scrollbar`, and so on — are classes in Java. You also find classes for kinds of information that do not appear directly on-screen such as `Date`, `String`, `AudioClip`, and `Image`. As we suggest in Chapter 2, we like to think of a class as a *blueprint*.

The developers of the Java language wrote many Java classes for you (including classes for the standard GUI features). And they made these classes available to you in the *Java Class Library.* The `import` statements at the beginning of the HelloWorld applet (see Chapter 2) make this *library code* available to the applet.

In the HelloWorld applet, `Label` is an example of a class that is included in the Java Class Library. As we mentioned previously, you also find library classes for all the standard GUI features (such as `Button` and `CheckboxGroup`) and for other kinds of information that you may need to use (such as `Date` and `Image`).

One of the main things we show you in this book is how to use the Java Class Library. That is, we show you how to avoid writing code unless absolutely necessary — one of the primary skills of a good programmer!

An *object* is a specific set of data, based on the description in a class. The scratch pad pages we discuss in Chapter 2 are objects. In the HelloWorld applet, `helloLabel` is an object.

You can have more than one object based on a given class. For example, an applet can use many `Label`s. But every object must be based on a class — either a library class or one that the programmer has written herself. To write the applet that appears in Figure 4-1, you use the `Button` class definition to create two objects, `oKButton` and `cancelButton`.

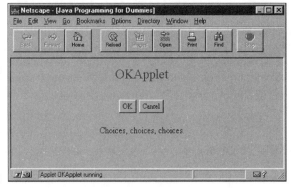

Figure 4-1:
How many
classes?
How many
button
objects?

When you write a Java applet, you must always define one class yourself. That class is the applet. For example, the only class defined in the HelloWorld applet code is class `HelloWorld`.

Can you have more than one `HelloWorld` applet object? Figure 4-2 shows you the answer. Some objects contain families of other objects. Each of these `HelloWorld` applet objects includes a `helloLabel` object.

Writers and programmers are not always consistent in their use of words to describe object-oriented programming features. In place of *class*, some people say *type* or *template*. In place of *object*, some say *instance*.

A Closer Look at a Class and an Object

We want to begin with something that may seem pretty trivial — the label in our HelloWorld applet. The computer needs to keep track of at least a dozen distinct facts in order to establish and maintain the display of the label on the screen. If you don't believe me, think for a moment about what you would have to tell someone in order for them to recreate an accurate representation of the label on graph paper:

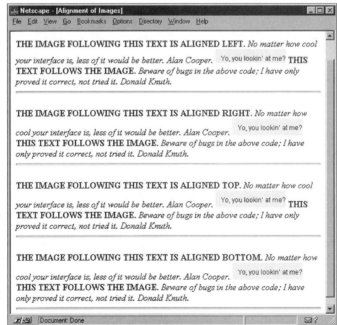

Figure 4-2: More than one HelloWorld applet object.

- ✔ Distance from left edge of screen (or graph paper)
- ✔ Distance from top of screen (or graph paper)
- ✔ Height of label
- ✔ Width of label
- ✔ Background color for the label
- ✔ Words to appear on the label
- ✔ Style of lettering
- ✔ Color of lettering
- ✔ And so on . . .

If you want to put a second label on the screen, the computer needs to keep track of another set of label facts. You can imagine that the computer is maintaining a notebook of label information; Table 4-1 shows how this notebook may look:

Table 4-1   The Computer's Notebook of Label Facts

Name	HelloLabel	GoodbyeLabel
Distance from left edge of screen	5	300
Distance from top of screen	5	300
Height	10	10
Width	100	100
Background color	yellow	blue
Content	"Yo, you lookin' at me?"	"So long."
Style of lettering	Times Roman	Times Roman
Color of lettering	black	white
And so on	. . .	. . .

In addition to this information about individual labels, the computer has a set of instructions on how to do various things with labels. For example, if you need to change the background color of a label, the `setBackground` *method* tells the computer how to look up the location and size of the label, locate and change the color of that area on the screen, and update the information in the notebook to indicate the label's new background color.

If an applet displays seven buttons, one for each day of the week, the computer must keep track of all the relevant details about each button — location, size, color, text, whether the button is released or depressed, and so on. However, the seven button objects share the same methods.

Similarly, when your computer displays a WWW page with four copies of the HelloWorld applet, it must keep track of all the information about each applet object — including a different `helloLabel` object in each of the four applet objects. However, the methods for each `HelloWorld` applet object, and for each `helloLabel` object, are the same.

Managing your objects: define, declare, instantiate

The computer's "notebook," with its list of information items and instructions, is the *class definition*.

Each time you create a new label, the computer must add another column of information about a specific label. If you want to do something to a specific label, you must identify which label you are interested in. The column of information with its identifying name is the object.

The important thing to notice is that you do not have to deal with all these details in order to create a label. After you define the `Label` class, the computer takes care of most of the work automatically.

You must do three key things to manage the life of objects:

✔ **Define a class.** Often you can use a class definition in the Java Class Library. Sometimes you may have to modify an existing class.

✔ **Assign a name for an object.** The technical term for this action is to *declare* an object. The code to declare an object consists of the name of the class followed by the name you are assigning to a particular object in that class. For example:

```
Label helloLabel;
```

✔ **Set up the actual data space for an object in computer memory.** The technical term for this action is to *instantiate* an object. The Java code you use to do this is called a *constructor*. The code to instantiate an object consists of the keyword `new` followed by the class name and often some additional information required for the setup of the object. For example:

```
new Label("Yo, you lookin' at me?")
```

You may often declare and instantiate an object at the same time:

```
Label helloLabel = new Label("Yo, you lookin' at me?");
```

Constructors and other methods

When you want to instantiate an object, you need to know the exact form of its constructor. The constructor code for each object is part of its class definition. You can look up the constructor code for library classes in the *Java Applications Programming Interface Reference* (the API reference, located on the Web at `http://www.javasoft.com/JDK-1.0/api/packages.html`). The class definition of `Label` includes the following two constructors:

- ✔ `Label(String label)`: Constructs a new label with the specified String of text. The notation `(String label)` tells you that what you put between the parentheses must be a String.

- ✔ `Label()`: Constructs an empty label. When you leave the parentheses empty, the label is empty.

In the following references, we show you both forms of the `Label` constructor in use. Notice that each code line ends with a semicolon.

In Chapter 2, `Label(String label)`:

```
Label helloLabel = new Label("Yo, you lookin' at me?");
```

In Chapter 3, `Label()`:

```
Label helloLabel = new Label();
```

Look for the declarations in the following code. Find where we call the constructor for `helloLabel`.

```
import java.applet.*;
import java.awt.*;
import java.lang.*;

public class HelloAgainWorld extends Applet {

    Label helloLabel = new Label();
    String infoString = null;

    public void init() {
        infoString = getParameter("info");
        helloLabel.setText(infoString);
        add(helloLabel);
```

```
        }
    }
```

If you want to write a line in the code for another class that can enable objects of that class to change helloLabel in some way, use one of the Label methods. Like constructors, the methods for each library class are documented in the Java API Reference. For example, the specification for the setText method of Label says the following:

setText(String)

Sets the text for this label to the specified text.

The grammar of Java requires you to name the object that you're addressing, followed by a dot, followed by the name of the method, followed by parentheses. If any additional information is needed to complete the desired action, you include that information between the parentheses. And of course, the whole statement ends with a semicolon. For example:

```
helloLabel.setText("This is my new text.");
```

Java's *dot notation,* as in the preceding example, is intended to be convenient and clear. If you find dot notation confusing, think of the object on the left side of the dot as a special parameter for the method on the right side of the dot.

Terse Verse

In the example we're using in this chapter, you go through several steps to send the "info" parameter value to the helloLabel object. You don't refer to the parameter value anywhere else, so you don't really need to give it a name by declaring it.

You can just write getParameter. . . where you want the "info" parameter to appear:

```
public class HelloAgainWorld
    extends Applet {
```

```
Label helloLabel = new Label();
public void init() {

helloLabel.setText(getParameter("info"));
        add(helloLabel);

    }

}
```

Whether you use shortcuts like this is a matter of style and preference. Both versions of the code work equally well.

The Shapes Applet — Using Inheritance

Shapes is an applet that illustrates the most important basic ideas and techniques of object-oriented programming in Java. This applet displays a variety of shapes on the screen. Each shape is accompanied by a label that states the name, perimeter, and area of the shape (see Figure 4-3).

Figure 4-3:
The Shapes
applet.

As we show you in the Shapes example, you can base one class definition on another and program only the differences using the inheritance process common to object-oriented programming. If you make changes in the original *parent* class (the "founder" of like classes), the changes are automatically *inherited* by the *child* class (the class derived from the parent and sharing features with it). Using this process saves an enormous amount of programming work. In Shapes, we set up a generalized Shape class and then use *inheritance* to create specific shapes. (We talk more about inheritance later in this chapter.)

In the Shapes example, we also show you that each object behaves like a *black box,* an important advantage of OOP. The class definition establishes what information the outside world provides to the object and what information the object provides to the outside world. You can use a class in your program without knowing the details of the object's private life. For example, the computation for the area of a circle is quite different from the computation for the area of a rectangle. To write a Circle class, you need to know how to calculate the area of a circle. But you do not need to know how to calculate the area of a circle in order to use the Circle class in the Shapes applet.

Following is the code for the Shapes applet. The code doesn't compile as it appears here; you need the other classes that we define in the following pages before the applet can run. We'll tell you when.

```java
import java.applet.Applet;
import java.awt.*;

/**        Shapes - an applet for exploring inheritance.
*          @author = dkoosis@iscinc.com
*          @version 0.1, 10 April 1996
*/

public class ShapeApplet extends Applet {

    public void init() {
        Rectgl r = new Rectgl(10,5,Color.red);
        Square s = new Square(10,Color.blue);
        Circle c = new Circle(20,Color.yellow);
        Square s2 = new Square(40,Color.green);
        add(r);
        add(s);
        add(c);
        add(s2);
        add(new ShapeLabel(r));
        add(new ShapeLabel(s));
        add(new ShapeLabel(c));
        add(new ShapeLabel(s2));
            }
}
```

Look for the classes and objects in the preceding code. You can pick out four obvious classes from the constructors: `Rectgl`, `Circle`, `Square`, and `ShapeLabel`. `Rectgl` and `Circle` are used to create only one object each, `r` and `c`. `Square` is used to create two objects, `s` and `s2`. `ShapeLabel` is used to create four objects, but the objects are not given names.

This applet also uses a `Color` object. You can tell that the object is used by the references to it — `Color.red`, `Color.green`, and so on. `Color.green` refers to all the information and instructions needed to make a green color appear on the screen.

`Rectgl`, `Square`, `Circle`, and `ShapeLabel` are *not* library classes. In order to run the Shapes applet, we must provide definitions of these classes.

Sorry we couldn't spell out the name of the rectangular shape properly, but another library class uses the name *Rectangle* for a purpose that does not match our needs for this class. The correct solution to this dilemma would be to put our `Shape` classes in their own package, which would allow us to use any names we want for our shapes. But for this simple demonstration, we prefer to take the quick-and-dirty approach by selecting an unused name (`Rectgl`) for our class of rectangular shapes.

Defining a Rectgl: Step-by-Step

The following code is a definition of the class `Rectgl`. We explain the code step-by-step later in this section.

```java
public class Rectgl extends Shape {
    /* Constructor */
    public Rectgl(int width, int height, Color c) {
        myDimension.width  = width;
        myDimension.height = height;
        setColor(c);
    }
    /* Draw the shape */
    public void paint(Graphics g) {
g.fillRect(0,0,myDimension.width,myDimension.height);
    }
    /* Return this shape's area */
    public double getArea() {
        return myDimension.width * myDimension.height;
    }
    /* Return this shape's perimeter */
    public double getPerimeter() {
        return (myDimension.width + myDimension.height) * 2;
    }
    /*  Return a string describing the shape */
    public String getKind () {
        return "Rectangle";
    }
}
```

Now, we discuss the preceding code in a series of steps. We first show you the segments of code to discuss, and we then discuss the code segments in the paragraph that follows each segment. We proceed from the top down.

```java
class Rectgl extends Shape {
```

The preceding code line is very similar to the line that begins the definition of your applet class. Just as the Hello examples extended the `Applet` class, we now extend the `Shape` class. *The brace { at the end of the line marks the start of the class definition contents.* The very end of the class definition has a matching close brace }. Everything in between the braces is the contents of the class definition for `Rectgl`.

```
/* Constructor */
public Rectgl(int width, int height, Color c) {
        myDimension.width  = width;
        myDimension.height = height;
        setColor(c);
}
```

This preceding segment of code is a *constructor*. The text in parentheses on the first line tells what information you must provide to instantiate a Rectgl — in this case, two integers and a color. The information between the braces tells what the computer is to do when the code instantiates a Rectgl object. That is, the computer assigns the first number to be the width element of the shape's dimension and assigns the second number to be the height element. The setColor instruction tells the computer to use the given color for any graphics that are put on the screen. The code line in the Shapes applet that instantiates Rectgl r matches this constructor:

```
Rectgl r = new Rectgl(10,5,Color.red);
```

If you try to put something other than two integers and a color between the parentheses of the constructor, the compiler gives you an error message and refuses to compile your code.

```
/* Draw the shape */
public void paint(Graphics g) {
        g.fillRect(0,0,myDimension.width,myDimension.height);
    }
```

The preceding and following lines of code are all *methods*. They represent things that a Rectgl object can do. The first method is the paint method. Everything that appears on-screen gets there via a paint method. The name g refers to the current graphics object — think of the graphics object as a paintbrush. Whenever the code of an applet or another object tells a Rectgl object "paint," the Rectgl tells the paintbrush to fill in a rectangular area myDimension.width wide and myDimension.height high.

Now we skip ahead in the code to the last method definition.

```
/* Return a string describing the shape */
    public String getKind () {
        return "Rectangle";
    }
```

The preceding method enables a `Rectgl` object to tell other objects (such as the applet and the `ShapeLabel`) what kind of shape it is. Whenever the code of an applet or another object tells a `Rectgl` object "getKind," the `Rectgl` sends back the string `"Rectangle"`. If our applet contains rectangle r and we want to make `myLabel` identify the kind of shape r is, we can use the `getKind` method.

```
myLabel.setText(r.getKind());
```

The `getKind()` method serves our purpose for this example. Generally, however, if we need to find out the identity of an object, we use the built-in methods `toString()`, `getClass()`, or `getName()`, or the operator *instanceof*.

Class and Method Definitions: Rules of Punctuation and Grammar

We want to point out some specific rules about definitions:

- ✔ **Every method (except a constructor) either returns something or is void.** Notice that the first line of each method definition that we discussed in the previous section tells you what type of information the method returns — in the case of `getKind`, a string. Other methods of `Rectgl` return `double`, which is a number that may be a decimal fraction. And the `paint` method does not return anything, so the method is labeled `void`.

- ✔ **Every method definition tells you, between parentheses, what information the method requires to do its thing.** The `Rectgl` constructor requires two integers and a color. The `paint` method requires a graphic object — the *paintbrush*. The methods that do not require any information from the outside world have empty parentheses — ( ).

- ✔ **Every class definition begins and ends with a brace —** { class definition }.

- ✔ **Every method definition inside the class definition begins and ends with a brace —** { method definition }.

- ✔ **Every statement ends with a semicolon** ; .

How to Work Less and Enjoy Programming More

You may have noticed that writing the code for a task as simple as putting a rectangle on the screen is a lot of work. And we still have to deal with a square and a circle.

Of course, you could probably copy much of the code you have written for Rectgl and then edit it. But you would run the risk of forgetting to make a necessary change or making a typo. Next, we want to show you a much more elegant way to build on the work you have already done.

Using inheritance to build on your work

As the Shapes applet demonstrated earlier in this chapter, Java has a feature called *inheritance* that allows you to base a new class definition on a class definition that already exists. In this way, you need to spell out only the differences, as we explain after you take a look at the class definition of Square:

```java
class Square extends Rectgl {
/* constructor */
    public Square(int side, Color c){
    super(side, side, c);
}
/* Return a string describing the shape */
    public String getKind () {
        return "Square";
    }
}
```

We now discuss the preceding code in a series of steps. We show you the segments of code to discuss and then discuss them in the paragraph that follows each segment.

```java
class Square extends Rectgl {
```

The preceding line of code tells you that a Square object is a special case of a Rectgl. When you construct a Square, you construct a Rectgl with some added or changed properties and methods specified in the class description.

```java
/* constructor */
    public Square(int side, Color c){
    super(side, side, c);
```

The constructor for a square requires only one integer. The super (for super-class — another name for parent class) method refers to the class Square is based on — Rectgl. Instantiating a Square is the same thing as instantiating a Rectgl with both height and width equal to the Square's side integer.

```java
/* Return a string describing the shape */
    public String getKind () {
```

(continued)

(continued)

```
        return "Square";
    }
```

Because `Square` is a different kind of shape, the method definition must return a different string to `getKind`. The computations for area and perimeter and the graphic operations to put a square on the screen are the same as for a `Rectgl`.

Planning ahead: using abstract classes

If displaying these shapes is a one-shot deal, you may want to go ahead and write completely separate code for `Circle` and be done with the project. However, experience shows that more often than not, you should expect to expand or modify your applet later. What about adding a triangle?

When you have a family of related objects and want to manage them in an organized way, creating an object that bundles everything they have in common is useful. This *grandfather* object is likely not to exist in the real world, so we call it an *abstract* class.

For our Shapes applet, the abstract class `Shape` is the starting point for all the individual shape classes. Notice that almost all the methods are empty. The one thing that the abstract `Shape` class actually does is to make sure that the shape's `preferredSize` and `minimumSize` are the same as the dimensions of the shape. This step is necessary to make any shape object display correctly on the screen.

```
public abstract class Shape extends Canvas {
    Dimension dimension_ = new Dimension();
    public void Shape() {
    }
    public Color getColor() {
        return getForeground();
    }
    public void setColor(Color c) {
        setForeground(c);
    }
    public void paint(Graphics g) {
    }
    public double getArea() {
        return 0;
    }
    public double getPerimeter() {
        return 0;
    }
    public String getKind() {
```

```
        return "unknown shape";
    }
    public Dimension preferredSize() {
        return myDimension;
    }
    public Dimension minimumSize() {
        return myDimension;
    }
}
```

Using this abstract class provides a framework to assure that all shapes have the same basic set of methods. All shapes can respond to `paint`, `getKind`, and so on. Making sure that the methods for the new shape are implemented in a meaningful way is up to the programmer who adds a new shape, but the abstract class provides the framework. And any other code that deals with shapes can handle the new shape without revision.

ShapeLabel

To see the benefits of the abstract class approach, look at the `ShapeLabel` class.

JAVA JIVE

A Few Tangled Details about Strings

In Java programming, text between quotation marks is always a string. Numbers used for computation are not strings and cannot be printed on the screen without first converting them to strings. So you must use a `.toString` method such as `Double.toString` before you can print a numerical result on screen.

To indicate that you want to start a new line in a string of text, use `\n` — the newline code. For example, consider the following line of code:

```
"\nMy area is " +
    Double.toString(s.getArea())
```

This line of code says:

1. Start a new line.

2. Begin with `My area is`.

3. Get the area of the object `s`, convert the numerical value to string form, and add the converted form to the string.

```
class ShapeLabel extends TextArea {
    public ShapeLabel(Shape s) {
      super( "I am a " + s.getKind()+ "\nMy perimeter is " +
        Double.toString(s.getPerimeter()) + "\nMy area is " +
        Double.toString(s.getArea()));
        }
    }
```

ShapeLabel applies to any Shape object. The programmer who wrote the
ShapeLabel class knows that every Shape has a getKind method that returns
a string, a getPerimeter method that returns a double, and so on.

And lest we forget it, Circle

In case you want to try writing a Circle class definition on your own (before
you look at our version), you need a few additional bits of information:

✔ Shape knows about height and width, but not about a radius. Your Circle
  class needs to declare a private integer variable to keep track of its own
  radius. At the beginning of the class definition, write a declaration like this:

```
private int radius_;
```

✔ To obtain the value of Pi, use the method Math.PI.

✔ To fill in a circle, use the method g.fillArc:

```
fillArc(int x, int y, int width, int height, int
      startAngle, int arcAngle)
```

where x and y are the location coordinates of the arc, width and height are
the maximum dimensions of the circle, and startAngle and arcAngle
give the angles of the two edges of a pie slice — for a circle, startAngle is
0 and arcAngle is 360.

And here is the code for our version of Circle.

```
class Circle extends Shape {
    private int radius_;
    /* constructor */
    public Circle(int radius, Color c) {
        radius_ = radius;
      dimension_.width = dimension_.height = 2 * radius;
      setColor(c);
    }
```

```
    /* Display the shape */
    public void paint(Graphics g) {
        g.fillArc(0,0,(2*radius_),(2*radius_),0,360);
    }
    /** Return this shape's area */
    public double getArea() {
        return Math.PI * (radius_ * radius_);
    }
    /* Return this shape's perimeter*/
    public double getPerimeter() {
        return 2 * Math.PI * radius_;
    }
    public String getKind () {
        return "Circle";
    }
}
```

Putting the applet all together

To compile and run the completed Shapes applet, all the classes must be available to the computer at the same time. For purposes of learning Java, you can simply put the source code for all the class definitions in the same file with the applet class definition.

If you create related groups of classes that you use in more than one applet, you can save space and achieve more flexible access by creating a *package* or a *library*. Building packages and libraries is an advanced topic.

If you have some programming experience with other languages, you may wonder whether problems happen when different classes and objects use the same names to mean different things. For example, getPerimeter (that is, computing the measurement of the perimeter of the shape) involves a computation with Pi in the case of a Circle and an entirely different computation in the case of a Rectgl. One of the great advantages of programming in Java is that each object minds its own business. As long as your code makes clear which object is doing the work, each object keeps track of its own data and methods and faces no danger of confusion, regardless of what vocabulary you adopt. Programming gurus refer to this feature as *polymorphism*.

The Cartoon Version of "Hello, World!"

When we (David, Don, and others who talk about programming) talk about Java programs, we often speak as though program objects were people. For example, we talk about objects keeping track of their own data and methods, sending messages and returning data.

Thinking this way makes programming more fun, but also reflects an important idea behind the design of Java and other object-oriented languages. The developers of these languages believe that the structure of a program should reflect the structure of the problems that the program intends to solve. By designing classes that represent the real-world things you are working with, you can write programs with fewer errors and programs that are easier to maintain, modify, expand, and reuse.

Don't be concerned that you need an in-depth understanding of all the classes you come across. The Java Class Library contains hundreds of classes — all of them derived by inheritance from one class named Object.

Many classes deal with issues that don't concern you unless you are deeply involved in computer science. (Are your dreams haunted by *ThreadDeath* and *MalformedURLException*?) Other classes, such as Color and Integer, deal with issues that you can hardly avoid.

If you use the objects that represent the things you need to deal with and ask these objects to do the things you need done, you find that (most of the time) you don't need to study the inner workings of these classes.

To encourage you to think like a professional programmer, I offer you the following dramatic interpretation of what happens when a WWW page down-loads the HelloWorld applet. Refer to the applet code as you read the script. Borrowing two hand puppets from a cooperative child (or at least putting an old sock on each hand) also helps. If you have neither children nor socks, look at the pictures in Figures 4-4 through 4-7.

```
public class helloWorld extends Applet{
    Label helloLabel = new Label ("Yo, you lookin' at me?");
    public void init (){
        setBackground(Color.yellow);
        add(helloLabel);
    }
}
```

Figure 4-4:
Public class
HelloWorld
extends
Applet { ...

WWW page: *(Offstage voice)* Hello World!

HelloWorld: *(Pops up on stage. Takes scrap of paper labeled Job Description out of his pocket and looks at it.)* Hmm. I am going to need a Label. (Figure 4-4.)

Figure 4-5:
new Label
("Yo, you
lookin' at
me?");

HelloLabel: *(Pops up on stage.)* Yes?

HelloWorld: I'm going to call you HelloLabel, OK?

HelloLabel: Sure.

HelloWorld: And your text information is "Yo, you lookin' at me?"

HelloLabel: *(Pulls a T-shirt from his pocket and writes "Yo, you lookin' at me?" on the T-shirt with a marking pen. Puts on the T-shirt.)* See Figure 4-5.

Figure 4-6:
set
Background
(Color.yellow);

Figure 4-7:
add
(HelloLabel);

WWW page: *(Offstage voice)* Time to initialize!

HelloWorld: *(Looks again at scrap of paper from his pocket.)* OK, first I have to turn my background yellow. *(Turns yellow,* Figure 4-6)

HelloWorld: *(Looks again at scrap of paper from his pocket.)* . . . And now I add HelloLabel! *(Reaches out and grabs HelloLabel to hold him up at the front of the stage.)* See Figure 4-7.

Part II
Javanese

The 5th Wave   By Rich Tennant

CHUCK BUTZLE BREAKS THE BATTERY BARRIER IN LAPTOPS BY ADAPTING HIS "POTATO CLOCK" TO A COMPUTER, THUS CREATING THE FIRST 100 MHz, 8M BYTE, 2 SPUD PORTABLE.

RICHTENNANT

In this part . . .

To make the most of your leap into Java object-oriented programming, we present the elements that let you control what the Java applet users see and how they can interact with the applet. We tell you some programmer's tools and tricks and give you some useful coding and testing advice.

Part II introduces the processes you use for making choices with your code, repeating steps, understanding the rules of program language grammar, and checking the logic of your choices. Finally, we take a closer look at the building blocks of the Java programming language. We show you how to use code that already exists and how to extend it (or build your own) to create the classes, objects, and methods that you need.

Chapter 5

Where's the Action?

. . . .

In This Chapter

▶ Using layouts to control where objects go on the screen

▶ Responding to mouse events

▶ Repainting an object

▶ Responding to the keyboard

▶ Using the library code for a GUI class

▶ Responding to a GUI event

. . . .

*W*hen you use Java, you can easily take for granted many of the things that the computer does for you. In fact, one of the great benefits of object-oriented programming is that you don't have to pay attention to all the tacky details in order to get a job done.

One of the tacky details that you have been able to take for granted so far is the arrangement of all your objects on the screen. You just write add, and an object appears on the screen. The object doesn't cover up what is already there or fall off the edge of the screen. At the risk of sounding like your mother, we say, "You should be grateful for this!"

Everything in Its Place

A family of objects called *Layouts* provides the service of organizing and arranging objects on the screen. When you say add, it is a layout that you are speaking to. The default layout — the one in charge if you haven't put another layout in charge — is FlowLayout. So, when you write add(HelloLabel) in your code, with no other information about layout, FlowLayout decides where the label appears.

Do you notice how easy it is to talk about objects as though they were personalities?

When you indicate nothing at all about how your visual components are to be displayed on-screen, the decisions about where to put things are made by FlowLayout. You can call on several other Layouts to arrange objects on-screen: BorderLayout, CardLayout, GridLayout, GridBagLayout. In this chapter, we show you two: FlowLayout and BorderLayout.

FlowLayout

FlowLayout arranges your objects on the screen in rows from left to right. When the current row has no more room for a new object, FlowLayout begins a new row. When the space that you allocated for your applet is full, nothing more appears until you make room for it by removing something else or resizing the applet (see Figure 5-1).

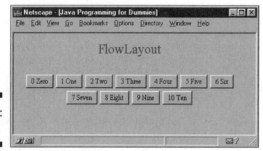

Figure 5-1:
FlowLayout.

Even though you may not have known it at the time, you used FlowLayout to arrange the shapes and labels of the Shapes applet in Chapter 4, as well as the label of the HelloWorld applet. (See Figure 5-2.) You can tell FlowLayout how you want to align and space the rows of objects.

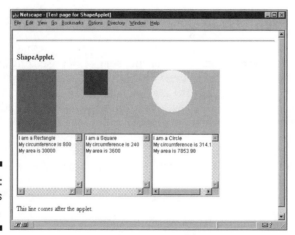

Figure 5-2:
Shapes uses
FlowLayout.

Class variables

The FlowLayout class includes its own special definitions of LEFT, RIGHT, and CENTER. Terms with special definitions are called variables. To clarify that we are referring to these definitions (variables), we must call on the class FlowLayout to handle this information. We can't just say LEFT or CENTER, but instead must use the object-oriented notation and say FlowLayout.LEFT, FlowLayout.RIGHT, or FlowLayout.CENTER.

FlowLayout has three possible constructors that you may use. One lets FlowLayout just do its own thing; one tells it how to align the objects; and one tells it both alignment and spacing. Following are examples of each:

```
new FlowLayout(FlowLayout.RIGHT, 5, 10)
```

With the preceding constructor, you can create a FlowLayout that starts each row at the right edge and allows 5 units of horizontal space and 10 units of vertical space between each object.

```
new FlowLayout(FlowLayout.LEFT)
```

With the preceding constructor, you can create a FlowLayout that starts each row at the left edge and makes its own decision about spacing.

```
new FlowLayout()
```

This last constructor creates a FlowLayout that makes its own decision about both alignment and spacing (the default alignment is CENTER).

See Figures 5-3, 5-4, and 5-5 for the results of using different alignments.

Figure 5-3:
FlowLayout
(Flow
Layout.
LEFT).

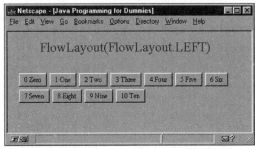

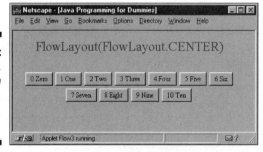

Figure 5-4:
FlowLayout
(Flow
Layout.
CENTER,
5,10).

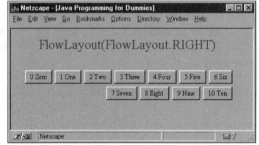

Figure 5-5:
FlowLayout
(Flow
Layout.
RIGHT,
10,5).

BorderLayout

BorderLayout is a class that gives you more control over where things go, by setting up a five-part screen (see Figure 5-6). The applet's screen real estate is divided into North, South, East, West, and Center.

To put an object on-screen with a BorderLayout, you need to tell the layout where the object goes. For some arbitrary reason, when you refer to BorderLayout regions, you use strings. So, for example, to create the border, you write

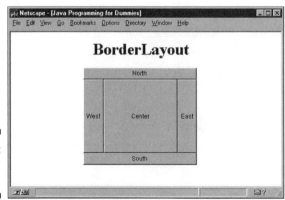

Figure 5-6:
Border
Layout.

```
new BorderLayout():
```

and then you must say

```
myPanel.add( "North", MyLabel)
```

`myPanel` refers to the object whose layout is managed by the `BorderLayout`.

Note the difference between the code to add an object to a `BorderLayout` and the code to instantiate a `FlowLayout`:

```
FlowLayout(FlowLayout.CENTER, 5,10)
```

but

```
myPanel.add( "Center", myLabel)
```

Building a screen layout

A typical way of organizing applet screen areas is to use a `BorderLayout` to set up some areas on the screen and then use a `FlowLayout` to fill each area with the objects that it needs. We use this approach in the example we work with in this chapter.

With `BorderLayout`, you can put more than one object in the same place. If you do this, the last object added covers up the previous objects.

When you use `BorderLayout` to put objects on-screen, `BorderLayout` gives the `North`, `South`, `East`, and `West` objects as much space as they require and then allocates what is left to `Center`.

If you think of the screen display for a typical personal computer program that uses a GUI, you get the idea of a `BorderLayout`. For example, a word processing program typically has a menu bar and some other user controls at the top. It has a status bar with other information at the bottom. Depending on the program, other controls often appear at the left and right edges of the screen. The space that remains in the center of the screen is the work space where the user's typing appears.

A *Panel* is an object whose main purpose in life is to contain other objects. A `Panel` may contain buttons or other GUI controls, or it may contain other `Panels` in order to organize a display. In Java, you can use `Panels` to set up a screen display like the one described in the preceding paragraph. You begin by using a `BorderLayout` of `Panels`. Then, you use a `FlowLayout` for each `Panel`, as follows:

```
        setLayout(new BorderLayout());
        Panel np = new Panel();
        add("North",np);
        Panel sp = new Panel();
        add("South",sp);
        Panel ep = new Panel();
        add("East",ep);
        Panel wp = new Panel();
        add("West",wp);
        Panel cp = new Panel();
        add("Center",cp);
        np.setLayout(new FlowLayout(FlowLayout.CENTER, 10,5)
        np.add(new Label("Here I am.")
```

and so on. After North, South, East, and West have taken their shares of
screen space, everything that is left belongs to Center.

So, What's the Big Event?

The user communicates with the applet by using a mouse or the keyboard.
Whenever something happens to the mouse or keyboard while an applet is
running, the applet and all of its objects are informed of this *event*. Imagine this
informing process as an announcement over the public address system inside
your computer. (An event is a Java programming tool that allows a variety of
objects to respond independently to the same bit of information. As you go
deeper into Java programming, you will learn about other types of events.)

All the objects hear about the event, and several objects may have methods for
responding to the event. But typically, one object is responsible at any given
moment. For mouse actions, the object responsible is the object located where
the mouse pointer appears.

For keyboard events as well, one object is on duty at any given time. Depending
on the platform, the object may be the one located where the mouse pointer
appears or the last object where a mouse click occurred. We say that this object
has the *keyboard focus*. The object that has the focus has the first responsibility
for responding to the keyboard event.

Several things can happen when an event is announced:

- ✔ The on-duty object may respond to the event and announce that the event has been taken care of. In this case, the other objects do not respond, even though they may also have methods for dealing with the event (see Figure 5-7).

- ✔ The on-duty object may respond to the event but not announce that the event has been taken care of. In this case, other objects that have methods for dealing with the event may also respond.

- ✔ The on-duty object may have no method for handling the event. In this case, responsibility for handling the event passes on to the nearest object that does have a method to handle the event (see Figure 5-8).

- ✔ Finally, the possibility exists for no object to have a method for handling the event. In that case, the event is ignored.

Figure 5-7:
The object that has the focus may respond to the event.

Monkeying with the mouse

The following is an example of the Java source code that you must write to deal with mouse events. If you include this method in the class code for an object on-screen, the object turns blue when the mouse pointer moves over the object.

```
public boolean mouseEnter(Event evt, int x, int y) {
    setBackground(Color.blue);
    repaint();
    return true;
    }
```

When the mouse moves into the screen area of the object, the object executes the steps in this method. In this specific example, the object sets its background color to blue and repaints itself. The final line in the method

```
return true;
```

is the way this object tells the rest of the world that it has taken care of the event and no one else should deal with this particular event.

In object-oriented programming jargon, we say that the object *receives the* mouseEnter *message.* When the method returns true, we say that it has *satisfied* the event.

Notice that the mouseEnter method expects to receive three bits of information — the three items within the parentheses. The first is identification of the event type, which you already know in this case. The other two are the x and y coordinates of the mouse cursor, which you may sometimes wish to use.

How about some code to change the color of the object to another color when the mouse leaves? This next code is a mouseExit method to turn an object cyan when the mouse leaves the object. (Cyan is a greenish blue. You recognize it when you see it, even if the name is not familiar.)

```
public boolean mouseExit(Event evt, int x, int y) {
    setBackground(Color.cyan);
    repaint();
    return true;
}
```

If you would rather have your object turn red and white, you have to write your own code.

Table 5-1 contains a list of mouse-related events.

Table 5-1	What Can a Mouse Do?	
Event	*What Happened*	*Method to Handle*
MOUSE_ENTER	The user moved the mouse cursor into the screen area of the object.	mouseEnter(Event evt, int x, int y)
MOUSE_EXIT	The user moved the mouse cursor out of the screen area of the object.	mouseExit(Event evt, int x, int y)
MOUSE_DOWN	The user pressed the mouse button.	mouseDown(Event evt, int x, int y)
MOUSE_UP	The user released the mouse button.	mouseUp(Event evt, int x, int y)

(continued)

Table 5-1 *(continued)*

Event	What Happened	Method to Handle
MOUSE_MOVE	The user moved the mouse cursor.	`mouseMove(Event evt, int x, int y)`
MOUSE_DRAG	The user moved the mouse cursor while holding down the mouse button.	`mouseDrag(Event evt, int x, int y)`

In addition to identifying itself, each of the events in Table 5-1 gives the x-and y-coordinates of the mouse at the moment the event happens. We don't need the x-and y-coordinates of the mouse for our specific example, but sometimes they are useful.

The x-and y-coordinates are especially useful when you are writing a `mouseDrag` or `mouseMove` method. The MOUSE_MOVE and MOUSE_DRAG events are constantly repeated as long as the mouse is moving. As a result, you get instant updates on the position of the mouse.

This next snippet of code draws a line wherever you drag the mouse:

```
public boolean mouseDrag(Event evt, int x, int y){
    Graphics g=this.getGraphics();
    g.setColor(Color.black);
    g.drawLine(start_x,start_y,x,y);
    start_x=x;
    start_y=y;
    return true;
}
```

Repaint is not advice from a decorator

When you write code that changes the intended appearance of an object, the code does not necessarily take effect immediately. If you want to be sure that the appearance of the object is updated to agree with its most current status, you need to use the `repaint ()` method.

If an object doesn't seem to respond at all to a message that you send it, try repainting the object at the end of the method.

Okay, so this code says

- ✔ `Graphics g=this.getGraphics();` Take charge of the paintbrush for the object.

- ✔ `g.setColor(Color.black);` Dip it in the black paint can.

- ✔ `g.drawLine(start_x,start_y,x,y);` Draw a line from the location `start_x, start_y` to the `x,y` location where the mouse is now.

- ✔ Record the new location of the mouse as the new `start_x, start_y` location.

- ✔ `return true;` Let everyone know that you have satisfied the event.

As long as the mouse drags, the event keeps repeating and so the line follows the path of the mouse. To use this code in an object, you must declare and initialize the integers `start_x` and `start_y` somewhere in the code for your object.

Keyboarding input

Next, we show you a sample of the kind of code you must write to deal with keyboard input.

```
public boolean keyDown(Event evt, int key) {
   target = (char)key;
   return true;
}
```

The tricky thing about keyboard input is that most of the information you get from the keyboard is not characters, as you might expect, but numbers.

I've got your number

All the traditional typing keys were assigned number equivalents long ago. These numbers are referred to as ASCII codes. (ASCII stands for the American Standard Code for Information Exchange, commonly pronounced AS-SKI.) Each letter of the alphabet, lowercase and uppercase, has an ASCII code. Special symbols such as @ # $ % ^ & * < > ? ! ~ also have ASCII codes. A few typing-related keys such as Enter, Tab, Esc, and Backspace also have ASCII codes. The complete list is given in Table 5-2.

Table 5-2				ASCII Codes			
numerical value	*char*	*numerical value*	*char*	*numerical value*	*char*	*numerical value*	*char*
1		28		55	7	82	R
2		29		56	8	83	S
3		30		57	9	84	T
4		31		58	:	85	U
5		32	Space	59	;	86	V
6		33	!	60	<	87	W
7		34	"	61	=	88	X
8	Back space	35	3	62	>	89	Y
9	H tab	36	$	63	?	90	Z
10	New line	37	%	64	@	91	[
11	V tab	38	&	65	A	92	\
12	Form feed	39	'	66	B	93	]
13	Enter	40	(	67	C	94	^
14		41	)	68	D	95	_
15		42	*	69	E	96	
16		43	+	70	F	97	a
17		44	'	71	G	98	b
18		45	-	72	H	99	c
19		46	.	73	I	100	d
20		47	/	74	J	101	e
21		48	0	75	K	102	f
22		49	1	76	L	103	g
23		50	2	77	M	104	h
24		51	3	78	N	105	i
25		52	4	79	O	106	j
26		53	5	80	P	107	k
27	Esc	54	6	81	Q	108	l

numerical value	char	numerical value	char	numerical value	char	numerical value	char
109	m	114	r	119	w	124	|
110	n	115	s	120	x	125	}
111	o	116	t	121	y	126	~
112	p	117	u	122	z	127	Del
113	q	118	v	123	{		

Fortunately, you do not have to commit the table of ASCII codes to memory. The expression (char)key converts the integer key to its corresponding ASCII character.

Some keys have an unpublished number

Look at the keyboard of your computer, and you see that some keys have no typing-related function. For example, you are likely to have 12 function keys labeled F1 through F12. You should also have cursor-positioning keys like Home, End, PgUp, PgDn, and the arrow keys. These keys have been assigned class variables in the class Event.

Class variables must be referred to by using the name of the class as well as the name of the variable.

The class variable codes for function keys and cursor-positioning keys are as follows:

```
Event.HOME
Event.END
Event.PGUP
Event.PGDN
Event.UP
Event.DOWN
Event.LEFT
Event.RIGHT
Event.F1
  ...
Event.F12
```

Table 5-3 provides a summary of events that can come from the keyboard.

Table 5-3	Keyboard Events	
Event	*What Happened*	*Method to Handle*
KEY_PRESS	The user pressed one of the ASCII typing keys.	keyDown(Event evt, int key)
KEY_RELEASE	The user released one of the ASCII typing keys.	keyUp(Event evt, int key)
KEY_ACTION	The user pressed a special function key.	keyDown(Event evt, int key) use function key codes Event.HOME or soon
KEY_ACTION_RELEASE	The user released a special function key.	keyUp(Event evt, int key) use function key codes Event.HOME or soon

When handling keyboard events, you need to look at the Event type, evt, to know whether the key that was pressed is a regular ASCII key, a positioning key, or a function key.

What is this *public Boolean* business?

Java needs to know two things about every method or variable in a class definition: scope and type. By keeping track of these two facts, Java protects you from writing the kind of code that might make your computer go out to lunch until you reboot.

Scope has to do with how widely information is shared between objects. If you want other objects to be able to use a method with code of the form yourObject.method, you must make the method public. Similarly, if you want other objects to use data from a class, as in Event.HOME or FlowLayout.LEFT, you must make the data item public.

Type has to do with the kind of data returned by a method. Some methods do not send out any result to the outside world. These methods are void. Other methods return a number of some type; for example, an integer — int. Then there are methods like the ones we use to handle mouse and keyboard events. The message they send back is true or false. The technical name for true/false data is *Boolean* data (named after George Boole, one of the developers of mathematical logic).

Methods for event handling are usually public and Boolean. We talk more about scope in Chapter 8, and more about type in Chapter 9.

> ✔ evt.id==Event.KEY_PRESS means that an ASCII key was pressed.
>
> ✔ evt.id==Event.KEY_ACTION means that a positioning or function key was pressed.

In Chapter 6, we show you more about how to write code that can make these comparisons and lead to appropriately different results.

Button, Button

A button is a typical GUI object. A button object reflects quite a bit of programming effort. Each platform and operating system has a built-in style of button that looks and behaves slightly differently from every other. Through some clever programming tricks that are too deep to explain in this book, Java allows you to use buttons in the native style of whatever system your applet happens to find itself in. If your applet is downloaded to a Web page on a UNIX workstation running Motif, the user sees a Motif-style button. On a Macintosh, the user sees a Macintosh-style button. On a PC running Windows 95, the user sees a Windows-style button.

As a Java programmer, you find that a ready-made button object in the Java Class Library saves you most of the work of creating buttons. The code to declare and instantiate a button is very similar to the code for a label:

```
Button okButton = new Button("OK");
```

When you click on a button with the mouse, the button generates an ACTION_EVENT, which you can handle with an action method:

```
public boolean action(Event evt, Object what) {
        String okString = new String("OK");
        if (okString.equals(what)) {
            MyObject.repaint();
            return true;
        }
    return false;
}
```

When the object clicked is a GUI button, the information the action method receives is ACTION_EVENT for the evt and the string that is the button's label for what. We go into the grammar of the if statement in Chapter 6. This if statement is a test to see whether the OK button is the button that was clicked.

The Programmer's Activity Box, Version 1.0

The following are specifications for a Java applet that pulls together all the various techniques we've covered so far for putting objects on the screen and making them respond to the user.

- ✔ The applet screen consists of five major panels: North, South, East, West, and Center.

- ✔ North, East, West and Center are each labeled with their names.

- ✔ An additional panel in the center of Center contains a label that says No News.

- ✔ On South, we put a button labeled South.

- ✔ All the panels are colored cyan. When the mouse enters any panel, the panel turns blue. When the mouse exits, the panel returns to cyan.

- ✔ When you type, the name of the panel that has the focus is replaced by the letters that you key. (Remember, depending on your system, you may have to click an object to give it keyboard focus.)

- ✔ When you type, the No news message in the center of the applet is replaced by the letters that you key.

- ✔ When you click on the South button, the No news panel turns blue and the text of the label goes blank.

See Figure 5-9 for a picture to make the screen layout easier to understand.

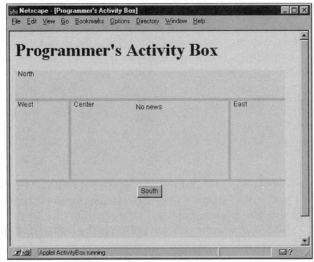

Figure 5-9:
The
Programmer's
Activity Box.

To get this applet right takes a little advance planning. We share some ideas.

- ✔ The overall layout is a typical BorderLayout. To make it look good, we probably have to give the component panels a preferred size, the way we did for the Shapes applet in Chapter 4.

- ✔ All the panels have the same behavior in response to the mouse and typing. It makes sense to create a special class with these behaviors and let each panel be an instance of that class.

- ✔ The button and the label in the center of the screen really belong to the applet as a whole, not to an individual panel. They interact with more than one of the objects on screen.

- ✔ Typing is handled in two places: the panel that has the focus and the label in the center. The method that handles typing in the panels must return false so that the other object knows that work still has to be done.

Conducting a beta test

To check that a program does everything that the specifications call for without problems, programmers create a version of the code for beta testing — a beta is a test version of the program. The following code does everything that the specifications call for. You may want to test this code on your system.

(In the following code we use an additional way to set off comments. A double slash at the start of a line indicates that the line is a comment, for documentation only.)

```
import java.awt.*;
import java.applet.*;

/* ActivityBox Applet*/
public class ActivityBox extends Applet {
//Declarations
    String infoString = new String("No news");
    MousePanel ccp = new MousePanel(40,60,infoString);
    String southString = "South";
    Button southButton = new Button(southString);
```

The MousePanel named ccp is the "Center Center Panel," the one that has the No news message on it.

```
//init
    public void init() {
        setLayout(new BorderLayout(5,5));
```

(continued)

(continued)

```
        MousePanel np = new MousePanel(50,50,"North");
        add("North",np);
        np.setBackground(Color.cyan);
        MousePanel sp = new MousePanel(100,100);
        sp.add(southButton);
        add("South",sp);
        sp.setBackground(Color.cyan);
        MousePanel ep = new MousePanel(100,100,"East");
        add("East",ep);
        ep.setBackground(Color.cyan);
        MousePanel wp = new MousePanel(100,100,"West");
        add("West",wp);
        wp.setBackground(Color.cyan);
        MousePanel cp = new MousePanel(100,100,"Center");
        add("Center",cp);
        cp.setBackground(Color.cyan);
        cp.setLayout(new FlowLayout());
        ccp.setBackground(Color.blue);
        cp.add(ccp);
    }
```

When we added `North`, `South`, `East`, `West`, and `Center`, we also added the button and the `Center Center` panel.

```
//action
    public boolean action(Event evt, Object what) {
        if (southString.equals(what)) {
            ccp.setBackground(Color.blue);
            ccp.blankNameTag();
            ccp.repaint();
            return true;
        }
        return false;
    }
```

This is the method that checks for a click on the button. Later, we may want to add another button so that we have the method return `false`, just in case some other object's method also needs to look for this event.

```
/*keyDown*/
    public boolean keyDown(Event evt, int key) {
        ccp.addToNameTag("" + (char)key);
```

```
        repaint();
        return true;
    }
```

This is how we get the typing into the Center Center message. If the same method in the panels returns true, this method never knows about the key press.

```
}
```

The last bracket marks the end of the applet definition.

```
/*MousePanel*/
class MousePanel extends Panel {
    String nameTag = "";
    Dimension dimension_ = new Dimension(15,15);
//Constructor 1 - no name tag
    MousePanel(int h, int w) {
        dimension_.height = h;
        dimension_.width = w;
    }
//Constructor 2 - with name tag
    MousePanel(int h, int w, String nt) {
        dimension_.height = h;
        dimension_.width = w;
        nameTag = nt;
    }
```

Two different constructors exist: one for giving the MousePanel a specific label when we instantiate it, the other for leaving the label blank, depending on our preference.

```
//paint
    public void paint(Graphics g) {
        g.drawString(nameTag,5,10);
    }
//preferredSize
    public Dimension preferredSize() {
        return dimension_;
    }
//minimumSize
    public Dimension minimumSize() {
        return dimension_;
    }
```

The size methods let the layout know what size these objects need to be to look
okay.

```
//addToNameTag
    public void addToNameTag(String s) {
        nameTag = nameTag +  s;
        repaint();
    }
//blankNameTag
    public void blankNameTag(){
        nameTag = "";
        repaint();
    }
```

The name tag methods let the applet send messages to change the name tag
information that appears on the individual panels.

```
//Events
//mouseEnter
    public boolean mouseEnter(Event evt, int x, int y) {
        setBackground(Color.blue);
        repaint();
        return true;
    }
//mouseExit
    public boolean mouseExit(Event evt, int x, int y) {
        setBackground(Color.cyan);
        repaint();
        return true;
    }
//keyDown
    public boolean keyDown(Event evt, int key) {
      blankNameTag();
        nameTag = nameTag + (char)key;
        repaint();
        return false;
    }
```

A return of `false` by the panel's `keyDown` method is important so that the
applet's `keyDown` method has a chance to do its work also.

```
}
```

This last brace marks the end of the `MousePanel` class definition.

To test this applet, you will have to put it into an HTML page. For example:

```
<HTML>
<HEAD>
<TITLE> A Programmer's Activity Box </TITLE>
</HEAD>
<BODY>
<H1>The Activity Box </H1>
<APPLET CODE="ActivityBox.class" WIDTH=500 HEIGHT=300>
</APPLET>
</BODY>
</HTML>
```

Try breaking the code

One of the dirty little secrets of programming is that bugs always occur. If you have time and access to a computer right now, you can find compiling this applet and playing with it for a while to be a useful exercise. You can surely find features that you would like to tweak — behavior that is not quite right.

When you find a problem, look back at the code and see whether you can locate where you need to make changes.

To get you started, one issue that you should explore is what happens when you press an ASCII key that does not put a character on-screen — for example, Esc or Backspace.

Try making some small changes in the code — one at a time — and see what happens.

Chapter 6 provides some additional Java language features that give you better control over your applets.

Chapter 6

Choices, Choices, Choices: if, else, and switch

- -

In This Chapter

▶ Why selection statements are used in programs

▶ Writing grammatically correct `if` statements and `if...else` statements

▶ Writing grammatically correct `switch` statements

▶ Recognizing typical situations that call for using `if`, `else`, and `switch` statements

- -

*Y*ou want to know Java because you want to add interactivity and dynamic behavior to your Web pages. The most basic Java language tools for making this happen are the `if` statement and the `switch` statement, which are called *selection* statements.

```
If(you already know how to use selection statements in a
            programming language){
    break; /* skip to the next section in
                this chapter */
}
else{
    /* read this following section */
```

Selection statements are the brains of your Java applet. The `if` statement and its close relative the `switch` statement let your Java applets include methods that discriminate between situations and behave accordingly. All practical programs have decision points in them — and an `if` or a `switch` can be found in almost all of them. We already used a few unavoidable `if`s in the preceding chapters.

This chapter is about three basic kinds of decisions:

- ✔ Your applet must decide whether to carry out an action — use `if`
- ✔ Your applet must choose between just two alternative actions — use `if...else`
- ✔ Your applet must choose among a number of alternative actions — use `switch`

Selection and Why You Need It

Before we get into the technical details of `if`, `else`, and `switch` statements, we offer a few examples of how we typically use them.

Listening to the user

Some programs do one thing and one thing only, with no need to respond to the outer world or changing circumstances. The HelloWorld applet in Chapter 2 and the Shapes applet in Chapter 4 are examples of such programs. But you probably agree with us that programs that respond to the user in some way are more interesting and more useful.

Events allow your program to receive communications from the user (see Chapter 5). For example, the `KEY_PRESS` event tells your applet that the user has pressed a key. And you can write a `keyDown()` method to respond to that fact.

But suppose that you want to do something different depending upon which key the user presses. To accomplish this, you must use a selection statement.

The `if` statement: When a simple "yes" will do

When you want your applet to perform one specific task after it receives one specific input, use an `if` statement.

Suppose that you want to modify "Hello, World" so that it responds to user input. When you start the applet, you want the applet to display "Hello world! Is anyone there?" Then if the user presses the letter *y* on the keyboard, the applet displays "Nice to meet you!"

The heart of the code to accomplish this is an `if` statement:

```
public boolean keyDown(Event evt, int key) {
    if ((char)key == 'y'){
        g.drawString ("Nice to meet you!", 10, 10);
    }
    return true;
}
```

If the user presses the *y* key, the program displays "Nice to meet you!" on the screen. Otherwise, nothing new happens. This is a small but constructive step toward a more responsive program.

An if statement creates a side-trip from the main line of your program statements. See Figure 6-1.

Figure 6-1:
An if
statement
makes a
yes / no
decision.

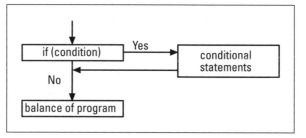

if . . . else: *When you want a choice*

You can make the program more intelligent by using an if . . . else construction. If the user presses the *y* key, the window displays "Nice to meet you!" But if the user presses any other key, the window displays "Please press y for yes."

The code to accomplish this is an if . . . else statement:

```
public boolean keyDown(Event evt, int key) {
    if ((char)key == 'y'){
        g.drawString ("Nice to meet you!", 10, 10);
    }
    else {
        g.drawString ("Please press y for yes.", 10, 10);
    }
    return true;
}
```

The if . . . else statement creates two alternative paths in the main line of your program statements (see Figure 6-2).

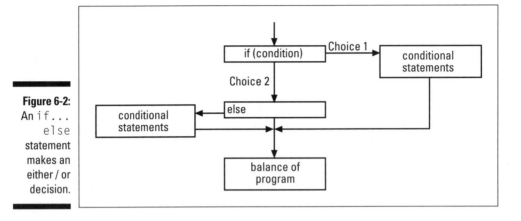

Figure 6-2:
An if...
else
statement
makes an
either / or
decision.

The switch statement: When you have many choices

The switch statement lets your program distinguish among a number of different alternatives. For example, the following code behaves differently according to which key is pressed. Inputs of *y, Y, n,* or *N* all call forth different displays. Any other key elicits the default response.

Look for the four special case responses and the default response in the code. Can you find them? (Hint: Look for the keywords case and default.)

```
public boolean keyDown(Event evt, int key) {
    switch ((char)key){
        case ('n'):
            g.drawString("Can't fool me.  I know
                                you are there!",25, 25);
            break
        case ('y'):
            g.drawString("Nice to meet you!",
                            25, 25);
            break;
        case ('N'):
            g.drawString("Can't fool me.  I KNOW
                                YOU ARE THERE!",25, 25);
            break;
        case ('Y'):
            g.drawString("NICE to meet you!",
                            25, 25);
```

```
        break;
    default:
        g.drawString("Please press y for
                        'yes' or n for 'no'.",25, 25);
    }
    return true;
}
```

The `switch` statement creates a number of alternate parallel paths (see Figure 6-3).

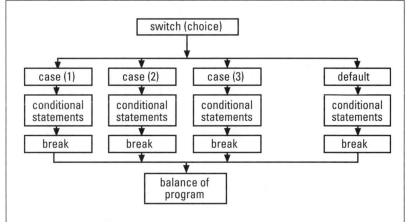

Figure 6-3: A `switch` statement makes a multiple-choice decision.

More Reasons for Being Selective

Experienced programmers learn to recognize a variety of situations that automatically call for one of the three types of selection statements. As you begin to write Java programs, you develop your own catalog of selection situations that are typical of your subject matter and programming needs. We give you a few examples to get you started.

You don't have to do everything the user tells you

Even though you set up your program to respond to user requests, you don't have to accept everything that the user sends. Selection statements let you make sure that users provide valid input to the program. That way, you don't get information that you can't use or that can mess up your program.

For instance, suppose that you have an online auction application. The WWW page contains descriptions and images of the items up for sale. Users can send bids in directly from the Web page. (An example of this technique appears in Chapter 16.)

But you discover that some clowns think that sending in 29-cent bids on hundred-dollar merchandise is fun. Handling these nonsense bids slows down your system. You would rather let the end user's computer do the work of filtering out this kind of bid.

A Java applet can filter out all bids below a built-in minimum. This applet contains an if statement that compares the user's bid with the minimum bid:

```
if(userBid.value < minimumBid.value){
    g.drawString ("You must be kidding!");
}
```

With this code, when the value of userBid is less than the minimum value you have established, the bid is rejected before it is sent on to the server. Users who want to play games can still do so, but they won't make your server do extra work. Serious bidders get a faster response because the server needs to process only serious bids.

Know when you're up against the wall

Selection statements let you create Java applets that mimic the behavior of physical objects. For example, suppose that you want to create a handball game. When the ball hits the wall (the boundary of the on-screen panel containing your game), the ball bounces back in the opposite direction. An if statement can provide the desired bounce.

In the following code, ball.xlocation is the on-screen location coordinate of the graphic handball, and court.xboundary is the on-screen location coordinate of the panel boundary. The expression (180 - ball.direction) represents the direction that the ball bounces when it hits the wall.

Don't worry about the geometry of this. (Would we make this up?) Chapter 14 contains a complete example of a graphic simulation.

```
if (ball.xLocation >= window.xBoundary){
    ball.direction = (ball.direction-180)
}
```

Whenever the ball's location is the same as the wall's location (that is, whenever the ball hits the wall), the ball changes direction (see Figure 6-4).

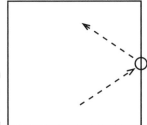

Figure 6-4:
Bounce.

When you write your own video games, you can use selection statements to give life to the animated objects on the screen.

Follow the rules

Selection statements let you write programs that apply rules to a variety of situations. Consider the following problem:

You publish an online visual anatomy reference and you want to exercise some control over who gets to visit which pages. You decide on the following access rules for the "sensitive" pages.

- ✔ Everyone aged 18 or over may have access
- ✔ Users 12 years and over may have access if they have registered parental permission

Assuming that you can figure out a way to find out users' ages and to register parental permissions, building these rules into your Java applet using selection statements is easy:

```
if (user.age >= 18) {
    //call our hypothetical method to grant access
    grantAccess();
else {
    if (user.age >= 12) {
        if (permission == true) {
            //call our hypothetical method to grant access
            grantAccess();
        }
    }
}
```

```
} // this closes the "else" at the start of this chapter.
        Read on to see why it is here.
```

Grammar Lessons

If you have experimented with writing and compiling Java code, you know that the Java compiler is very picky. A missing or misplaced semicolon, parenthesis, or bracket is guaranteed to cause a bad result — usually an error message from the compiler; occasionally a misbehaving program. Each type of selection statement has very specific rules of form and punctuation.

The grammar of a simple Java if statement

Use the simple if statement described in this section when you want to deal with some special condition and keep on going. Figure 6-5 is a grammatical diagram of an if statement.

Suppose that you want to convert all positive numbers to the equivalent negative value. For example, 1 is to be converted to –1 and 15 is to become –15. You would use the following if statement:

```
if (value >0) {
    value = - value;
}
```

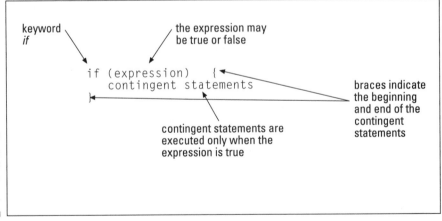

Figure 6-5:
Anatomy of
an if
statement.

A few bracing words

In this book, we always enclose the conditional statements following an if or an else in braces. The rules of Java grammar allow you to omit the braces when there is only one statement, but we find that using the braces consistently makes the code easier to read and guards against those foolish little programming errors that are so hard to find and fix because they are so basic.

If... *or* else

Use an if...else statement when you want to create two alternative paths, and take one or the other depending on the condition you test with the if expression.

Figure 6-6 is a grammatical diagram of an if...else statement.

Suppose that you want to display all negative numbers in red and all other numbers in black. You might use the following if...else statement:

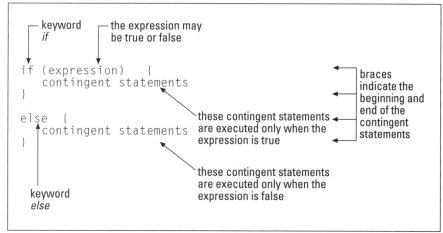

Figure 6-6: Anatomy of an if...else statement.

```
if (value <0) {
    text.color = Color.red;
}
else {
    text.color = Color.black;
}
```

For another example, suppose that:

- ✓ Price is the price of the items ordered
- ✓ Limit is the customer's credit limit

When the price of the items ordered is greater than the online customer's credit limit, you want to use a method called requestDeposit. When the credit limit is greater than or equal to the price of the items ordered, instead use a method called holdAgainstLimit.

The code to accomplish this uses an if...else statement.

```
if (price>limit) {
    requestDeposit(price);
}
else {
    holdAgainstLimit(price);
}
```

Boxes within boxes, ifs within ifs

When you want your Java program to make more complex decisions, you are likely to use *nested* ifs. That is, if statements appear among the conditional statements of other if statements. Consider the following variation on an example taken from the previous section.

Suppose that you want to display all negative numbers in red and all other numbers in black. In addition, you want to call special attention to numbers that fall outside established safety limits by causing the text to flash. Your program calculates a lower and an upper safety limit, either of which may be positive or negative. Values that are dangerously low flash slowly and values that are dangerously high flash rapidly. You might accomplish this with the following code:

```
if (value <0) {
/* The following happens when the value is negative */
   if (myNumber.value < lowlimit ){
      myNumber.showNum("slowFlash", Color.red);
   }
   else {
      if (myNumber.value > highlimit ){
         myNumber.showNum("fastFlash", Color.red);
      }
      else {
         myNumber.showNum("noFlash", Color.red);
      }
   }
}
/* The following happens when the value is positive */
else {
   if (myNumber.value < lowlimit ){
      myNumber.showNum("slowFlash", Color.black);
   }
   else {
      if (myNumber.value > highlimit ) {
         myNumber.showNum("fastFlash", Color.black);
      }
      else {
         myNumber.showNum("noFlash", Color.black);
      }
   }
}
```

A, B, C, D, or None of the Above

The if statement lets you deal with true/false situations. But often you want to write code that responds to multiple-choice situations. The switch statement gives you this capability. Figure 6-7 shows you the anatomy of the switch statement.

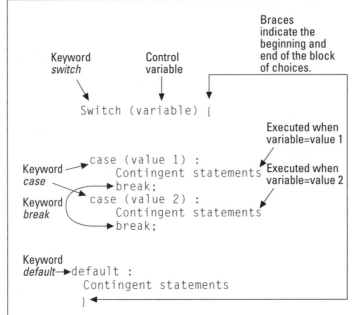

Keyword
switch

Control
variable

Braces
indicate the
beginning and
end of the block
of choices.

```
Switch (variable) {
```

Executed when
variable=value 1

```
      case (value 1) :
Keyword ──→      Contingent statements
case                                    Executed when
           ──→break;                    variable=value 2
Keyword        case (value 2) :
break           Contingent statements
           ──→break;
```

Executed when
variable=value 2

Figure 6-7:
Anatomy of
a case
statement.

Keyword
default──→

```
default :
      Contingent statements

}  ◄───
```

Matters of style

Don and David agree that using braces with a consistent style of indenting helps you to read the code. Put the closing brace for each `if` at the same level of indentation as the `if` it closes. To do this, you have to leave each closing brace on a separate line.

You don't have to follow this advice. It is legal to omit the braces when there is only one statement, as in the following:

```
if (value <0) red;
```

```
else black;
```

And indentation is never required. You could write the code that apperars in the section "Boxes within boxes, ifs within ifs" like this instead:

```
if(value <0){if(Number.value<lowlimit){Number.showNum(slowFlash,
   Color.red);}else{if(Number.value>highlimit){Number.showNum(fastFlash,
   Color.red);}else{Number.showNum(noFlash,Color.red);}}}
```

```
else{if (Number.value<lowlimit){Number.showNum(slowFlash,
   Color.black);}else{if(Number.value>highlimit){Number.showNum(fastFlash,
   Color.black);}else{Number.showNum(noFlash,Color.black);}}}
```

The style with no indentation or whitespace is pretty dreadful to read, but it saves space.

One common use of the switch statement is to evaluate and respond to user input from a GUI (graphical user interface). For example, when the user of your Java applet makes a menu selection or clicks on a radio button, you can convert the result into a choice number that your applet may then evaluate with a switch statement to decide what to do next.

Here is an example. Suppose that you created a multilingual word processing applet with the following choices appearing on a Tools menu:

> **W**ord count
>
> **S**pell check
>
> **G**rammar check
>
> **T**ranslate

If you make item No the reference number of the menu choice, the code that responds to this menu could look something like this:

```
switch(itemNo){
    case 1 : //word count
        Doc.wordcount();
        break;
    case 2 : //spell check
        language=currentLanguage;
        Doc.spellcheck(currentLanguage) (currentDoc);
        break;
    case 3) : //grammar check
        language=currentLanguage;
        Doc.gramcheck(currentLanguage);
        break;
    case 4 : //translate
        fromLanguage=currentLanguage;
        showGetlanguageDialog(toLanguage);
        Doc.spellcheck(fromLanguage, toLanguage);
        break;
    default :
        showError();
}
```

In this code, the keywords are switch, case, break, and default.

> ✔ switch identifies the variable that the program watches to decide where to go next.
>
> ✔ case identifies the beginning of each branch.

- ✔ break identifies the end of each branch.
- ✔ default is the branch to follow if the switch variable does not match any of the cases.

The variable that you use for a switch must be one of the following:

- ✔ char
- ✔ int
- ✔ short
- ✔ byte

Specifically, you may not use a string or a floating-point number as a switch.

You find that many Java class variables are integers that have special names. This makes setting up a switch to handle them easy. For example, the event IDs described in Chapter 5 are integers. Each event has its own ID. You can tell whether a key press is an ASCII key or a function key, whether a GUI event is a button or a menu click, and so on by referring to the event ID. And you can use a switch statement to sort out the different types of events and respond to each type appropriately.

Couldn't I do the same thing with ifs?

Yes, anything that you can do with switch you can also do with if statements. One great advantage of switch is that it helps to make your code easy to read.

Sometimes you may want to use if statements to set the value of a switch variable. For example:

```
if (value>1000) {
    branch = 1
}
```

Another example:

```
if (instring == "yes") {
    branch=y
}
```

And another:

```
if (menuString.equals("Word Count")) {
    itemNo = 1;
}
```

Whose default is it, anyway?

default is the keyword for the conditional statements that are executed when none of the case values match the switch variable.

```
switch (letter) {
case 'a' :
    g.drawstring("You chose 'a'.", 25, 25);
    break;
case 'b' :
    g.drawstring("You chose 'b'.", 25, 25);
    break;
case 'c' :
    g.drawstring("You chose 'c'.", 25, 25);
    break;
case 'd' :
    g.drawstring("You chose 'd'.", 25, 25);
    break;
default :
    g.drawstring("You chose none of the above.", 25, 25);
    break;
}
```

Between equals

Two different ways exist to express equality in an if statement, as follows:

If the things you are comparing are objects, you must use the equals method of the object. For example, *menuString.equals("Word Count")*.

If the things you are comparing are numbers, characters, or Boolean values, use the double equal sign ==, which means *is equal to*.

Caution: Using a single equal sign = means *change so that it is equal to*. Do *not* use a single equal sign inside the parentheses of an if statement.

The impossible branch

When you are using a `switch` to evaluate the response to a menu or to some other user interface control, you might be very sure that your program can never reach the `default` branch of a `switch`. Nevertheless, it is a good idea to leave an explicit error branch in your code to make troubleshooting easier.

If you write completely error-free code, this practice is unnecessary. Send your resume with supporting testimonials to the address on the authors' WWW site.

You don't have to take a break

The `break` that ends each branch of a `switch` sends you to the first statement that follows the complete `switch`. If you omit the `break`, the conditional code for the next `case` can also be executed. In a few special situations, you may want to make use of this feature.

For example, suppose that your applet contains the dialog in Figure 6-8. The privileges that go with age are cumulative; any selection includes all the privileges of all selections lower down on the list.

Figure 6-8:
A dialog.

Java Programming for Dummies

In which age group do you fall?

- ⊙ Over 21
- ○ 17-20
- ○ 13-16
- ○ Under 13

OK

In this example, you might use code like this:

```
Switch (buttonNumber) {
    case 1 :
        drink=true;
    case 2 :
        drive=true;
    case 3 :
        pgfilms=true;
    case 4 :
        gfilms=true;
        break;
    default :
        noteError();
        break;
}
```

In Java, the expression in an if statement is fully evaluated, including all side effects. If you are a hotshot C programmer, don't count on partial evaluation of expressions to speed your code or provide useful side effects.

Logic Chopping (or Chopping for Logic)

Java, like most other programming languages, provides you with *logical operators*, the symbols that indicate the logical relationship between two quantities or concepts.

The logical operators:

Operation	*Symbol*
and	&&
inclusive or (a or b or both) See Figure 6-9.	||
not	!
equal	==
less than	<
greater than	>

For completeness, we've included a diagram for the other kind of *or* — the exclusive *or*. See Figure 6-10.

Figure 6-9:
A ‖ B —
inclusive
or.

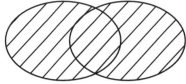

Figure 6-10:
((A ‖ B) &&
!(A && B))B
— exclusive
or.

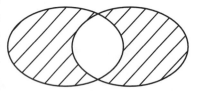

These operators allow you to write expressions like the following:

Expression	What It Means
if (a&&b)	if both a and b are true
if ((n<12)&&(b>5))	if n is less than 12 and b is greater than 5
if ((val1==21)||(val2<95))	if val1 equals 21 or val2 is less than 95 or both are true
if ((!fish)&(!fowl))	if not fish and not fowl (fish and foul are assumed to be of type boolean)

Often, a well-thought-out logical expression can take the place of a complicated series of nested if and else statements.

For example, consider once again the question of who may visit the "mature" areas of your Web site. To gain admission, a user must be 18 years of age or older, or 12 or older and have parental permission.

You can write all these restrictions as one logical expression (see Figure 6-11).

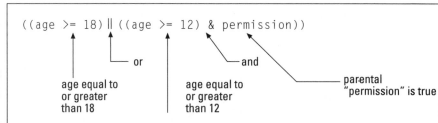

Figure 6-11:
Some logic.

Then you can put the logical expression in one simple if statement:

```
if ((age >= 18) || ((age >= 12) && permission)) {
    // a hypothetical method to grant access
    grantAccess();
}
else {
    // a hypothetical method to deny access
    denyAccess();
}
```

When you find yourself writing complex if statements and copying the same selection statements to several different spots in your code, try writing your rules as one logical expression. You often find the resulting code more elegant.

Chapter 7

Round and Round: for and while

Computers are very fast and, as far as we know, they don't get bored very quickly. Because computers have these two great virtues, you can set them to doing repetitive tasks that you could never assign to a human being.

Iteration and Why You Need It

Iteration statements are the tools you use to put the computer to work on repetitive tasks. Java provides you with two kinds of iteration statements, `for` and `while`. Use iteration statements when you face these typical situations:

- A task must be repeated a specific number of times.
- A task must be repeated until a specific condition is met.

The `for` statement is the tool you use when a specific number of repetitions is needed. The `while` statement calls for repetition until a specific condition is met.

I'd like a dozen of those, please

Often you find situations where a set of steps must be repeated a specific number of times. For example, suppose you want to create a card-playing applet. To deal five cards, you can tell the applet to repeat the steps to select a card at random from the deck five times. The following code does exactly that. (We explain the detailed programming grammar shortly.)

```
for (int i =1; i <= 5; i++){
    dealCard();
}
```

A video game applet requires your applet to construct ten rocket bases on screen. A `for` statement will build all ten without requiring you to repeat the code.

```
for (int i =1; i <= 10; i++){
    add(new rocketBase());
}
```

Whenever you see this kind of repetition, think of the `for` statement.

The `for` statement uses a counter to keep track of how many loops through the code are needed (see Figure 7-1).

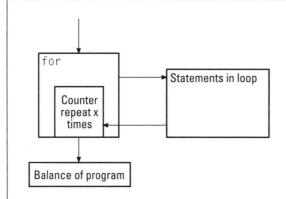

Figure 7-1:
The `for` statement uses a counter.

Loops

Programmers talk about `for` and `while` *loops* because the program completes a series of steps and then starts over again at the top of the series, looping throughout the same code over and over again.

Any object with a standard repeated structure is a candidate for the use of `for` loops. Spreadsheets and game boards are two examples of objects that have a standard repeated structure in two dimensions. The standard way to create these objects is by using a loop inside another loop. First you write the code to create a column of squares, cells, or whatever. Then you write code to create a table by repeatedly creating columns.

For example, a checkerboard is eight columns wide and eight rows deep. You can use a loop to create a row eight columns wide. Then you can use another loop to create a board eight columns deep. The loop to create a row would be nested inside the loop to create the board.

How many would you like?

You can get user input to control a `for` loop. As long as the object knows the number of times to go around the loop before it starts repeating, a `for` loop is fine. For example, if you write an applet to play cards with visitors to your WWW page, you may need to deal the number of cards the user requests.

```
inputNum = getValidNum();
for (int i=1; i=<inputNum; i++){
    dealCard();
}
```

You'll know when it's done

In many cases, you don't know in advance how many times it will be necessary to go around the loop. The video game keeps firing rockets as long as the user has bases left to defend. Depending on the skill of the user, the program may go around the loop to fire a rocket many times or just a few.

Instead of using a counter, the `while` loop uses a logical test to know when to stop (see Figure 7-2).

If you have created an online shopping application in which users establish a line of credit and then place orders against their credit, you might use a `while` loop to accept orders as long as they have not used up the credit.

```
while( creditAmount >= purchaseTotal){
    getNextPurchase();
```

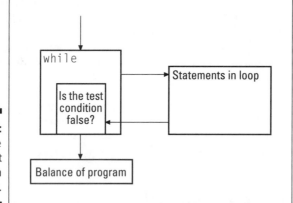

Figure 7-2:
The `while`
statement
uses a
logical test.

More Grammar Lessons

Just like selection statements, iteration statements must follow rules of form and punctuation closely. If you leave out a parenthesis, brace, or semicolon, the Java compiler will complain. In addition, the counters and test conditions that tell when to exit from the loop must follow precise rules.

The grammar of a Java `for` statement

Use the `for` statement described in this section when you want to perform a series of steps a specific number of times. Figure 7-3 is a grammatical diagram of a `for` statement.

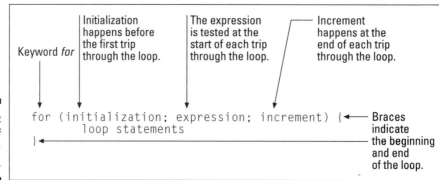

Figure 7-3:
Anatomy of
a `for`
statement.

The code that sets up the for loop appears within parentheses after the keyword for. It consists of the following:

- ✔ An initialization statement that sets the starting value of a counter
- ✔ A test expression that checks the value of the counter each time the loop is completed
- ✔ An incrementing statement that changes the value of the counter each time the loop is completed

Following this setup, the statements within braces (called the *body of the loop*) are executed until the expression is no longer true.

An example of a for loop

Here is a detailed example to work through. It puts the letter X into a string a variable number of times. The example may not represent something that you will want to do every day, but you can type the code and experiment with it quickly.

```java
import java.applet.*;
import java.awt.*;
import java.lang.*;

public class Loop1 extends Applet {
    Label LoopLabel = new Label();
    String InfoString = null;
    int r = 0;
    public void init() {
        InfoString = getParameter("info");
        r = Integer.parseInt(getParameter("repetitions"));
        for (int i=1; i <= r; i++) {
            InfoString = InfoString + "X";
        }
    }
    public void paint(Graphics g) {
            g.drawString(InfoString, 5, 10);
    }
}
```

To test this applet, you have to put it into an HTML page. For example:

```
<HTML>
<HEAD>
<TITLE> Loop Test </TITLE>
</HEAD>
<BODY>
<H1>Loop Test </H1>
<APPLET CODE="Loop1.class" WIDTH=500 HEIGHT=300>
<PARAM NAME=info VALUE="4">
</APPLET>
</BODY>
</HTML>
```

Before you try out the code, read it carefully. Begin by locating the `for` loop.

The initialization statement is

```
int i=1;
```

This statement declares a variable named *i* and sets it equal to 1 at the beginning of the loop. This statement is executed only one time, when the loop begins.

```
i <= r;
```

This is the test condition. As long as this test condition is true, the computer will execute the statements in the body of the loop — the statements within the braces of the `for` statement. In this particular case, the loop will be repeated as long as i is less than or equal to r. When i is found to be greater than r, the loop will end.

```
i++
```

This statement is read "increment i." It means increase i by 1. (You could also write i=i+1.) This statement is executed each time that a pass through the loop is completed.

Here is what happens if the value of r is 3:

1. **When the loop begins, i is set to 1. The test is performed — 1 is less than 3, so the test condition is true.**

   The body of the loop is executed, so that infoString becomes "3X." Then i is incremented. At the end of the first pass, i=2.

2. **The test is performed again — 2 is less than 3, so the test condition is true.**

   The body of the loop is executed, so that `infoString` becomes "3XX." Then `i` is incremented. At the end of the second pass, `i=3`.

3. **The test is performed again — 3 is equal to 3, so the test condition is true.**

   The body of the loop is executed, so that `infoString` becomes "3XXX." Then `i` is incremented. At the end of the third pass, `i=4`.

4. **The test is performed again — 4 is greater then 3, so the test condition is false.**

   The loop ends.

The road from parameter "repetitions" to int r

As noted in Chapter 3, parameters from the HTML page begin life as a series of typed characters, a string. If you want to do math with a parameter, you must convert it into an appropriate kind of number. Two lines of code in the example are devoted to transforming the parameter "repetitions" into an integer `r` that can be compared with the integer `i`.

```
int r = 0;
...
r = Integer.parseInt(getParameter("repetitions"));
```

`int r = 0` sets up an integer variable.

`getParameter("repetitions")` brings in the string from the HTML page. The string might be "1", or "3", or "25".

Lazy fingers

A family of keying shortcuts exists that started out in life as part of the C programming language and have been adopted in Java. Using these keyboard shortcuts is never required, but you certainly need to understand them when you look at code because these shortcuts have become standard among programmers.

```
i++ means i=i+1
i-- means i=i-1
i+=2 means i=i+2
i-=3 means i=i-3
```

`r = Integer.parseInt(...)` takes the string between parentheses and tries to convert it to an integer number. If successful, the statement stores the resulting number as `r`. (If the string is something like "B4U" or "please pass the salt", an error condition will result because these strings can't be converted to intergers.) You can read more about `Integer.parseInt`. in Chapter 10.

A nesting ground of fors

When you read Java code, one typical pattern that you will notice is nested `for` loops — that is, one `for` loop inside another.

```
for (int row=1; row<=ROWS; row++) {
  // for each row...
    for (column=1; column<=COLUMNS; column++) {
      // for each column...
        g.drawString("Row: "+Integer.toString(row)+
            ", Col:"+Integer.toString(col));
    }
}
```

In this code, you go through the column loop `COLUMNS` times for every time that you increment `row`. When row=1, the result will look like Figure 7-4.

When row=3, the result will look like Figure 7-5.

Figure 7-4:
row = 1.

Row: 1 Col: 1	Row: 1 Col: 2	Row: 1 Col: 3	Row: 1 Col: 4

Figure 7-5:
row = 3.

Row: 1 Col: 1	Row: 1 Col: 2	Row: 1 Col: 3	Row: 1 Col: 4
Row: 2 Col: 1	Row: 2 Col: 2	Row: 2 Col: 3	Row: 2 Col: 4
Row: 3 Col: 1	Row: 3 Col: 2	Row: 3 Col: 3	Row: 3 Col: 4

Counting by twos

It is perfectly legal, and sometimes useful, to change the counter in steps greater than one. For example, if you want to change the color of alternate columns in a table, your code might say (all on one line):

```
for (column=1; column<=COLUMNS; column+=2) {
```

Similarly, you could start with a large counter number and work your way down with code like this:

```
for (column=MAX; column>=MIN; column-) {
```

We do not recommend that you change the value of your counter with code inside the loop. For example, do not write something like this:

```
for (column=MAX; column>=MIN; column-) {
   ...
   if (MIN>0){
      MIN=0;
   }
   ...
}
```

The Grammar of while

Use the while statement described in this section when you want to perform a series of steps as long as a particular condition is true. Figure 7-6 is a grammatical diagram of a while statement.

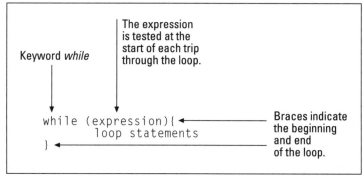

Figure 7-6: Anatomy of while.

The code that sets up the while loop appears within parentheses after the keyword while. It consists of a test expression that checks the controlling condition before each pass of the statements that make up the loop.

Following this set-up, the statements within braces (the body of the loop) are executed until the test expression is no longer true.

Decoding a label

Suppose that you are writing an applet that helps the online customer order replacement parts for home appliances. The customer types in the model number of the appliance and then uses a visual interface to select the exact part that is needed. In order to display a graphic that closely matches the customer's real product, you want to know the color of the product.

Color information is coded into the model number. The first 5-7 characters in the model number identify the product type and where it was assembled. Then the letter C is followed by a two-character code that indicates the color. For a human who knows the code, it is easy to scan for the letter C and then pick out the two characters that follow. You can tell the Java applet to do the same thing using a while statement and the substring method of the String object.

The substring( ) method picks out a group of characters (a *substring*) from a string using the position numbers of the first substring character and the character that follows the end of the substring. By the way, the first position number in a string is 0. For example, if modelNum is 27318CRED6580, the position number of the character 2 is 0. And modelNum.substring(6,9) is RED, because character number six in modelNum is R and character nine is 6 — the character following D. This is just a preview of String methods; for more information about Strings and their methods, see Chapter 10.

Here is the sample code:

```
String letter = null;
String colorCode = null;
int n = 0;

while (letter.equals("C")==false) {
    letter = modelNum.substring(n,1);
    n++;
}
n++;
colorCode=modelNum.substring(n,2);
```

The applet checks the value of letter. It is not equal to "C", so the loop begins. Now the applet sets letter to be the first character in modelNum — the substring from position 0 to position 1 in modelNum. And it bumps up the value of n by 1.

The loop now checks the value of letter again. If letter is still not equal to "C", you go through the loop again, setting letter equal to the next position in modelNum.

When letter equals "C", the loop stops. The next two characters are the colorCode.

Give me a call

As you may have noticed, people like their phone numbers nicely broken up with a hypen (-) and parentheses and so on. Computers do not. You may use a while statement to get rid of the hyphen in a phone number.

We use `substring()` again in this code. If we leave out the second position number when we use `substring()`, it returns a substring that ends at the end of the string. We also use another `String` method — `indexOf()`. The `indexOf()` method returns the position number of a given character or substring. If the target is not found, it returns -1. In this example, we use `indexOf("-")` to find the position of the first hyphen in the phone number.

```
String phoneNumber = "212-477-8800";
while (phoneNumber.indexOf("-") >= 0) {
   phoneNumber =
   phoneNumber.substring(0,phoneNumber.indexOf("-")) +
   phoneNumber.substring(phoneNumber.indexOf("-")+1);
}
// now phoneNumber == "2124778800"
```

Here is what happens in this `while` loop.

1. **When the loop begins, the first - is at position 3, which is greater than 0.**

   The computer takes the substring in positions 0-2 — `phoneNumber.substring(0,phoneNumber.indexOf("-"))` — and adds to the end of it the substring from position 4 to the end of the string — `phoneNumber.substring(phoneNumber.indexOf("-")+1)`. This becomes the new working version of `phoneNumber`. We have eliminated the first -, and we are ready to start the loop again.

2. **Now the first - is at position 6. The test expression is still true.**

   We repeat the substring trick to get rid of the next - , and we are ready to start the loop again.

3. **At the start of the third trip around the loop, we find no more - characters in** `phoneNumber.indexOf("-") returns -1`. **The test expression is false and the loop ends.**

Keeping score

Your video game keeps score of how many Klingons you have exterminated and how many Tribbles survive on your side. Although the number of Tribbles is at least 1/10 the number of Klingons, hope remains. If the number gets too small, a cloud of doom settles across the landscape.

The code is:

```
while ( (Tribble.count() / 10) >= Klingon.count() ) {
    playerThread.continue();
}
// no hope left...
cloudOfDoom.activate();
```

Locating the nearest exit

Loops are a vital tool for every programmer, but they must be handled with respect. You want to be sure that there is a way out of every loop. One of the most common programming mishaps is to lose track of the test in a `for` loop or a `while` loop in such a way that the loop just keeps going forever. For example, you might write:

```
for (i=1; i <= max; i++)
```

This will work fine if `max` is a positive number. But what if `max` is 0? The test is never false, and the computer will stay in the loop indefinitely. This condition is known as *infinite loop.*

The computer may simply hang there, unresponsive to the outside world. If you wait long enough, you may eventually get an interesting error message such as `out of memory`.

If you encounter these symptoms, try to reconstruct what the applet was doing, step by step, as it executes your code. Chances are high that you will find a point where there is an error or an overlooked situation in the test for a loop.

A personal confession

In the dark ages when all computer output was on paper, one of the authors (who will remain otherwise anonymous) wrote an elegant program to compute a table of mathematical functions for n from 1 to 1000. Being slightly dyslexic and thoroughly overconfident, he keyed > rather than < at a strategic point in the program. A 3-foot-high stack of computer printout decorated with five columns of zeros resulted, and he hasn't run out of scratch paper yet.

Chapter 8
Anatomy of a Class

• •

• •

*T*his chapter gives you a more formal overview of the parts that go together to make the code of a Java applet. Every applet consists of at least one class definition. Most useful applets use a number of other classes, some defined in the Java Class Library and others custom built for the individual applet or for a family of applets.

When you read Java code, you can read more intelligently if you know what to expect. And as you begin to write Java code that uses a variety of classes, knowing how classes are organized is important.

Classes with Class

As we discussed in Chapter 4, a class definition usually includes several main chunks of code in addition to the name of the class:

✔ **Declarations of class variables or properties:** The declarations give object variables — bits of information about the object — names so that the variables can be used or tracked. Usually the variables are instantiated and given a starting value as well.

✔ **Constructors:** A class includes one or more constructors that tell what information must be provided from outside when an object of this type is instantiated and how that information is to be used in setting up the object.

✔ **Methods:** The methods are the object's job description. Each method is an action that the object understands, an instruction to which it can respond.

See Figure 8-1.

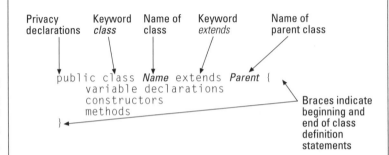

Figure 8-1:
Anatomy of
a class
definition.

No Trespassing

You have seen the keyword word `public` a number of times in Java code by now. When a class, variable, or method is *public,* it is accessible to any other Java code that is running in the same machine at the same time. It is also possible for a class or some of its variables or methods to be *private.* When a class, variable, or method is *private,* it is not accessible to any other code.

```
public class Rectangle extends Shape {
    public Rectangle(int width, int height, Color c) {
```

Any other code can make use of the `Rectangle` class created in this definition.

The following code, however, declares `Circle` public but makes `radius_` private:

```
public class Circle extends Shape {
    private int radius_;
```

Any code can use the `Circle` class. For example, we can write another class called `CircleFactory`. `CircleFactory` may call on the `Circle` class to instantiate a circle and add it to the screen. And `CircleFactory` can determine in advance the size of the circle's radius by using the desired value in the constructor. But the new program cannot directly change the radius of the circle after it has been created. For example, you could *not* successfully write an applet that says

```
myCircle.radius_ = 27;
```

In Java, you can establish four different levels of privacy. (See Table 8-1.) For most purposes, you need know only that anything labeled `private` simply does not exist outside the class in which it is declared. If you try to access private data or use a private method from an outside class, will receive an error message from the compiler.

If you want to be able to communicate with other objects, to allow them to access data or otherwise send messages to an object, you must make the relevant methods or data `public`.

Table 8-1	Rules of Privacy
Declaration	*Visibility*
`public`	Visible to everyone
`private`	Visible to no one
`(no declaration)`	Visible to everyone in the same file or package
`protected`	Same as (no declaration) but visible for inheritance purposes only to everyone in the same file or package

Variables

Variables that record some basic property of an object are usually declared at the top of the class definition. For each variable, you tell the computer what type of variable it is so that the computer can set aside the appropriate scratch pad space in memory to keep track of it. You may also assign a value right away, or you may leave the variable set to the default value for that type until you give it some new value later in the code.

Minimizing errors

In Java, making an error and changing the data of an object unintentionally would be difficult because you normally address each object by name. In other programming languages, being unclear about which bit of information belongs to which piece of code is much easier. In some cases, the same piece of information may be unintentionally changed in two different places. This can result in hard-to-find bugs that you remember fondly (or not) for many years.

A variable declaration includes:

- ✔ A type or class name
- ✔ A name used to refer to the specific variable
- ✔ Optionally, a statement that assigns an initial value

Instance variables

Most of the variables that you use are *instance* variables. That is, every object based on the class template can have a different value for the variable, so the computer must set up scratch pad space for the variable each time that an instance of the class is created.

For example:

```
class ArcCanvas extends Canvas {
    int startAngle = 0;
    int endAngle = 45;
    boolean filled = false;
    Font font;
    . . .
```

Every `ArcCanvas` that you create has its own `startAngle`, `endAngle`, filled condition, and font.

Class variables

Sometimes a variable represents basic information that applies to a class as a whole. You have already seen a few typical examples:

- ✔ `PI`, which applies to all `Circles`
- ✔ `LEFT`, `RIGHT`, `CENTER`, which apply to all `FlowLayouts`

These variables are actually constants whose values you type into the code of the class definition. Traditionally, such constants are identified by entering their names as all capitals. RED, BLUE, YELLOW, ...which are variables of the class `Color`. The numbers that correspond to these standard colors may differ from system to system, but they do not vary from color object to color object. All color objects created on a given system have the same definition of RED.

Class variables are identified by the keyword `static` in the declaration. For example:

```
public class Chart extends java.applet.Applet {
    static final int    VERTICAL = 0;
    static final int    HORIZONTAL = 1;
    static final int    SOLID = 0;
    static final int    STRIPED = 1;
```

Telling the world about variables

You may see classes in which all the variables are private. One standard approach to setting up communications between a Java object and the outside world is to give the object a set of public methods that respond to `getValue` requests for information about the object and that receive `setValue` instructions from the outside world. For example, my `Radius` is private data, but `radius` can be revealed to other objects by the method:

```
public double getRadius()
```

Similarly, you may have a radius-setting method that sends in the desired new radius value by means of a method call, instead of directly changing the value of the variable:

```
public void setRadius(double r)
```

The advantage of this approach is that it allows you to deal with special situations only in the object that those situations affect. For example, you can write code to deal with negative values of r or other special situations as part of the `Circle` object. You may want to convert negative values to their positive equivalents, or to use a default value, or possibly to return an error message. The other objects that interact with `Circle` do not need to know about its inner workings.

In this way, if you discover some unanticipated circumstances after writing a class, you need only revise the code in one place.

Object under Construction

Constructors contain instructions on how to create a new object of this class. A class may have more than one constructor.

A constructor consists of:

✔ The name of the class

✔ The information required from outside to set up an object of this class

✔ Any necessary setup steps, such as putting initial values into the object's scratch pad variables

Figure 8-2 shows the elements of a constructor.

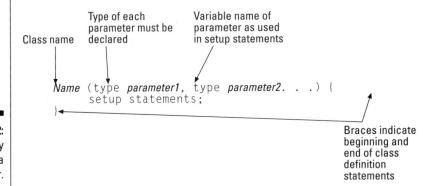

Figure 8-2:
Anatomy
of a
constructor.

For example:

```
MousePanel(int h, int w, String l) {
        dimension_.height = h;
        dimension_.width = w;
        label = l;
    }
```

Any time that you list an item in the parentheses following the class name of a constructor, you must first identify its type and then give it a name. The name that you give the item is used in the statements in braces to put the value into the appropriate places in the new object.

The pattern consisting of the name plus the information that appears in parentheses is called the *signature* of the constructor. The signature of the preceding MousePanel constructor is MousePanel(int, int, String).

A second MousePanel constructor must have a different signature. For example, you may define a constructor that leaves the string set to some default value.

```
MousePanel(int h, int w) {
      dimension_.height = h;
      dimension_.width = w;
   }
```

The signature of this constructor is `MousePanel(int, int)`.

How Do You Do That?

The third element in a class definition is *methods*. Methods are the job description of the class. An object responds to every message that refers to a method defined for its class (or the parent of its class). If you ask an object to do something that is not included in its methods, your request is refused. (That is, you get a compiler error.)

The most common way for objects to communicate with each other is for one object to address another by its name and the required method.

```
Waiter.passThe(salt)
```

Like variables, methods may be public or private. Only methods that are not private may be used to communicate with the object. A private method is some computation that is a step in the object's internal work.

Just as you normally expect some response when you speak to a person, you expect some response when you send a message to an object. The method declaration tells what kind of response to expect.

Often, a method returns an item of data — a number or a string. Sometimes a method returns a yes/no response — Boolean `true` or `false`. And some methods return nothing at all — `void`.

A method definition consists of:

   ✔ Privacy declarations, if any

   ✔ The expected return of the method

   ✔ The name of the class

   ✔ The information required from outside to complete the instructions

   ✔ The setup of any scratch pad space used only for this method

   ✔ The steps to complete the action

Figure 8-3 shows the elements of a method.

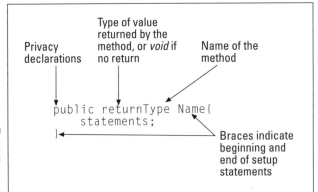

Figure 8-3:
Anatomy of
a method.

This next example is similar to one that we discussed in Chapter 5:

```
public boolean mouseEnter(Event evt, int x, int y) {
        setBackground(Color.blue);
        repaint();
        return true;
    }
```

This is a public method whose name is mouseEnter. It happens to be a method of the class MousePanel. A MousePanel object, such as southPanel, may receive a method call that says something like this:

```
southPanel.mouseEnter(MOUSE_ENTER ,10, 12);
```

When southPanel receives this method call, it executes the steps in braces. That is, it sets its own background color to be blue, it repaints itself, and it returns true to the object that sent the method call.

More than one way to circle the globe

Just as a class may have more than one constructor, it may have more than one method of the same name. When different ways exist to do the same thing, a class can have more than one method definition with the same name. The computer knows to apply the correct method by looking at the signature of the method. Of course, this means that you can't have two different methods with the same name and the same signature.

Many methods have a blank signature; that is, they take no information from the object that calls them. In this case, the method definition has an empty pair of parentheses. But the parentheses are still required so that the computer recognizes that it is dealing with a method definition. For example:

```
void init()
```

Table 8-2 shows a number of method calls and definitions.

Table 8-2	Some Method Calls and Definitions
Method call in displayPanel	*Method definition in myShape class*

`Square.showName();`
`Row 2, Column i`
`Label says"Generic Shape"`
	`void showName (){`
	`    myLabel.setText("Generic Shape");`
	`    add(myLabel);`
	`    repaint();`
	`}`

`Square.showName("Irving");`
`Label says "Irving"`
	`void showName (String fullName) {`
	`    myLabel.setText(fullName);`
	`    add(myLabel);`
	`    repaint();`
	`}`

So's your old man — laws of heredity

Classes inherit the methods of their parents. Inherited methods do not show up in the class definition of the child class, but they are available to call on as needed. Methods such as `setBackground()`, `repaint()`, and `add()` are inherited by many classes. Much of the time, you rely on a family of basic methods that are common to most of the classes with which you work.

A common programming trick is to override one of the inherited methods with a more specific method that serves a purpose of your applet.

The event-handling behaviors with which you work to attend to mouse and keyboard events are an example of overriding an inherited method with a custom method. These methods exist in the parent class `Component`, but you don't see them do anything visible until you override the inherited do-nothing method with a method that produces the result you want.

Managing a Large Family

As you begin to write more complex applets, you may find that you need to manage groups of related classes. Several techniques exist to help you keep large families of classes organized so that they don't become unruly.

Two techniques can help you make sure that, within a particular group, all classes (and their objects) speak the same language; that is, they have the same methods. These techniques are as follows:

▸ Creating an abstract class

▸ Creating an interface

A third technique makes sure that a group of classes are packaged together so that all are available at the same time: This third technique is creating a package.

Abstract classes and interfaces

We already discussed an example of an abstract class in the Shapes applet of Chapter 4. An *abstract class* is a class that has children but no instances of its own.

Shape is an abstract class. It sets up a structure of data and methods that its children can inherit and extend. You know that all the children of Shape — Circle, Rectangle, and Square — have methods to return a perimeter, an area, and a name, for example. But you still have to go ahead and implement these methods for each specific type of object.

```java
public abstract class Shape extends Canvas {
    Dimension dimension_ = new Dimension();
    public void Shape() {
    }
    public Color getColor() {
        return getForeground();
    }
    public void setColor(Color c) {
        setForeground(c);
    }
    public void paint(Graphics g) {
    }
    public double getArea() {
        return 0;
    }
    public double getPerimeter() {
        return 0;
    }
    public String getKind() {
        return "unknown shape";
    }
    public Dimension preferredSize() {
        return dimension_;
```

```
        }
    public Dimension minimumSize() {
        return dimension_;
    }
}
```

Occasionally, you want to assure that a number of classes have the same bundle of methods, even though they are not all children of the same parent class. For example, suppose that your game includes a variety of different classes of droids, bots, and actors. Each group of classes has some distinctly different methods and properties. Figure 8-4 shows some varieties of these elements.

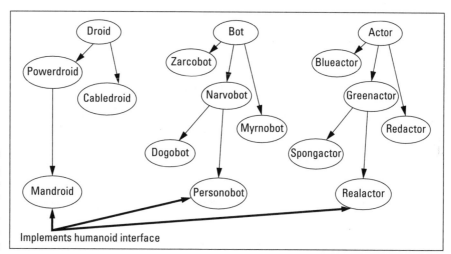

Figure 8-4:
The many varieties of droids, bots, and actors.

Furthermore, some droids, some bots, and some actors are humanoid, whereas others of each class are spongiform. You can tell a humanoid droid, bot, or actor to *jump* or *run*. But all you can tell a spongiform to do is *assimilate*.

In this case, you may enforce a humanoid set of behaviors on all classes by declaring a humanoid interface. Then when you define a humanoid class, regardless of whether it inherits from the droid family tree or the actor family tree, you declare that it implements interface *humanoid,* and the Java compiler requires you to provide all the necessary behaviors.

When you use an *interface* declaration, you must still write specific procedures to implement all the behaviors in the interface for each class that implements the interface. The interface declaration puts the Java compiler to work only as a watchdog to make sure that you do the work. It does not do the work for you. An abstract base class can provide default behaviors that you change only where necessary, but an interface leaves all the work to you.

Packaging

So far, you have made sure that all the classes you need for your applet are available by putting them all in the same file. When you begin to build more complex programs and to use the same classes in more than one applet, this approach is inconvenient. You may find it easier to build a package instead.

A *package* is a group of classes that work together. When you are writing Java code, you can put a class into a package by declaring the package name in the first line in the file — package mypackage. After classes are written and packaged, you call on classes in a package by using an import statement. You are already familiar with some packages — java.applet, java.awt, and so on.

When you run the code as an applet, the browser or applet viewer needs to know where all the class files are located. The browser already knows where the class files for the Java library classes are located, but looks for classes that belong to a package in a subdirectory with the same name as the package name.

The following steps show what you need to do when you want to create your own package:

1. **Declare the package.**

   Write the code for each class in the package. Add a package declaration as the first line of each code file. For example:

   ```
   package mypackage;
   import java.awt.*;
   public class Droid extends Object {
   ...
   ```

2. **Put the compiled .class files in a directory named for the package.**

   Compile the code for each class in the package. For example, you may have a group of class files:

   ```
   droid.class
   bot.class
   actor.class
   ```

Put all these files into a subdirectory named `mypackage`.

While you are developing your applet, the `mypackage` subdirectory may be a subdirectory of your current working directory (for example, `cafe\projects\mypackage\`) or you may add the directory that you have created to the CLASSPATH declaration. (See Appendix B, C, or D for instructions on setting the class path for your system.)

Codebase

When you publish your applet on the WWW, you may keep the applet code and package subdirectories in the same directory as the HTML file for the page that contains the applet. But you may want to organize your applet code in a directory separate from the HTML code. You can tell the HTML page where to look for Java code by adding a `CODEBASE=` statement to the HTML `<APPLET>` tag. For example:

```
<APPLET CODEBASE= http:\\www.iscinc.com.\appletcode\
CODE="HelloAgainWorld.class"  WIDTH=100 HEIGHT=100 ALIGN=left>
<PARAM NAME="info" VALUE="Hello.">
</APPLET>
```

In this case, when the Web browser reads the HTML page, it goes to the indicated URL to look for the applet code instead of looking in the same place where the HTML page is located. The browser looks for packages as subdirectories at the CODEBASE URL.

Chapter 9

Recycle This Code

● ●

In This Chapter

▶ Using the AWT graphic user interface tools

▶ Responding to the user's interaction

▶ Working with GUI layout structures

▶ Reading Java Class Library documentation

● ●

The Java Class Library provides a number of prewritten classes that you can use directly to create useful applets. Among the most useful are the basic graphic user interface objects, such as buttons, check boxes, and drop-down lists. This chapter gives you a guided tour through these GUI objects and through the Java Class Library documentation that you will refer to when you use them.

Getting Started

To set up a graphical user interface for an applet, you must take care of two issues:

✔ Putting the GUI objects on the screen

✔ Responding to user input

Chapter 5 gives you an example of how to display and respond to a button. The Java Class Library documentation tells you everything that you need to know to do it again.

Looking it up

To use a class that someone else has written for you, you need to know its constructors, its public methods, and something about what it does. For classes in the Java library, you can find all this necessary information in the

Java API (applications programming interface) documentation. The Java documentation is available online at `http://www.javasoft.com/doc.html`. It is also provided as a component of some programming toolkits.

The documentation is organized by package. A class index exists for each package. The GUI classes are located in the `java.awt` package. So, to find out about the `Button` class, for example, look it up in the class index of the AWT (Abstract Windowing Toolkit) package.

The Java Class Library documentation is an HTML hypertext document. You move around in the documentation by clicking on the hypertext links. This documentation was created by using Javadoc to pull comments from the source code of the Java class libraries.

If you follow the references for `Button`, you find the following:

✔ A family tree diagram

✔ A list of constructors, briefly explained

✔ A list of methods, briefly explained

The family tree diagram tells you the parent classes of `Button`. This is important information, because `Button` inherits the methods of its parents. Although the methods you are most interested in are usually the methods defined in the class itself, sometimes you need to check what other methods are available. The family tree diagram lets you check on the methods of parent classes.

Setup

To set up the button, you are primarily interested in its constructors. Keep following the hypertext links and you can find the information you need to instantiate a button with a label.

```
public Button(String label)  Constructs a Button with a string label.
                              Parameters: label - the button label
```

The constructor code goes in the definition of the applet or object where the GUI control appears.

```
String southString = "South";
Button southButton = new Button(southString);
```

Response

When a GUI object exists, user interaction with the object causes events. Events are posted to all the objects in your applet. Whichever object is to do the responding must have a method that responds to the appropriate event message.

More often than not, the response to the GUI event does not happen in the GUI object. Instead, it is the applet itself, or some other component of the applet, that responds to the click on the button or whatever. For example, in the Programmer's Activity Box applet in Chapter 5, the applet is in charge of responding to a button press. The applet's action method checks for an event containing the label of the button and passes on instructions telling it what to do to the object that actually responds — the Center Center Panel —

```
public boolean action(Event evt, Object what) {
     if (southString.equals(what)) {
         ccp.setBackground(Color.blue);
         ccp.blankNameTag();
         ccp.repaint();
         return true;
     }
     return false;
}
```

The documentation of the Event class includes a list of the static variables that represent all the standard kinds of events. The list is long, but we show you a few examples:

Static Variable	Kind of Event
ACTION_EVENT	An action event
DOWN	Pressing the down arrow key
END	Pressing the end key
F1	Pressing the F1 function key
GOT_FOCUS	A component gained the focus
KEY_PRESS	The key press keyboard event
LIST_SELECT	
MOUSE_DOWN	The mouse down event.
MOUSE_DRAG	The mouse drag event.
MOUSE_ENTER	The mouse enter event
SCROLL_LINE_DOWN	The line down scroll event.

The component class, which is a parent of everything that appears on-screen, has methods for responding to events. These placeholder, do-nothing methods are the ones that must be replaced when you want a particular object to respond to one or more types of events. Again, the list of methods is long. A number of methods handle only one specific type of event. Others, such as `action,` respond to a variety of event types. Some examples follow:

Method	Event Handled
`action(Event, Object)`	Called if an action occurs in the Component.
`gotFocus(Event, Object)`	Indicates that this component has received the input focus.
`handleEvent(Event)`	Handles the event.
`keyDown(Event, int)`	Called if a character is pressed.
`mouseDown(Event, int, int)`	Called if the mouse is down.
`mouseDrag(Event, int, int)`	Called if the mouse is dragged (the mouse button is down).

An Activity Box for More Mature Programmers

By referring to the AWT documentation, you can put together an applet that demonstrates each type of GUI user control. One block of code creates the controls and adds them to a panel. Another block of code responds to the events generated by the GUI controls. The finished product looks something like Figure 9-1.

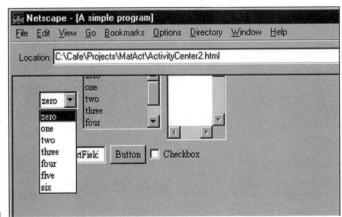

Figure 9-1: Activity box for more mature programmers.

Button

A button generates an event when the user clicks on it with the mouse (see Figure 9-2). We've already used examples of the code to instantiate a button and the code to respond to a user's click on a button — in the "Setup" section of this chapter and in Chapter 5.

Figure 9-2:
A button.

Check box

A check box may be either checked or blank (see Figure 9-3). When the user clicks on the check box, the check box changes its state. If the check box is blank, it becomes checked; if the check box is checked, it becomes blank.

Figure 9-3:
A blank
check box.

An applet can refer to the check box variable that keeps track of the state of the check box. An applet can also respond to the event generated when a check box changes state.

Variable	Activity
Checkbox()	Constructs a check box with no label, no check box group, and initialized to a false state.
Checkbox(String)	Constructs a check box with the specified label, no check box group, and initialized to a false state.

When you first create a check box, its state is always `false` — that is to say, not checked.

```
Checkbox myCheckbox = new Checkbox("Checkbox");
```

If you want to make it begin life on the screen with a check mark in it, you must use the `setState` method to change its state:

```
myCheckbox.setState(true);
```

When the user clicks on a check box, the check box changes state and generates an ACTION_EVENT. You can watch for a checkbox event and display a message in the status bar of the browser with code like the following. The `showStatus()` method displays a string in the status bar of the browser.

```
public boolean action(Event evt, Object what) {
    if (what == myCheckbox) {
        if (myCheckbox.getState()==true) {
            showStatus("Checkbox: True");
        }
        else {
            showStatus("Checkbox: False");
        }
        return true;
    }
    return false;
}
```

Check box group, AKA radio buttons

The check box group GUI control is often referred to as *radio buttons* because the group behaves like the buttons on a car radio. Whenever one button in the group is selected, it turns off or deselects whatever other button in the group is currently selected. The check box group enforces a single choice among a group of options (see Figure 9-4).

Figure 9-4:
A check
box group.

To use a check box group, you must instantiate a check box group as well as each of its check boxes.

`CheckboxGroup()`	Creates a new check box group.
`Checkbox(String, CheckboxGroup, boolean)`	Constructs a check box with the specified label, specified check box group, and specified boolean state.

The following code sets up a check box group:

```
CheckboxGroup myCheckboxGroup = newCheckboxGroup();
...
Checkbox[] checkList = new Checkbox[5];
...
    public void init() {
        add(checkList[0] = new
          Checkbox("zero",myCheckboxGroup,true));
        add(checkList[1] = new
          Checkbox("one",myCheckboxGroup,false));
        add(checkList[2] = new
          Checkbox("two",myCheckboxGroup,false));
        add(checkList[3] = new
          Checkbox("three",myCheckboxGroup,false));
        add(checkList[4] = new
          Checkbox("four",myCheckboxGroup,false));
    ...
    }
```

By now, you should be comfortable enough with Java to handle the following code for responding to a check box group event. Read it carefully. The code has two noteworthy features:

- A monster OR condition, denoted by the ‖ symbol
- A chained method call — checkboxGroup.getCurrent().getLabel(), which means "Get the label of the current selection of the check box group."

```
public boolean action(Event evt, Object what) {
    if ((what == checkList[0]) || (what == checkList[1]) ||
        (what == checkList[2]) || (what == checkList[3]) ||
        (what == checkList[4])){
                showStatus("Radio button
                "+checkboxGroup.getCurrent().getLabel());
                return true;
    }
    return false;
}
```

Thing [0] and Thing [1]

This title and the following code snippet for handling check box groups both use array notation. Arrays may be new to you if you have never done any programming.

The use of square brackets following a name in a variable declaration indicates that you are setting up a series of parallel items. Rather than give them separate names, you treat them as a group and refer to them by number — checkList[0], checkList[1], and so on.

In a variable declaration, [ ] indicates an array. A number inside the brackets indicates how many items are in the array. For example, Checkbox[5] means an array of five check boxes. The meaning of the following code is "Instantiate an array of five check boxes and name it checkList."

```
Checkbox[] checkList = new
    Checkbox[5];
```

You may refer to the individual check boxes as checkList[0], checkList[1], and so on. You may even refer to checkList[n] and compute a value of n someplace to tell the computer which particular check box in the array interests you.

Oh, by the way, one of the charming little quirks that Java has inherited from its Bell Labs ancestors is that it begins counting at zero. So, the first item in an array is always item [0].

"Should array indices start at 0 or 1? My compromise of 0.5 was rejected without, I thought, proper consideration." - Stan Kelly-Bootle

You have a choice

The Choice GUI object looks different from a check box group but has the same effect of forcing a single selection from a group of alternatives (see Figure 9-5).

Figure 9-5:
A choice.

To set up a choice, you declare and instantiate the Choice object; then you add items to it and add the object to the applet.

```
. . . .
Choice myChoice = new Choice();
. . . .
public void init() {
    . . .
    myChoice.addItem("zero");
    myChoice.addItem("one");
    myChoice.addItem("two");
    myChoice.addItem("three");
    myChoice.addItem("four");
    myChoice.addItem("five");
    myChoice.addItem("six");
        add(myChoice); //this adds the choice component to the
                applet panel
    . . .
}
```

To respond to the list selection, the object that is responding to your applet needs to read the name of the choice returned by the event.

```
public boolean action(Event evt, Object what) {
    if (what == myChoice) {
        showStatus("Choice "+evt.arg);
        return true;
    }
    return false;
}
```

You have more than one choice

List is another GUI control that resembles Choice, but its capabilities are quite different (see Figure 9-6).

Figure 9-6:
A list.

When you use a list, you may set up the list to permit the selection of more than one item. Also, using the List class provides you with a number of methods to manipulate the contents of the list after it has been instantiated. Just to give you an idea of what can be done, here is a selected list of methods (refer to the AWT documentation for the full list):

Method	Action Performed
`addItem(String)`	Adds the specified item to the end of scrolling list
`clear()`	Clears the list
`countItems()`	Returns the number of items in the list
`delItem(int)`	Deletes an item from the list
`delItems(int, int)`	Deletes multiple items from the list
`deselect(int)`	Deselects the item at the specified index
`getItem(int)`	Gets the item associated with the specified index
`getRows()`	Returns the number of visible lines in this list
`getSelectedIndex()`	Gets the selected item on the list or -1 if no item is selected
`getSelectedIndexes()`	Returns the selected indexes on the list
`getSelectedItem()`	Returns the selected item on the list or null if no item is selected
`getSelectedItems()`	Returns the selected items on the list
`isSelected(int)`	Returns true if the item at the specified index has been selected; false otherwise
`makeVisible(int)`	Forces the item at the specified index to be visible
`replaceItem(String,int)`	Replaces the item at the given index
`select(int)`	Selects the item at the specified index
`setMultipleSelections (boolean)`	Sets whether this list should allow multiple selections or not

User interaction with a `List` object generates three different kinds of events. When a user double-clicks on a list item (as you might when selecting a file to run or open in a typical Windows application), the list generates an `ACTION_EVENT`. In addition, each time that the user clicks on an item to select it or deselect it, the list generates a `LIST_SELECT` or `LIST_DESELECT` event with the index number of the selected item.

If you wish to respond to `LIST_SELECT` or `LIST_DESELECT`, you can't use the action method. But another method allows you to handle any event. Cleverly enough, it is called `handleEvent`.

handleEvent

When you are handling a variety of events in one place, it is more elegant to write one `handleEvent` method that catches all kinds of events at once and then uses contingent statements to sort out what to do. When you use handleEvent, you must write a separate expression to test Event.arg, the event-specific information that tells you exactly what happened. This next code is an example of a handleEvent method.

```java
public boolean handleEvent(Event event) {
    switch(event.id) {
        case Event.ACTION_EVENT:
            if (event.target == myButton) {
                showStatus("Button: OK");
            }
            else if (event.target == myCheckbox) {
                if (myCheckbox.getState()) {
                    showStatus("Checkbox: True");
                }
                else {
                    showStatus("Checkbox: False");
                }
            }
            else if ((event.target == checkList[0]) ||
                    (event.target == checkList[1]) ||
                    (event.target == checkList[2]) ||
                    (event.target == checkList[3]) ||
                    (event.target == checkList[4])) {
                showStatus("Radio button " +
                myCheckboxGroup.getCurrent().getLabel());
            }
            else if (event.target == myChoice) {
                showStatus("Choice "+event.arg);
            }
            else if (event.target == myList) {
                showStatus("List "+event.arg);
            }
        case Event. LIST_SELECT:
            showStatus("List item " + toString
                            (event.arg) + "selected" );
        case Event. LIST_DESELECT:
            showStatus("List item " + toString
                            (event.arg) + "deselected" );
        }
    return false;
}
```

Put it in writing

Two Java GUI controls allow the user to input text: the text field and the text area. A text field accepts only one line of text. When the user presses the Enter key, the text field generates an ACTION_EVENT that reports the text string in the field.

The ACTION_EVENT and text string generated by a text field in which the user types **OK** is exactly the same as the ACTION_EVENT and text string generated when the user clicks on a button labeled OK. You need to check the event.target that is a property of the event to make sure that you are responding to a button, not a text field.

```
if (event.target == myButton) {
              showStatus("Button: OK");
}
```

A text area accepts multiline input. It does not generate an action event when the user presses the Enter key. Instead, it simply moves on to a new line in the text area as shown in Figure 9-7.

Figure 9-7:
A text field
and a text
area.

The usual way for an applet to find out the contents of a text field or text area is to wait for a cue from some other control and then use the getText() method.

For example:

```
if (event.target == button) {
    showStatus(textField.getText());
}
```

Go to the Library Often

Building on the examples in this chapter, you should be able to assemble a user interface that includes any of the standard GUI components. If you want to do something that is not included in our examples, look in the Java API documentation under the name of the class with which you want to work — button, check box, text area, and so on. Browse for a method that sounds like the one you want and read the description. Then do some experimenting.

Look out for the window

Our examples have been built on applets and panels. As you look at the class library, you will see that Window and Frame are also available. These objects have the typical GUI close buttons, as well as the other features you would expect. For example, a Frame has a title bar and may have a menu. The procedures for adding GUI controls to a Frame are exactly the same ones already covered in this chapter. You can add a MenuBar with Menus consisting of MenuItems to a Frame. But we have a caution to add.

A Frame or a Window introduces an additional layer of complication in handling events and passing them on to other objects. Also, Frames and Windows expect you to be able to iconify or minimize the object and to close it. For applets that reside on a WWW page, the added benefits often do not justify the added complexity. In any event, before you undertake working with windows and frames, make sure that you are fluent working with GUI controls on applets and panels.

More layouts

As you explore the contents of Java.awt, you will find three more Layouts — GridLayout, GridBagLayout, and CardLayout. GridLayout lets you set up a simple table of rows and columns. You can then place components in any given cell (see Figure 9-8).

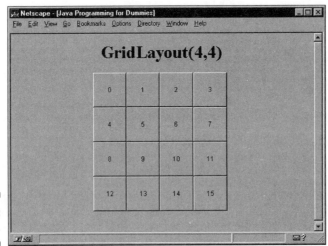

Figure 9-8:
GridLayout.

GridBagLayout lets you build a complex layout based on combinations of grid cells (see Figure 9-9). You will find an extensive explanation of GridBagLayout in the Java API docmentation.

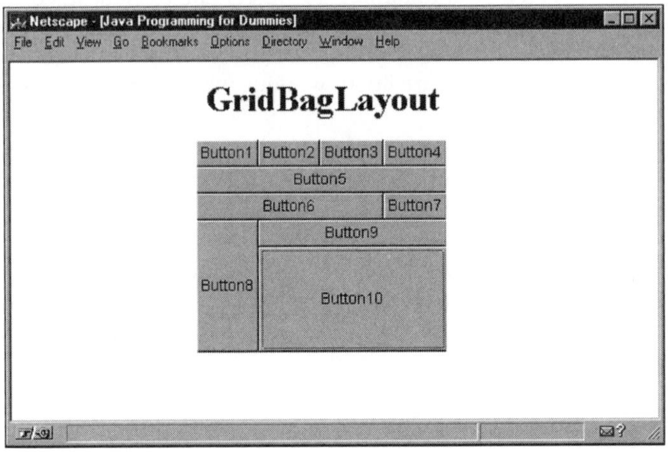

Figure 9-9:
GridBagLayout.

CardLayout lets you fill a space with multiple layers, like a tabbed notebook (see Figure 9-10).

Figure 9-10:
CardLayout.

A Little Code For Dessert

Here is some sample code to get you started in using GUI objects. Experiment
with the effects of giving your applet different dimensions on the HTML page.
You might also want to try out some different layouts. And, test the `resize()`
method that will allow you to adjust the size of components so that the Layout
does not exercise complete control of the size of components on-screen.

```
/** This is an activityCenter for more mature Java program-
          mers.
 */
import java.awt.*;
import java.applet.*;

public class ActivityCenter extends Applet {
    Button myButton = new Button("Button");
    Checkbox myCheckbox = new Checkbox("Checkbox");
    Choice myChoice = new Choice();
    List myList = new List(5,false);
    TextArea myTextArea = new TextArea(5,10);
    TextField myTextField = new TextField("TextField");
    CheckboxGroup myCheckboxGroup = new CheckboxGroup();
    Checkbox[] checkList = new Checkbox[5];
```

(continued)

(continued)

```
public void init() {

    add(checkList[0] = new
        Checkbox("zero",myCheckboxGroup,true));
    add(checkList[1] = new
        Checkbox("one",myCheckboxGroup,false));
    add(checkList[2] = new
        Checkbox("two",myCheckboxGroup,false));
    add(checkList[3] = new
        Checkbox("three",myCheckboxGroup,false));
    add(checkList[4] = new
        Checkbox("four",myCheckboxGroup,false));

    myChoice.addItem("zero");
    myChoice.addItem("one");
    myChoice.addItem("two");
    myChoice.addItem("three");
    myChoice.addItem("four");
    myChoice.addItem("five");
    myChoice.addItem("six");
    add(myChoice);

    myList.addItem("zero");
    myList.addItem("one");
    myList.addItem("two");
    myList.addItem("three");
    myList.addItem("four");
    myList.addItem("five");
    myList.addItem("six");
    add(myList);

    add(myTextArea);
    add(myTextField);

    add(myButton);
    add(myCheckbox);
}

    public boolean handleEvent(Event event) {
        switch(event.id) {
            case Event.ACTION_EVENT:
```

```
                if (event.target == myButton) {
                    showStatus("Button: OK");
                }
                else if (event.target == myCheckbox) {
                    if (myCheckbox.getState()) {
                        showStatus("Checkbox: True");
                    }
                    else {
                        showStatus("Checkbox: False");
                    }
                }
                else if ((event.target ==
                                checkList[0]) ||
                         (event.target ==
                                checkList[1]) ||
                         (event.target ==
                                checkList[2]) ||
                         (event.target ==
                                checkList[3]) ||
                         (event.target ==
                                checkList[4]))    {
                showStatus("Radio button
"+MyCheckboxGroup.getCurrent().getLabel());
                }
                else if (event.target == myChoice) {
                    showStatus("Choice "+event.arg);
                }
                else if (event.target == myList) {
                    showStatus("List "+event.arg);
                }
                else if (event.target == myTextField) {
                    showStatus("TextField
                        "+event.arg);
                }
                else if (event.target == myTextArea) {
                    showStatus("TextArea
                        "+event.arg);
                }
            }
        return false;
    }
}
```

Chapter 10

Finding Your Type

· ·

In This Chapter

▶ Describing data types for numbers and letters

▶ Using `integers`, `longs`, `floats`, and `doubles`

▶ Converting numbers among the number data types

▶ Using math library functions

▶ Using class wrappers

▶ Dividing letters into characters and strings

▶ Identifying characters and special codes

▶ Editing, comparing, and analyzing strings

· ·

*A*n important fact of human communication (and miscommunication) is that the meaning of a statement depends on what type of object the statement is about. When you say "Don't mix apples and oranges," essentially, you are talking about *data types*. In their famous vaudevillian routine "Who's on First . . ." Abbott and Costello were experiencing a data-typing problem. (The expression *Who* referred to an object of data type *name of baseball player*, instead of an object of data type *interrogative pronoun*.)

Java insists on knowing the type of every item of data at all times. For example, Java requires you to name the data type for every variable at the time you set up the variable. This feature makes Java what programming gurus call a *strongly-typed* language.

In other sections of the book, we touched on several of the standard Java data types in passing. In this chapter, we review all the basic types.

About Data Types

As you know, the computer represents all data as patterns of ones and zeros. But sometimes the ones and zeros are interpreted as a number, sometimes as a letter, and so on. If you or the computer lose track of how a particular pattern of ones and zeros is to be interpreted, the resulting interpretation may be amusing or catastrophic, but it's rarely what you intended.

The following sections tell you all about describing your data types. We divide our discussion into two primary categories of data, numbers and letters. Within these primary categories, we talk about specific data types and the methods that you can use to work with them. And we hope the discussion helps you get the data interpretation results that you intend!

Categorizing Your Numbers

Most computers are built around the idea of using a standard amount of memory space for each number. This design enables computers to do mathematical computations very quickly, but it also imposes some limitations on how large or how accurate a number may be. You find two basic types of numbers to work with in Java, as in most computer languages.

- **Whole numbers:** When working with whole numbers, we never round things off. Instead, we always use exact numbers. The financial industry likes to use whole numbers because the results are then accurate to the last penny (if you are counting in pennies). The disadvantage of working with whole numbers is that you may run out of space to represent numbers and some fractions and other numbers can't be represented with reasonable accuracy using only whole numbers.

- **Fractional numbers:** With fractional numbers, we represent numbers as a whole number plus a decimal fraction. The fractional number type enables you to handle much larger and smaller numbers, but only to a certain number of decimal places of accuracy.

Java has four different types of whole numbers and two types of fractional numbers. The data types differ in whether they are whole numbers or fractional numbers and in how much memory space is allocated to each number.

Describing whole numbers

Java uses the following data types for whole numbers:

- byte: An 8-bit whole number; a byte can only be a whole number between –128 and +127.

✔ **short:** A 16-bit whole number; a short number can be a whole number between –32768 and +32767 only.

✔ **int:** A 32-bit whole number; an int number can be a whole number between –2147483648 and +2147483647 only.

✔ **long:** A 64-bit whole number; a long number can be a whole number between –9223372036854775808 and +9223372036854775807 only.

To give you a sense of scale, you can't quite compute the national debt accurate to the penny as an int, but you can comfortably do so by using a long. The data types byte and short are rarely used. For most purposes, you can use int even when you could get away with using a byte or short.

Describing fractional numbers

Java uses the following data types for fractional numbers:

✔ **float:** A 32-bit floating point number as large as + or –3.40282347 times 10 to the 38th power. A float number can be exactly zero or a fraction as close to zero as + or – 1.40239846 times 10 to the –45 power.

✔ **double:** A 64-bit floating point number as large as + or –1.79769313486231570 times 10 to the 308th power. A double number can be exactly zero or a fraction as close to zero as + or – 4.94065645841246544 times 10 to the –324 power.

Unless you are doing scientific calculations that require an unusually high degree of precision or exceptionally large numbers, you are not likely to use doubles. And unless you make other arrangements, when a number has more than six digits the computer displays floats and doubles in a special notation, as follows:

1.239874E5 means 1.239874 times 10 to the fifth power. That is, 1.239874 × 100,000 = 12,39874.

2.431502E-2 means 2.431502 times 10 to the –2 power. That is 2.431502 × 0.01 = 0.02431502.

5.632714E9 means 5.632714 × 1,000,000,000 = 5,632,714,000.

1.354321E-4 means 1.354321 × 0.0001 = 0.0001354321

If you want to avoid this *scientific notation,* you must write your own method to convert the number to a string of the form you desire.

What you can do with numbers

You can perform all the basic arithmetic operations with any of the six number types describe in the previous sections. That is, you can add, subtract, multiply and divide; you indicate these operations in the code by using the operators +, -, *, and /, respectively. You cannot mix different number data types in the same computation.

A warning about division. When you divide fractional numbers — float and double, the result is carried out to as many decimal places as are available and then rounded off. When you divide whole numbers — byte, short, int, long — the result is not rounded off. Instead, any remainder after division is simply dropped.

For example, 5/2==2. Programmers call this action *truncation*. If you want to find the remainder, you can use a special operator called the *remainder operator* (%) that calculates the remainder only, for example, 5%2==1. That is, when you divide 5 by 2, the remainder is 1. Also, 13/4==3, and 13%4==1.

Table 10-1 gives a short summary of the operations that you can perform with numbers.

Table 10-1   A Summary of Mathematical Operations in Java

Operator	Code Line	What It Means
+	`intx = inta+intb;` `floatx = floata+floatb;`	Set x equal to a + b.
-	`intx = inta-intb;` `floatx = floata-floatb;`	Set x equal to a - b.
*	`intx = inta*intb;` `floatx = floata*floatb;`	Set x equal to a * b.
/	`intx = inta/intb;` `floatx = floata/floatb;`	Set x equal to a / b. For int, short, and long, the result is truncated.
%	`intx = inta%intb;`	Set x equal to the remainder of a / b. Applies only to int, short, and long.
+=	`intx += inta;` `floatx += floata;`	Add a to the old value of x and save the result as x.
-=	`intx -= inta;` `floatx -= floata;`	Subtract a from the old value of x and save the result as x.
*=	`intx *= inta;` `floatx *= floata;`	Multiply a by the old value of x and save the result as x.
/=	`intx /= inta;` `floatx /= floata;`	Divide the old value of x by a and save the result as x.

Remember, the grouping of mathematical operations makes a difference. Consider the following example:

```
(4 × 5) + 3 = 23
```

but

```
4 × (5 + 3) = 32
```

You should always use parentheses to group mathematical operations to clarify what is going on in your mind and to make sure that the calculations are executed in the correct order.

Numbers in an object wrapper

You cannot mix the data types for numbers together in computations, but you can always convert from one type of number to another. As a general rule, you should specifically convert all numbers in a computation to the same type before you perform the computation, for example, adding up a column of numbers.

The Java Class Library includes a group of number classes in the `java.lang` package. The parent class for all these classes is called `Number`. Each of the classes that extends `Number` has a similar set of methods that take care of a variety of useful conversions. If you expect to need any of these number conversions, you declare and instantiate an object *wrapper* instead of relying on the basic "unwrapped" number type.

If your number is instantiated in an object wrapper, that is, if you declared an instance of the appropriate number class, you can use these forms of conversion:

Object Method	*What It Does*
`myNumber.doubleValue()`	Returns a number in the `double` data type.
`myNumber.intValue()`	Returns a number in the `int` data type.
`myNumber.floatValue()`	Returns a number in the `float` data type.
`myNumber.longValue()`	Returns a number in the `long` data type.
`myNumber.toString()`	Returns a string representing the printed value of the number.

If you have not instantiated an object wrapper, you can use the class methods to make conversions. For example:

Class Method	What It Does
`Integer.doubleValue(myNumber)`	Converts `myNumber`, which happens to be an `Integer`, to its `double` value.
`Long.doubleValue(myNumber)`	Converts `myNumber`, which happens to be a `Long`, to its `double` value.
`Double.intValue(myNumber)`	Converts `myNumber`, which happens to be a `Double`, to its `int` value.

When a number is represented as a string — for example, when used as an applet parameter — you can convert the string back to a number:

Class Method	What It Does
`Integer.parseInt(myString)`	Translates `myString` to its `integer` form.
`Long.parseLong(myString)`	Translates `myString` to its `long` form.

Using Special Mathematical Functions

If you are in need of special mathematical functions or values, study the Java API (Application Programming Interface) documentation for `java.lang.math`. This class has a number of class methods that make standard mathematical functions and constants available to you. The next listing shows you a few samples:

Math Class Function	What It Does
`Math.E`	Enables you to use the constant **e**.
`Math.PI`	Enables you to use the constant π.
`Math.abs(myNumber)`	Returns the absolute value of `myNumber`.

Math Class Function	What It Does
`Math.max (myNumber, yourNumber)`	Returns the greater of two numbers.
`Math.pow(myNumber, exponent)`	Raises a number to a power, for example, `pow(4²)= 42=16`.
`Math.random()`	Generates a pseudorandom number between 0.0 and 1.0.
`Math.sqrt(myNumber)`	Returns the square root of `myNumber`.

You also find a full set of trigonometric functions, and so on. Check out the `java.lang.math` documentation!

Categorizing Your Letters

When dealing with letters and words, we need some different data types. Java has two basic data types that enable us to work with letters and words, rather than numbers.

Describing characters

The data type `char` is for a single character. Java uses the *Unicode* standard to represent characters. That is, Java allows 16 bits to represent each character. Unicode represents not only the Latin alphabet, but also a wide variety of other scripts and character sets. In this book, we work only with the ASCII - Latin alphabet subset of Unicode, because most hardware systems offer only minimal support for other alphabets as yet. In theory, you could write your Java applet to handle strings in Armenian or Thai or Han ideographs.

To represent a `char` value, type the character within single quotation marks — `'a'`. A few special `char` values represent special codes that you cannot type directly — backspace, tab, and so on. You can represent each special code by using an *escape sequence* that consists of the \ character followed by another character. See Table 10-2 for these special characters, their associated escape sequences, and ASCII character numbers.

Table 10-2   Representing Special char Values in Java

Special Function	*Escape Sequence*	*ASCII Number*
backspace	\b	8
horizontal tab	\t	9
newline	\n	10
formfeed	\f	12
carriage return	\r	13
double quote	\"	34
single quote	\'	39
backslash	\\	92

Suppose that you want to test whether myChar is a backspace character; you can write the testing code like this:

```
if (myChar=='\b') {
    do something;
}
```

Also, an object wrapper for char, named Character, offers some useful class methods:

Method	*What It Does*
Character.isDigit(myCharacter)	Returns true if myCharacter is a digit — 0123456789.
Character.isUpperCase(myCharacter)	Returns true if myCharacter is an uppercase letter.
Character.isLowerCase(myCharacter)	Returns true if myCharacter is a lowercase letter.
Character.isSpace(myCharacter)	Returns true if myCharacter is white space (space, tab, or so on).

The following sample code snippet uses some `Character` methods. Suppose that you want to evaluate a keyboard response to a multiple-choice question. The user's response is saved as:

```
char userInput
If (Character.isUpperCase(userInput)) {
    switch (userInput) {
        case 'A': statements; break;
        case 'B': statements; break;
        ...
        default: statements; break;
        }
    }
If (Character.isLowerCase(userInput)) {
    switch (userInput) {
        case 'a': statements; break;
        case 'b': statements; break;
        ...
        default: statements; break;
        }
    }
```

Working with strings in Java

The second data type for letters, `String`, works with letters as a series of characters — from one letter to many words. `Strings` have a special status in Java; they are allowed to break the rules of object-oriented style. `Strings` can be manipulated with the + operator and do not require formal instantiation. These departures from the normal Java style for handling objects are a concession to the millions of programmers who are used to handling strings in a certain way and who must work with strings every day.

`String` is a class that instantiates itself whenever needed. The formal way to declare and instantiate a string is perfectly acceptable:

```
String myString = new String ("Foo!");
```

However, simply saying the following is equally acceptable:

```
String myString = "Foo!";
```

Also, you can combine two strings by using the + operator. For example, if AString equals "Hello " and Bstring equals "World," you can combine them with this next statement:

```
CString = AString + Bstring;
```

The resulting string is "Hello World."

The technical term for combining two strings is *concatenate*. When used with strings, the + sign is the *concatenation* operator.

By the way, if you want to be an object-oriented purist, you can use a method called concat that does exactly the same thing as the operator + for strings. For example, you can say either of the following:

```
CString = AString.concat (BString);
```

or

```
CString = AString + BString;
```

The String *methods*

A number of methods enable you to do interesting things with strings. You can find descriptions of all these methods in the Java API documentation, but the following overview can help orient you to the kind of methods available.

- ✔ **Edit:** One family of methods lets you make changes to strings. You can convert a string to all uppercase or all lowercase. And you can substitute one character for another everywhere that character appears in the string.

- ✔ **Compare:** Another family of methods lets you make comparisons between strings. You can test whether two strings have the same contents, whether they start or end with the same characters, and so on.

- ✔ **Analyze:** A last family of methods lets you identify and pull out the letters from particular positions in a string. For example, you can pull out the first letter, or the third letter, or the second through tenth letters of a string. And you can find where in a string a particular character appears.

Editing methods

You can use edit methods to change or format a string. For example, you may want to make sure that user input is consistently received in all uppercase or all lowercase letters. That way, you can make consistent comparisons and enforce consistent appearance of text. To convert a string to all uppercase or all lowercase, use the appropriate method:

```
newString=myString.toLowerCase;
newString=myString.toUpperCase;
```

You can also replace a given character with another one. For example if you want to replace all appearances of the letter A with the number 1, you might write this line of code:

```
newString=myString.replace('A', '1');
```

If you want to get rid of white space at the beginning and end of a string, you can use the trim method:

```
newString=myString.trim()
```

Comparison methods

Comparison methods return a true or false answer and may be used in selection and iteration statements.

You must use the `equals` method to compare strings. Java enables you to make a comparison of strings by using the == operator, but the result may be misleading. To Java, == means that both strings have the same location in computer memory, which may be true for some strings that are identical, but is not true for all strings.

The following are `equals` methods that you may use; they're pretty self-explanatory, but remember that they each return a logical value (that is, true or false).

```
(myString.equals(AString))
(myString.equalsIgnoreCase(AString))
(myString.endsWith("ed"))
(myString.StartsWith("http://"))
```

Analyze methods

You can pick a string apart character by character with the analyze methods. For example, suppose that you are analyzing a URL, an Internet address. You want to find the first dot and then pick out the character immediately following it. The following code finds the *index* — the position number in the string — of the first dot and then finds the character at that-position-plus-one.

```
key = tempAddress.charAt(1+indexOf('.'))
```

Other methods let you find *substrings* (that is, part of a string), the last index of a particular character or substring (if that element appears more than once), and so on. Another handy method tells you the length of a string.

```
n=myString.length()
```

You had a preview of working with these methods in Chapter 7.

Other Data Types

As you become more a more sophisticated programmer, you develop a library of classes of your own that impose rules about what operations are permitted and how to convert between one class and another. Keep in mind the model of how the basic Java types behave. For example, you may develop a class called `Prospect` that organizes name and address information about people, and you may also develop a class called `Customer`. You probably want to write a `Prospect.toCustomer` method that enables you to make the conversion in a planned way.

As you read the remaining chapters of this book, keep the data type model in mind as one way to reach a deeper understanding of the classes designed by the applet programmers.

Part III
Caffeinated Pages

The 5th Wave By Rich Tennant

"They're fruit flies, Rog. For gosh sake, how many Applets have you written today?!"

In this part . . .

*P*art III shows you how Java programming can be really fun and useful, too! In this part, we present a bevy of applets that help you practice your programming skills. This part gives you great, simple applets to expand upon that can stimulate your own creativity in the process.

The applets in Part III include a calendar that you can use in a variety of ways, scrolling ticker tapes and bouncing animations, framed input forms and lists of choices, fractals, and online shopping carts. Along with each specific example, we give you ideas for other ways to apply that applet's elements, techniques, and structures.

Chapter 11

A Calendar Class

*N*ow that we've covered some fundamentals, we want to take a look at a more sophisticated Java applet. If you ever use a computer program to track your personal finances, manage a project, or tally up your billable hours, you probably have to input dates — the date you write a check, the date you expect a project to be completed, the date you start your vacation.

Can We Meet Next Friday?

Some programs require you to input a date directly. To select November 7, 2000, you might type 11/7/2000, for example. Typing dates this way is fairly convenient for the computer but often inconvenient for people. Knowing what day a particular date falls on is helpful. You might remember that you wrote a check on Monday or that your best client prefers not to meet on Fridays. November 7 in the year 2000 may not mean much to you, but if we point out that it's the first Tuesday in November, you might recognize the date as another presidential election day in the United States.

To accommodate our human foibles and to reduce data-entry errors, current computer programs that require date input usually provide calendar-like interfaces — like the one pictured in Figure 11-1 — for selecting dates.

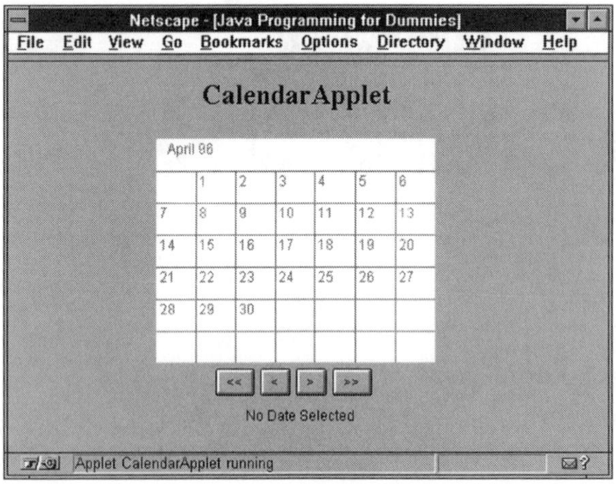

Figure 11-1:
A calendar-
style date
selector.

In the next few pages, we show you how to implement a calendar class that can be used to select dates using the familiar calendar-style interface. It's not a finished product, but it is a beginning upon which you can build to create an applet that you can use in your own Web sites.

The class that we envision has the following job description:

   ✔ It must display dates in a calendar format, one month at a time.

   ✔ It must allow the user to move backward and forward in steps of a month or a year by clicking on buttons.

   ✔ It must allow the user to select a date by clicking on it with the mouse.

With these modest ambitions, we move ahead.

Strategy

Spending a little time thinking about the big picture is a good idea before you get too involved in writing detailed applet code. Issues that are wise to consider include the following:

   ✔ What existing classes provide the behaviors that you want in your applet?

   ✔ What new classes do you need to create and where can you use existing classes unchanged?

   ✔ How will the user interact with the applet?

   ✔ How will the applet interact with the WWW page?

   ✔ What kinds of revisions can you anticipate and how can you make them easy?

Choosing your ancestors wisely

As the designer of a new Java class, you can choose the parents. What's more, you can have the class inherit whichever of your parents' capabilities and qualities that you want. To a large extent, your ability to get things done with Java, at least at first, is a measure of your ability to choose your ancestors wisely; that is, to find an existing Java class that meets — or nearly meets — your needs.

The basic Java Class Library includes hundreds of classes that provide the nuts and bolts of any Java applet. With time, you may buy or borrow additional Java classes that do the particular things your programs need to do. Sometimes you may need to build your own classes, as we do in these chapters.

As you might expect, related classes are usually grouped together in a *package*. You can't learn the entire Java Class Library at once, nor do you need to. Instead, you can work with one related group of classes at a time.

Where does our calendar fit in the family tree? Already, we know a lot. The calendar appears on-screen and responds to user input. In this regard, our calendar behaves a lot like some other objects we've seen: `Button`, `TextField`, and `Choice` come to mind. See the branches of the family tree in Figure 11-2.

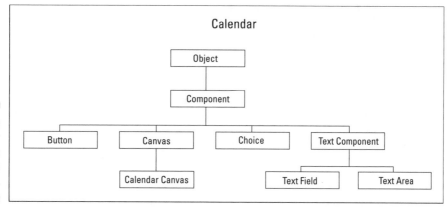

Figure 11-2: Calendar and its immediate family.

If you study the Java Class Library, you discover that all the objects that appear on screen and respond to user input are derived from the `Component` class. It would seem reasonable, then, to derive our calendar from `Component`. If you look further, however, you see that the `Canvas` class, derived from `Component`, is the one intended for use in constructing special-purpose GUI controls. We can derive our Calendar class from `Canvas`.

Don't write code if you don't have to

The buttons and labels in the standard Java AWT are sufficient for our purposes in this applet. The standard graphics methods are also plenty to create a calendar. All we need is to draw some straight lines and possibly fill in the color of some areas.

On the other hand, the buttons are intended to step forward and back a month and a year. The built-in Java date object does not have these capabilities. In this case, we need to extend the class by adding methods that allow us to step forward and back in units of a month or a year.

Talking with the user

Because we may want to use this code as a component in a larger applet, making the calendar behave in a way that is similar to other GUI components would be convenient. Objects such as `Button` and `Checkbox` communicate their outputs by posting events. A smart strategy is to use the same approach for the calendar. Then, using the `Calendar` object in combination with other GUI components, or as a replacement for another GUI component, is easy.

Making yourself (or your applet) at home on a page

An applet is a funny sort of computer program, really, because it lives as a guest within a Web page. Like any guest, your applet will be more welcome if it is considerate of its host. In particular, giving the host WWW page control over the appearance of your applet on-screen is a good idea. In this chapter, I show you how to let users specify your applet's size and color. This gives a Web page designer (perhaps you) an easy way to use your applet in a variety of pages, with different colors and different layouts, without having to modify Java source code to accommodate each change.

You can provide additional parameters to control background and foreground color. You can make the calendar large or small, red, blue, yellow or green, according to the needs of the particular Web page you are creating, just by using different parameters in the `<APPLET>` tag.

Code Me Some Code

The complete code for the Calendar applet appears in the section titled "The Complete and Unexpurgated Code." Before you look at the complete applet code, review these highlights.

Listening to the WWW page

The way that applet users communicate their preferences to an applet is with parameters embedded in the HTML <APPLET> tag. As you may recall, the APPLET tag requires at least a HEIGHT and WIDTH attribute as part of the basic tag. You can grab the values of the applet height and width as parameters, the same way you would grab any other applet parameters:

```
int height = Integer.parseInt(getParameter("height"));
int width = Integer.parseInt(getParameter("width"));
```

To work with the height and width values as numbers, you have to convert the string, returned by getParameter(), to an integer. The Integer class provides a static method, parseInt(), that does exactly that.

Remember that static methods, which are indicated by the keyword static in the method declaration, are special. They work even when you have not instantiated an object of their class. In other words, saying Integer height = new Integer is not necessary.

In the Calendar example, we just parse the "height" and "width" applet parameters. You see how to set background color and foreground color with parameters in the section called "Finishing Touches," but we leave the job of writing the final code to you.

Painting a pretty face

A large part of the calendar code is taken up with painting the calendar on the screen. Whenever we present a new month on screen, we display the month's name and we lay out the dates so that each date appears in the proper day column. Following are the graphics functions that we use:

- drawLine(x1, y1, x2, y2)
  This function is used draw lines that divide the canvas into a grid of seven rows and seven columns.

- clearRect(x, y, width, height)
  This function is used to clear the region at the top of the canvas to display the month name.

- drawString(string, x, y)
  This function is used to write out the month name and to display each date number in the appropriate column and row.

The applet uses two `for` loops to draw the lines on the calendar:

```
public void paint(Graphics g) {
        // paint the row dividers
  for (int i=rowHeight; i<r.height; i+=rowHeight) {
        g.drawLine(0, i, r.width, i);
    }
        // paint the column dividers
        for (int i=columnWidth; i<r.width; i+=columnWidth) {
            g.drawLine(i, rowHeight, i, r.height);
    }
```

The following code clears the area at the top of the calendar and writes out the month name. Notice that we must add a blank space — " " — between the MonthName and the Year. The last two parameters of the g.drawString ( ) method are the horizontal and vertical coordinates where the string will appear.

```
// paint the month name
g.clearRect(0, 0, r.width, rowHeight);
g.drawString(curDate.getMonthName() + " " +
        curDate.getYear(), 10, (rowHeight/2));
```

Handling current events

The applet has four buttons and a label for communicating with the user of the WWW page. The applet's `action` method tells how to handle button presses and mouse clicks, and how to communicate with the user. If you copy the monthCanvas class and install it in another applet, you need to put similar event-handling code in the new applet. For example, if you create an ExpenseAccount applet, the code you see below must be added to the action method of the ExpenseAccount class, along with any other code for handling other action events. See Chapter 5 and Chapter 9 for models of how to handle many events in one `action` or `handleEvent` method.

```
public boolean action(Event evt, Object arg) {
        if (arg.equals(" << ")) {
            monthCanvas.decrementYear();
        }
        else if (arg.equals(" < ")) {
            monthCanvas.decrementMonth();
        }
        else if (arg.equals(" > ")) {
            monthCanvas.incrementMonth();
        }
        else if (arg.equals(" >> ")) {
            monthCanvas.incrementYear();
```

```
    }
    else if (evt.target == monthCanvas) {

            selectLabel.setText("Selected: " +
            (String)evt.arg);
    }

        else { // if we don't handle this event, pass it on...
            return false;
        }
        return true;
    }
}
```

The selected date is passed on to the rest of the world in the form of an event. This allows another applet to easily use the date information in whatever way is appropriate to its needs. The Canvas posts the date selection event in its mouseDown method.

```
public boolean mouseDown(Event evt, int x, int y) {
        Date d = positionToDate(x, y);
        dateEvent.arg = (Integer.toString(d.getMonth()+1) +
            "/" + d.getDate());
        postEvent(dateEvent);
        return true;
    }
```

Java's date and my date

The basic work of the Calendar class requires calculations with dates. We need to calculate on which day of the week a particular date falls and to determine whether the year is a leap year. Or we need to get someone else to do it for us.

Fortunately, the Java util package includes a Date class that does most of what we want. The Date class provides the following methods:

✔ getTime(long)
    This function provides the current value of a date.

✔ setTime(long)
    This function sets the current value of a date.

To get the additional methods we need, we can extend the Java date class. The ISCdate class inherits the methods of the Java date class and spares us the work of researching how to identify leap years, and so on. But ISCdate

TIP

Labeling the Dates

To label the dates:

1. **Find the first day of the week.**

   The applet needs to know which column is the right place to begin putting in dates. That is, the applet needs to know what day of the week is the first of the month. The first block of code in this group locates the first day in the month and then backs up the date counter to whatever date is the Sunday before the first of the month.

   Reset the current date to the first of the month:

   ```
   curDate.setDate(1);
   ```

2. **Record the name of the current month:**

   ```
   int curMonth = curDate.getMonth();
   ```

   Back up the date to the first day in the row. For example, if the first of the month is on a Tuesday, back up two days so that the current date is the Sunday before the first of the month:

   ```
   curDate.decrement(curDate.getDay());
   firstDayInCalendarView.setTime (curDate.getTime());
   ```

3. **Paint the date for each day.**

   Nested `for` loops go through the cells of the calendar, painting the dates as they go. Note that dates outside the current month are skipped:

```
int column;
   for (int row=1; row<ROWS; row++) { // for each row...
       for (column=0; column<COLUMNS; column++) {
       // for each column... don't write date if not in current month
           if (curDate.getMonth() == curMonth) {
               g.drawString(Integer.toString(curDate.getDate()),
                   (column * columnWidth) + 3,
                   (row * rowHeight) + (rowHeight / 2) );
           }
           curDate.increment();
       }
   }
```

provides a way to increment and decrement the day without having to calculate in milliseconds each time. The class variable MILLISECONDS_PER_DAY lets us convert from time stated in milliseconds to units of a more convenient size.

```
private final static long MILLISECONDS_PER_DAY = 1000 * 60
        * 60 * 24;

/** increment to tomorrow */
public void increment() {
    increment(1);
}



/** increment by a specified number of days */
public void increment(int i) {
    setTime(getTime() + (MILLISECONDS_PER_DAY * i));
}
/** decrement to the first day of the current month last
        year.
        Sun's Date class, hence this class, start at UNIX
            Year Zero: 1970
*/
public void decrementYear() {
    setYear(getYear()-1);
    setDate(1);
}
```

Another feature we want for this calendar applet is to be able to label months by their names. So, we add a getMonthName() method.

Java dates

The Java Date class counts milliseconds since 12 a.m. Jan 1, 1970. A date in this form is very precise, but it is a very big number. Incidentally, no valid Java date exists before 1970 or after 2035. This date class is fine for many purposes, but for many others, you need to create your own class.

```
public String getMonthName() {
    String monthNames[] = {        "January", "February",
                                "March", "April", "May",
                                "June", "July", "August",
                                "September", "October",
                                "November", "December" };
    return monthNames[getMonth()];
}
```

If your applet is used in areas where English is not spoken, you may want to modify this method to adapt to local preferences.

The Complete and Unexpurgated Code

In this section, we give you the complete code for the applet class and each of the other classes it uses that are not part of the standard Java Class Library.

Calendar applet

```
/** CalendarApplet - an applet to demonstrate MonthCanvas.
    MonthCanvas displays a calendar-style interface to dates.
    @author <a href="mailto:dkoosis@iscinc.com">
    David Koosis</a>
    @version  0.1, 13 Feb 1996
    &copy; 1996 by <a href="http://www.iscinc.com/">
    ISC Consultants Inc.</a>, all rights reserved.
*/
import java.applet.Applet;
import java.awt.*;
import java.util.*;
import java.lang.*;
/** A simple applet which demonstrates the Calendar class */
public class CalendarApplet extends Applet {
    MonthCanvas monthCanvas = null;
    Label selectLabel = new Label("No Date Selected");

    public void init() {
      int height = Integer.parseInt(getParameter("height"));
      int width = Integer.parseInt(getParameter("width"));
      monthCanvas = new MonthCanvas(width,height-60);
```

```
        add(monthCanvas);
        add(new Button(" << "));
        add(new Button(" < "));
        add(new Button(" > "));
        add(new Button(" >> "));
        add(selectLabel);
    }


/** CalendarApplet handles two kinds of events:
        1) the button clicks which increment or decrement the
            current month
        2) the user-defined event which indicates that the user
            clicked on a date
    */
    public boolean action(Event evt, Object arg) {
        if (arg.equals(" << ")) {
            monthCanvas.decrementYear();
        }
        else if (arg.equals(" < ")) {
            monthCanvas.decrementMonth();
        }
        else if (arg.equals(" > ")) {
            monthCanvas.incrementMonth();
        }
        else if (arg.equals(" >> ")) {
            monthCanvas.incrementYear();
        }
        else if (evt.target == monthCanvas) {
            selectLabel.setText("Selected: " +
            (String)evt.arg);
        }
        else {
// if we don't handle this event, pass it on...
            return false;
        }
        return true;
    }
}
```

MonthCanvas class

```
/** MonthCanvas is a component to display dates with a
          calendar-style interface. */
class MonthCanvas extends Canvas {
    final static byte ROWS = 7; // rows in calendar
    final static byte COLUMNS = 7; // columns in calendar
    private ISCDate curDate = new ISCDate();
    private ISCDate tmpDate = new ISCDate();
    private ISCDate todayDate = new ISCDate();
    // date of the first Sunday (possibly from the preceding
          month)
    // in this calendar view
    private ISCDate firstDayInCalendarView = new ISCDate();
    private int rowHeight;
    private int columnWidth;
    private Rectangle r;
    private Dimension dimension = new Dimension(150,150);
    // a dateEvent is "posted" when the user clicks on a
    date.
    public Event dateEvent = new Event(this,
          Event.ACTION_EVENT, "dateEvent");
// Constructors
 public MonthCanvas() {
      initialize();
 }
public MonthCanvas(int width, int height) {
      reshape(0,0,width,height);
      initialize();
 }

    /** all constructors call this initialization method */
    private void initialize() {
        setBackground(Color.white);
        setForeground(Color.gray);
        r = bounds();
        columnWidth = r.width / COLUMNS;
        rowHeight = r.height / ROWS;
        // resize so that columns and rows fit evenly
        reshape(0,0,(columnWidth * COLUMNS),(rowHeight *
            ROWS));
        r = bounds();
        // save the height and width as a Dimension
        // for use by getPreferredSize() and getMinimumSize()
        dimension.width = r.width;
        dimension.height = r.height;
    }
```

```
public void incrementMonth() {
    curDate.incrementMonth();
    repaint();
}

public void decrementMonth() {
    curDate.decrementMonth();
    repaint();
}

public void incrementYear() {
    curDate.incrementYear();
    repaint();
}

public void decrementYear() {
    curDate.decrementYear();
    repaint();
}

public void paint(Graphics g) {
    // paint the row dividers
    for (int i=rowHeight; i<r.height; i+=rowHeight) {
        g.drawLine(0, i, r.width, i);
    }
    // paint the column dividers
    for (int i=columnWidth; i<r.width; i+=columnWidth) {
        g.drawLine(i, rowHeight, i, r.height);
    }
    // paint the month name
    g.clearRect(0, 0, r.width, rowHeight);
    g.drawString(curDate.getMonthName() + " " +
        curDate.getYear(), 10, (rowHeight/2));
// find the 1st (Sun)day in this calendar view
    tmpDate.setTime(curDate.getTime());
  curDate.setDate(1);
  int curMonth = curDate.getMonth();
    curDate.decrement(curDate.getDay());
    firstDayInCalendarView.setTime(curDate.getTime());
    // paint the dates
    int column;
```

(continued)

(continued)

```
        for (int row=1; row<ROWS; row++) { // for each row...
            for (column=0; column<COLUMNS; column++) {
            // for each column...
            if (curDate.getMonth() == curMonth) {
            g.drawString(Integer.toString(curDate.getDate()),
            (column * columnWidth) + 3,
            (row * rowHeight) + (rowHeight / 2) );
          }

                curDate.increment();
            }
        }
    // restore the date
    curDate.setTime(tmpDate.getTime());
}


    /** this internal routine returns the date corresponding
            to a position (x and y coordinate) in the current
            calendar view
    */
    private Date positionToDate(int x, int y) {
        int column = x / columnWidth;
        int row = (y / rowHeight) - 1;
        ISCDate returnDate = new ISCDate();
        returnDate.setTime(firstDayInCalendarView.getTime());
        returnDate.increment( (row * COLUMNS) + column );
        return returnDate;
    }


    /** When the user clicks on a date, "post" a dateEvent
            containing the selected date in M/D format.
            For example:  "12/15"
    */
    public boolean mouseDown(Event evt, int x, int y) {
        Date d = positionToDate(x, y);
        dateEvent.arg = (Integer.toString(d.getMonth()+1) +
            "/" + d.getDate());
        postEvent(dateEvent);
        return true;
    }


    /** Return the calendar's preferred size */
    public Dimension preferredSize() {
        return dimension;
```

```
    }

    /** Return the calendar's minimum size */
    public Dimension minimumSize() {
        return dimension;
    }

}
```

ISCDate class

```
/** A Date class with a few convenient routines not provided
            in Sun's date class.  To avoid name conflicts
            while retaining clarity,it would be best to put
            this class in a package and call it, say,
    COM.ISCInc.JPFD.Date.  Instead, we just call it ISCDate.
*/
class ISCDate extends Date implements Cloneable {

    private final static long MILLISECONDS_PER_DAY = 1000 * 60
            * 60 * 24;

    /** increment to tomorrow */
    public void increment() {
        increment(1);
    }

    /** increment by a specified number of days */
    public void increment(int i) {
        setTime(getTime() + (MILLISECONDS_PER_DAY * i));
    }

    /** decrement to yesterday */
    public void decrement() {
        decrement(1);
    }

    /** decrement by a specified number of days */
    public void decrement(int i) {
        setTime(getTime() - (MILLISECONDS_PER_DAY * i));
    }
```

(continued)

(continued)

```
/** increment to the first day of next month */
public void incrementMonth() {
    if ( getMonth() == 11 ) {
        setMonth(0);
        setYear(getYear()+1);
    }
    else {
        setMonth(getMonth()+1);
    }
    setDate(1);
}


/** decrement to the first day of last month */
public void decrementMonth() {
    if ( getMonth() == 0 ) {
        setMonth(11);
        setYear(getYear()-1);
    }
    else {
        setMonth(getMonth()-1);
    }
    setDate(1);
}


/** increment to the first day of the current month next
        year */
public void incrementYear() {
    setYear(getYear()+1);
    setDate(1);
}


/** decrement to the first day of the current month last
        year.
    Sun's Date class, hence this class, start at UNIX
        Year Zero: 1970
*/
public void decrementYear() {
    setYear(getYear()-1);
    setDate(1);
}


public String getMonthName() {
    // for international versions, one could use native
        methods to
```

```
        // get appropriate locale information from the oper-
            ating system
        String monthNames[] = {
                            "January", "February", "March",
                            "April", "May", "June", "July",
                            "August", "September", "October",
                            "November", "December" };
        return monthNames[getMonth()];
    }


    /** This overides Object.clone() */
    public Object clone() {
        try {
            return super.clone();
        }
        catch (CloneNotSupportedException e) {
            // this shouldn't happen, since we are Cloneable
            //throw new InternalError();
            return null;
        }
    }
}
```

Finishing Touches

Two methods that you ought to implement before you set your applet loose on
the world are the following:

- ✔ String[][] getParameterInfo()
  This method documents your classes' parameters. The [][] that you see
  tells you that getParameterInfo() returns a two-dimensional array of
  strings. We tell you more about arrays in Chapter 9. Put simply,
  getParameterInfo() returns the name, type, and description of each
  parameter that your applet understands. Look at this sample implementation:

```
String[][] getParameterInfo() {
String parameterInfo[][] = {
// name type   description
            "volume",  "1-100",  "how many fish",
            "speed",   "1-10",   "swimming speed",
            "hunger",  "boolean","are the fish hungry?"
                            };
return parameterInfo;
}
```

✔ `String getAppletInfo()`
This method is intended to provide information about the author, version, and copyright of the applet. Another sample implementation:

```
String getAppletInfo() {
String appletInfo = "FishTank, v2.0, by Robert Ahab";
return appletInfo;
   }
```

You can invoke `getAppletInfo()` and `getParameterInfo()` from the appletviewer menu.

Controlling the color

Now that plain gray Web pages are giving way to a variety of colors, Web designers appreciate having control over an applet's color. This control is a nice touch that is easy to implement using an applet parameter.

The HTML document that references your applet may look like this:

```
<HTML>
<HEAD><TITLE>Testing Color Settings</TITLE></HEAD>
<BODY BGCOLOR=0000ff >
<APPLET CLASS=FishTank.class HEIGHT=100 WIDTH=100 >
<PARAM NAME=bgcolor VALUE=#0000ff >
</APPLET>
</BODY>
</HTML>
```

The `BODY` tag uses the (not yet standard) `bgcolor` parameter to set the Web page background to the color blue. The value `0000ff` is the hexadecimal number representing blue. Keeping with convention, we provide our `FishTank` applet with a `bgcolor` parameter as well. As you can see, the Web designer wants to set the applet background to match the Web page background.

This next snippet of code illustrates how to fetch the applet parameter and set the background color:

```
int bgcolor = Integer.valueOf(getParameter("bgcolor"));
setBackground(new Color(bgcolor));
```

A comment about comments

If Java is your first programming language, now is a great time to develop some good programming habits. Get in the habit of writing programs for people, not for computers. Strive to write code that is easy to read and understand.

Making your programs easy to understand is so important that Java provides three ways to denote comments in your code, as illustrated here:

/*   This comment style, which is familiar to C programmers,
        can span multiple lines.
*/

//   This style, as in C++, runs until the end of the line

/**   Use this style for text that you want to appear in automatically
        generated documentation.

No performance penalty occurs for using comments in Java. The compiler strips comments from your code when it generates the class file.

Comments in Java cannot be nested. In other words, you can't place one comment inside another. The only time that you're likely to be annoyed by this is when you want to temporarily disable, or *comment out*, a block of code that contains comments.

That third style of comment (/**), as we mentioned previously, deserves further discussion. The Java Development Kit (JDK) includes a simple documentation tool, called Javadoc, which can help you document your classes. Javadoc parses declarations and specially marked comments from your Java code files and generates reference documents in HTML format. Consider the following snippet of code, from the Button class:

```
/**    A class that produces a labeled button component.
@version 1.16 08/17/95
@author  Sami Shaio
*/
public class Button extends Component {
```

Figure 11-3 shows a portion of the corresponding HTML page generated by Javadoc.

Besides showing an inheritance diagram, Javadoc displays a class's public and protected methods along with any documentation comments that appear in the code. The special tags `@version` and `@author`, when used in a documentation comment, are displayed as you see in the figure.

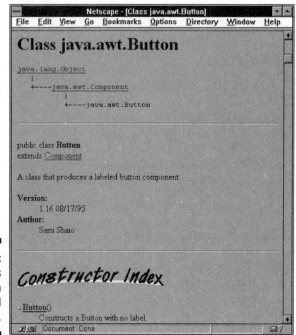

Figure 11-3:
Class
documentation
generated
by Javadoc.

Chapter 12
A Ticker Tape Class

- -

In This Chapter

▶ Making a minimal ticker tape

▶ Getting files from a remote server

▶ Dealing with exceptional occurrences

▶ Working with threads

- -

*I*n this chapter, you build an applet that fetches the contents of a text file and displays it in a scrolling ticker tape. The contents of the text file can be the bargain special of the hour, today's cafeteria menu, the local weather report, or anything else you'd like.

To build this applet, you need to know how to open and read a file and how to paint scrolling text on-screen. As with the `Calendar` component in Chapter 11, we *subclass* (that is, we derive characteristics of) the `TickerTape` class from the `Canvas` class.

I/O, I/O, into the Streams We Go

I/O is shorthand for Input/Output, which is programmer-speak for "getting data in and out of programs." We've already shown you some very important kinds of input: key presses and mouse clicks. And we told you how to work with output to the screen in the form of the Java `paint()` method. (See Chapters 5 and 8.)

Some common places to which one might send data (output) or from which one might fetch data (input) include

✔ A file on your DOS PC disk

✔ A tape drive on your UNIX machine

✔ A Web server on the Internet

We're sure that you can think of many other examples. (We're also sure that, in a few years, you'll find storage devices and network server programs of which you haven't even dreamt.) From the application programmer's point of view, data sources and data sinks are all the same. You either want to write data or read data and you'd rather not be bothered with the differences between files, network connections, tape drives, keyboards, and so on.

In other words, you don't care how many cylinders the car has, you simply want it to start when you turn the ignition key.

Streams provide the abstraction you seek. That is, the `Streams` classes provide a common way of accessing various I/O devices, whether these devices are files, network connections, keyboards, or something else. To open and read a file, our code uses several of the `Streams` classes: `InputStream`, `DataInputStream`, and `BufferedInputStream`.

Fetching a File from the Server

The data source for the ticker tape applet is a plain text file residing in the same directory as the applet. The message in this plain text file is the message displayed on the ticker tape. The text file could be on your local directory, on a company Web server — or anywhere you can get to with your Web browser. (If it's on the Internet, it must be on the same server as the applet.) Fetching a file is surprisingly easy. Include the code fragment that follows in your appplet to fetch a file; we go over the code in detail in the next section.

```
private final static char URLSeparator = '/';
private String messageFile = "message.txt";

/** fetch the message file into a string */
private String fetchMessageString() {

        String messageString = new String();

        // construct the URL of the message file
        String urlString = getDocumentBase().toString();
        urlString =
            urlString.substring(0,urlString.lastIndexOf(URLSeparator))
            + URLSeparator + messageFile;

        // fetch the message file
        try {
            URL url = new URL(urlString);
            InputStream inStream = url.openStream();
```

```
        DataInputStream dataStream =
        new DataInputStream(new
        BufferedInputStream(inStream));

        // stuff the message into messageString
        String inLine = null;
        while ((inLine = dataStream.readLine()) != null)
        {
            messageString += inLine;
        }
    }
    catch(MalformedURLException e) { // catch bad URL's
        showStatus("Invalid URL: " + urlString);
    }
    catch(IOException e) { // catch IO errors
        showStatus("Error " + e);
    }
    return messageString;
}
```

Examining the parts

Now we want to look at the various parts of the code. Near the beginning of the preceding code, you find a useful method worth remembering —
`Applet.getDocumentBase()`

This method returns the URL of the HTML file that includes your applet. We use `getDocumentBase()` to construct the URL of a file called *message.txt*, which is in the same directory as the HTML file (your Document Base).

If you want to ensure that an applet can be run only from a particular Web page, you can put a test in your code that looks something like this:

```
final String myURLString = "http://www.mycompany.com/
        mypage.html";
        if (
        getDocumentBase().toString().equals(myURLString)
        == false) {
    showStatus("Please run this applet from " +
        myURLString);
}
```

(continued)

(continued)

```
else {
    runMyApplet();
}
```

The `getDocumentBase()` method has a close cousin with which you should also become familiar — `Applet.getCodeBase()`

This method returns the URL of your applet's class file (your Code Base).

Opening the input text file

If you return to the example code, you notice some blocks of code labeled `try` and `catch`. We explain `try` and `catch` in a moment, but first, we need to open the input text file:

```
URL url = new URL(urlString);
InputStream inStream = url.openStream();
DataInputStream dataStream =
    new DataInputStream(new BufferedInputStream(inStream));

// stuff the message into messageString
String inLine = null;
while ((inLine = dataStream.readLine()) != null) {
    messageString += inLine;
}
```

These few preceding lines of code open a network connection, fetch our text file over the Internet (or from the local file system), and put the file contents in the String variable `messageString`. That's a lot of work for such a small amount of code.

The URL class provides an object wrapper for a valid Internet URL. The methods `getProtocol()`, `getFile()`, `getHost()`, and `getPort()`, return the different parts of the URL. The method `openStream()`, which we use in our code, opens a network connection to the URL. The method `openStream()` returns an `InputStream`, which in itself is not very useful. Because `InputStream` is an abstract class, you have to subclass it to do anything useful. We subclass `InputStream` twice.

✔ For the first subclass, we construct a `BufferedInputStream`. The `BufferedInputStream` class implements file buffering: Instead of reading from the file at each read request, which can be relatively slow, the `BufferedInputStream` reads big chunks of text into memory and services subsequent read requests from this memory image.

✔ For the second subclass, we use the `BufferedInputStream` to construct a `DataInputStream`, which provides us with a method, `readLine()`, to read entire lines of text at once.

Because the Ticker Tape applet will most likely be used to display short messages, using `BufferedInputStream` is not really called for. In more typical situations, however, you may be reading larger files and may want to follow the example we provide.

If you've ever had the pleasure of writing network programs in the past, you'll be impressed by the simplicity and power of Java's networking classes. Java includes — in the package *java.net* — a group of powerful, yet easy-to-use, networking classes which make building Internet applications easier than ever before.

Handling Exceptional Occurrences

Next we want to discuss exceptional occurrences; that is, now we want to talk about `try` and `catch`. (We said we'd get back to them!) These constructs of the Java language are intended to help you deal cleanly with those errors that commonly occur while your program is running. Perhaps your program fails to establish a network connection, or a user enters an invalid file name. Java's approach to dealing with errors — which is the same as in C++ and Delphi — is called *exception handling*. Exception handling enables you to expect the best and prepare for the worst. You may read the example code like this:

```
try
    to construct a valid URL from the variable named
        urlString
    to open a buffered input stream to the URL
    to read the contents of the URL into the variable named
        messageString
catch the exceptional condition when the URL is invalid
catch the exceptional condition when we can not open and read
        the file
```

Exception handling is a robust and fairly easy-to-use idiom for dealing with errors. The implementation of exception handling can also be confusing. For now, we explain just what you need as a beginning Java programmer.

Some of the more useful Java classes handle error conditions by *throwing an exception.* When you use a method that throws an exception, you're required to provide a way to *catch* that exception. Even as a beginner, you need to know enough about exception handling so that you can make good use of classes — like URL, InputStream, and Thread — that throw exceptions.

The constructor declaration for the URL class looks like this:

```
public URL(String spec) throws MalformedURLException
```

Notice that this method *throws* a particular exception named MalformedURLException. As you may guess from the name, the exceptional circumstance that MalformedURLException refers to happens when you try to construct a URL with a string that can't possibly be a valid URL. In order to use this method, we have to provide a catch for the MalformedURLException. The following code shows how:

```
try    {
        URL url = new URL(urlString);
}
catch(MalformedURLException e) {
        showStatus("Invalid URL: " + urlString);
}
```

If the urlString parameter contains a valid URL, like http://www.idgbooks.com/, then showStatus() isn't called. If, on the other hand, urlString contains some nonsense, like hohoho, showStatus() displays the message Invalid URL: hohoho.

If you call the URL constructor without providing a catch, your program doesn't compile. You get a compiler error something like the following:

```
error message 'uncaught.exception' not found
```

Exception handling is an advanced topic. For now, just be careful to follow the examples we give you and include try and catch code blocks when we use them with certain Java classes.

Running Your Tasks by a Thread

As you type away at your computer, perhaps a clock program discreetly displays the current time in a corner of your screen. With every passing second, the clock program redraws itself, or at least, redisplays the time in the corner of your screen. A clock program is a handy utility. But if this utility prevented you from doing other work, it would be pretty useless. After all, if you just wanted to tell time, you would buy a clock instead of a computer.

Fortunately, your computer system can handle multiple tasks at once. You can crunch numbers in your spreadsheet, listen to music on your computer's CD player, and download your e-mail from the Internet all at the same time.

Just as we like our computers to run more than one program at a time, we often like our programs to handle more than one task at a time. For example, a word processor should prepare output for the printer without interrupting your typing. Your Web browser should display text and accept mouse clicks even while it's still busy downloading that 100K picture of your company's CEO.

In Java, we can run separate tasks in separate threads of execution, or simply, *threads.* The next code is an example of a thread:

```java
class MyExample extends Canvas implements Runnable {
    private Thread thread;
    private boolean isRunning = false;
    // constructor
    public MyExample() {
        thread = null;
    }
    // methods
    public void start() {
        if (thread == null) {
            thread = new Thread(this);
        }
        isRunning = true;
        thread.start();
    }

    public void run() {
        while (isRunning) {
            doTheWork();
            try { Thread.sleep(sleepTime); }
            catch(InterruptedException e) {
            /* don't do anything */ }
        }
    }

    public void stop() {
        if((thread != null) && thread.isAlive()) {
            thread.stop();
```

(continued)

(continued)

```
            isRunning = false;
            thread = null;
    }
}
```

The class in the preceding code implements the Runnable interface (see Chapter 8 for more about interfaces), which provides the basic plumbing we use to run some code in its own thread.

All the preceding code is a framework around the method doTheWork() — just a made-up name for this example. This framework sets up doTheWork() to run as a separate thread. When run as a thread, this specific method can share computer resources with other tasks in a way that may be managed by the applet programmer, the browser, and the operating system. For example, the applet programmer can tell the thread to sleep for some milliseconds every interation of the code, or the programmer can assign the thread a priority relative to other activities of the computer.

The heart of the setup for a thread is one method, run(), which is invoked by the run-time system whenever the computer yields time for this thread to perform its work. Besides the actual doTheWork() activity, the run() method must include try and catch blocks like the ones we show you in the sample code.

If the run-time system yields time to some other thread, our thread catches an InterruptedException. We don't take any action when our thread is interrupted in the preceding code, and action isn't generally needed. But we are required to provide code to catch the exception, even when we don't do anything with it.

The start() and stop() methods are housekeeping activities used to make sure that a thread does not become duplicated in computer memory and take up computing resources unnecessarily. The start() method checks to make sure the thread is not already running. The stop() method eliminates all references to the thread which we instantiated by setting the thread to null, thus enabling the run-time system to reclaim the resource.

The Complete and Unexpurgated Code

The following is the complete code for the applet class and the TickerTape class that it uses. To use this applet as it is written, you must have a file (named *message.txt*) that contains the desired message and is located in the same directory as the applet class file. Figure 12-1 shows what the Ticker Tape applet looks like on a Web page. Remember, in real life, the message scrolls across the screen.

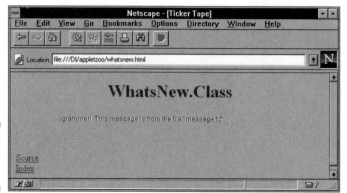

Figure 12-1:
The Ticker
Tape applet.

```
/**
 *   @version 0.2
 */

import java.awt.*;
import java.applet.Applet;
import java.net.*;
import java.io.*;

/** TickerApplet */
public class TickerApplet extends Applet {

    private final static char URLSeparator = '/';
    private String messageFile = "message.txt";
    private TickerTape tickerTape = new TickerTape();

        /** fetch Message Dtring */
        private String fetchMessageString() {

        String messageString = new String();

        // construct the URL of the message file
        String urlString = getCodeBase().toString();
        urlString =
            urlString.substring(0,urlString.lastIndexOf(URLSeparator))
            + URLSeparator + messageFile;
```

(continued)

(continued)

```java
        // fetch the message file
        try {
            URL url = new URL(urlString);
            InputStream inStream = url.openStream();
            DataInputStream dataStream =
            new DataInputStream(new
            BufferedInputStream(inStream));

            // stuff the message into messageString
            String inLine = null;
            while ((inLine = dataStream.readLine()) != null){
                messageString += inLine;
            }
        }
        catch(MalformedURLException e) { // catch bad URL's
            showStatus("Invalid URL: " + urlString);
        }
        catch(IOException e) { // catch IO errors
            showStatus("Error " + e);
        }
        return messageString;
    }

    /** init */
    public void init() {
        add(tickerTape);
        tickerTape.setText(fetchMessageString());
        tickerTape.start();
    }


    /** stop */
    public void stop() {
        tickerTape.stop();
    }

/* TickerTape class */
class TickerTape extends Canvas implements Runnable {

    private Dimension preferredDimension = new Dimension(400,10);
    private int messageWidth;
    private int messageX;
    private int messageY;
    private int currentX;
```

```
private int sleepyTime = 50;
private int scrollStep = 2;
private final static int INSET = 2;
private String messageString = "Default Message";
private Thread thread;
private boolean isRunning = false;

/** constructor */
public TickerTape() {
    thread = null;
    setBackground(Color.blue);
    setForeground(Color.white);
    setFont(new Font("TimesRoman", Font.BOLD, 14));
}

/** run */
public void run() {
    while (isRunning) {
        scroll();
        try {
            Thread.sleep(sleepyTime);
        }
        catch(InterruptedException e) {
            // caught an exception
        }
    }
}

/** stop */
public void stop() {
    if((thread != null) && thread.isAlive()) {
        thread.stop();
        {thread = null;
        isRunning = false;
    }
}

/** start */
public void start() {
    resize(preferredDimension);
    messageX = bounds().width;
    //System.out.println("startx="+messageX;//db
    if (thread == null) {
        thread = new Thread(this);
```

(continued)

(continued)

```
            thread.setPriority(Thread.MIN_PRIORITY);
        }
    isRunning = true;
    thread.start();
}


/**scroll*/
private void scroll() {
    // if the message has scrolled off the edge of the
        canvas, wrap it around
          if(messageX < (-messageWidth)) {
      messageX = bounds().width ;
    }
    else {
      messageX = messageX - scrollStep;
    }
    repaint();
}
}


/**setext*/
public void setText(String s) {
    messageString = new String(s);
    FontMetrics fontMetrics =
        getGraphics().getFontMetrics();
    messageWidth =
        fontMetrics.stringWidth(messageString);
    messageY = fontMetrics.getHeight() -
        fontMetrics.getDescent() + INSET;
    preferredDimension.height = fontMetrics.getHeight() +
        (INSET * 2);
}


/** Return the Ticker's preferred size */
public Dimension preferredSize() {
    return preferredDimension;
}


/** Return the Ticker's minimum size */
public Dimension minimumSize() {
    return preferredDimension;
}
```

```
/**paint*/
public finalvoid paint(Graphics g) {
    g.drawString(messageString,messageX,messageY);
}

/*

}
```

Chapter 13

Sprites: Faster than a Speeding Rabbit

*S*prite is a generic term for an image that you can move around the screen independently of the other elements on the screen. Sprites are typically an important element of graphical computer games or animations. A sprite object is an elegant example of how object-oriented programming allows you to reuse code.

When you run the applet represented by this chapter's code sample, you see bouncing squares and someone else bouncing around, also. See Figure 13-1 for a look at our sprites. Each sprite object has the following properties:

❙ ✔ A direction or *heading*

❙ ✔ A speed

❙ ✔ An image

In this chapter, we show you how to create a Sprite class. Then we show you how to use sprite objects in a simple applet that you can easily modify to try different techniques. In Chapter 15, we use the same sprite objects to create a more complicated simulation game.

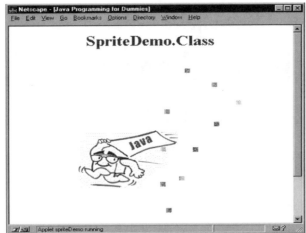

Figure 13-1:
Sprites.

The Strategy for Displaying Moving Graphics

Avoiding screen flicker

When you build an applet that involves displaying a moving component on-screen, like the ticker tape applet in Chapter 12, you need to consider the issue of screen flicker. Depending on your computer system, the ticker tape may blink unpleasantly as the message moves across the screen. And a reason for this flicker exists. The update() method of on-screen display can set the entire component region to the current background color before calling paint() to draw the component from scratch. This process takes time and can result in a flickering effect.

The component's default update() method looks like this:

```
public void update(Graphics g) {
    // fill the on-screen graphics region with the current
           background color
    g.setColor(getBackground());
                g.fillRect(0, 0, width, height);
    // call paint to render the component from scratch
    g.setColor(getForeground());
    paint(g);
}
```

Using the preceding algorithm can result in pretty obnoxious screen flickering, especially if your applet paints itself frequently. For the ticker tape applet, we left in the flicker to avoid complicating the code.

But for a sprite, whose purpose is to provide smooth animations, we have to do a better job of eliminating screen flicker. The best way to reduce flickering is through a technique called *double buffering*. See what you think of this idea: Instead of clearing and painting the on-screen image, we do all of our dirty work off-screen, on a scratch pad. Then in one efficient step, we copy the completed off-screen scratch pad to our visible on-screen workspace.

Following is a code snippet for the double-buffering process:

```
// create a scratch pad the same size as our on-screen image
Image scratchPad = createImage(this.size().width,
          this.size().height);
// get a Graphics object for our scratch pad
Graphics scratchPadGraphics = scratchPad.getGraphics();

public final void update(Graphics g) {
    // paint to our off-screen scratch pad - the messy stuff
          happens here
    paint(scratchPadGraphics);
    // copy our scratch pad to the screen
    g.drawImage(scratchPad,0,0,null);
    }
```

Instead of drawing directly to the screen, the double-buffering version of update() passes the scratch pad to paint(). When the paint() method completes its work, update() copies the finished image from the scratch pad to the screen.

As a final touch, we declare our update() method to be *final*. And because final methods cannot be inherited, Java doesn't have to figure out which update() method to call at run time. The compiler can take advantage of this preknowledge to generate code that runs slightly faster (or as the programmers simply say, *faster code*).

If you intend for a method not to be inherited, declare it *final* by including the word final in the declaration statement. Making this declaration enforces your intentions and provides the bonus of slightly faster code.

Displaying graphics files

Displaying graphics files is very simple in Java. The next code segment shows how your applet loads the picture joe.gif, residing in the same directory as the applet class file:

```
img = getImage(getCodeBase(), "joe.gif");
```

Then you may draw the image by placing the following line in the paint() method:

```
g.drawImage(img, x, y, null);
```

In the preceding code, img parameter is an image object and x and y are the coordinates where the image is to appear on-screen. (The fourth parameter, which is null in this case, allows you to declare something called an ImageObserver object that collects data about the downloading of images. We won't go into the advanced topic of ImageObservers here.) So the code boils down to specifying what image and where.

That's really all there is to it!

Bouncing the image around

How do you make the drawn images bounce around on-screen? You need to test for where the sprite is on-screen and then change the sprite's direction if it is at an edge of the applet's on-screen space. The following code shows the method for testing the sprite's location:

```
if (inside ((int)demoSprites[i].positionX,
            (int)demoSprites[i].positionY)) {
   if (((demoSprites[i].positionX - demoSprites[i].radius) <=
            0) ||
      ((demoSprites[i].positionX + demoSprites[i].radius) >=
            size().width))
      demoSprites[i].bounceVertical();
   if (((demoSprites[i].positionY - demoSprites[i].radius) <=
            0) ||
      ((demoSprites[i].positionY + demoSprites[i].radius) >=
            size().height))
      demoSprites[i].bounceHorizontal();
   }
```

And this next code shows how to change the sprite's direction, that is, the bounce methods:

```
public void bounceVertical() {
      direction = (0 - direction) % 360;
   }


   public void bounceHorizontal() {
      direction = (180 - direction) % 360;
   }
```

If you want the sprites in your application to do something other than bounce (explode, come in the opposite side of the applet window, or whatever) you can modify this code.

The Complete and Unexpurgated Code

You find two components to this code — a Sprite class and an applet that uses Sprite objects. The following is the complete code for the Sprite class. Please don't miss the comments and explanations that we include in the midst of this code!

```
/** Sprite class allows you to create moving objects on the
          screen */
class Sprite extends Panel {
    // constants that can be used outside the class
    final static int NORTH = 180;
    final static int SOUTH = 0;
    final static int WEST = 270;
    final static int EAST = 90;
    final static int MAXSPEED = 12;

    //constants accessible only to children of the class
    protected final static int DELTA = 4;
    protected final static int DEFAULTSIZE = 10;

    //some geometrical information
    float positionX = DEFAULTSIZE;
    float positionY = DEFAULTSIZE;
    float width = 0;
    float height = 0;
    protected double speed = 0;
```

(continued)

(continued)

```
    protected float radius = 0;
    protected int direction = SOUTH; //in degrees from SOUTH

    //everything else
    protected boolean isMoving = false;
    protected Image myImage = null;

    /**
     * protected contructor is only accessible to derived
            classes
     * derived class is expected to set myImage and dimen-
            sions
     */
    protected Sprite() {}

    /** this constructor creates a default graphical repre-
            sentation */
    Sprite (Component c) {
        myImage = c.createImage(DEFAULTSIZE, DEFAULTSIZE);
        Graphics gr;
        gr = myImage.getGraphics();
        gr.setColor(Color.red);
        gr.fillRect(0, 0, DEFAULTSIZE, DEFAULTSIZE);
        setDimensions();
    }
```

As you can see, the default appearance of a sprite is a red square 10 x 10 pixels. (DEFAULTSIZE has a value of 10.) Not very interesting. Also, you see that myImage is the off-screen scratch pad used to implement double buffering. The heading (the sprite's direction) can be specified in degrees or, as a convenience, using the NORTH, SOUTH, EAST, and WEST constants.

Apply these direction constants (NORTH, SOUTH, EAST, and WEST) like you're looking at the computer screen as a road map. That is, NORTH is toward the top of the screen, SOUTH is toward the bottom of the screen, and so on.

```
    /** this constructor accepts an image to be used for
            drawing Sprite on screen */
    Sprite (Image img) {
        myImage = img;
        setDimensions();
    }
```

```
/**
 * this constructor accepts an image to be used for
 * drawing Sprite on screen and its coordinates
 */
Sprite (Image img, int posX, int posY) {
    myImage = img;
    positionX = posX;
    positionY = posY;
    setDimensions();
}


protected void setDimensions() {
    // wait until image is loaded
    while (myImage.getHeight(this) == -1) {
    }

    width = myImage.getWidth(this);
    height = myImage.getHeight(this);
    radius = (float) (Math.sqrt(Math.pow(height, 2) +
        Math.pow(width, 2)) / 2);
}
```

What's going on here? Java's image-handling classes are smart enough that they don't keep you waiting while they download a potentially large image from a potentially slow data source. Instead, when you request an image, the Java classes start loading the image in a separate thread (see the Chapter 12 discussion about threads) and let you continue with your work.

But in this case, we need to know the dimensions of an image before we can do anything with it — in this particular snippet of code, you want to determine the radius of the image to display. Because you can't determine the radius of an image until it's completely loaded, we inserted a while loop that waits for the image to load completely. If you have many large images to load, and other things to do while they're loading, certain advanced techniques enable you to continue with other work while the images are loading. (These techniques make use of the capabilities of the ImageObserver objects that we mentioned previously.)

```
/** sets the direction of Sprite */
public void heading (int dir) {
    direction = dir;
}
```

(continued)

(continued)

```
/** Sets the speed between 1 and MAXSPEED)   */
public void setSpeed (double sp) {
    if ((sp >= 1) && (sp <= MAXSPEED))  {
        speed = sp;
    }
}


/** Causes the sprite to move   */
public void startMovement () {
    isMoving = true;
}


/** Causes the sprite to stop moving  */
public void stopMovement () {
    isMoving = false;
}


/** tick method is called by parent on every time tick.
 *    It moves the Sprite along its direction if necessary
 */
public void tick () {
    if ((isMoving) && (speed > 0)){
        positionX += ((float)speed / MAXSPEED) * DELTA
            * Math.sin((2 * Math.PI * direction) / 360);
        positionY += ((float)speed / MAXSPEED) * DELTA
            * Math.cos((2 * Math.PI * direction) / 360);
    }
}


/** causes Sprite to bounce off the vertical wall */
public void bounceVertical() {
    direction = (0 - direction) % 360;
}


/** causes Sprite to bounce off horizontal wall */
public void bounceHorizontal() {
    direction = (180 - direction) % 360;
}


/** draw is called by the tick method with parent's
       graphics object   */
void paint(Graphics g) {
    g.drawImage(myImage, (int)(positionX - width/2),
```

```
                (int)(positionY - height/2), null);
        }
    }
```

One sprite alone is not that much fun. But this next applet uses Sprites to create a little excitement.

```java
import java.awt.*;
import java.applet.*;
import java.lang.*;

/** This applet demonstrates sprite objects
      @author Anatoly Goroshnik   */
public class SpriteDemo extends Applet implements Runnable {
    final int quantum = 10;
    final int numSprites = 11;
    final boolean showTraces = false;

    Image offScreenImage = null;
    Graphics offScreenGraphics = null;
    Dimension offScreenSize = null;

    Thread demo;
    Sprite demoSprites[] = new Sprite[numSprites];

    public void init() {
        Image img = null;

        showStatus("loading images...");

        /** load the first Sprite image*/
        img = getImage(getDocumentBase(), "dan.gif");
        demoSprites[0] = new sprite(img, 60, size().height -
            60);
        demoSprites[0].heading(150);
        demoSprites[0].setSpeed(9);
        demoSprites[0].startMovement();

        /** load the rest of the Sprite images*/
        for (int i = 1; i < numSprites; i++) {
            img = getImage(getDocumentBase(), "image" + i +
                ".gif");
            demoSprites[i] = new sprite(img, 10, 10);
```

(continued)

(continued)

```
            demoSprites[i].heading(sprite.EAST - i * 5);
            demoSprites[i].setSpeed(3+i*0.9);
            demoSprites[i].startMovement();
        }

    showStatus("");
    }


    public void run() {
        while (true) {

            for (int i = 0; i < numSprites; i++) {
                demoSprites[i].tick();
                // check for boundary bounce conditions
                if (inside ((int)demoSprites[i].positionX,
    (int)demoSprites[i].positionY)) {
                    if (((demoSprites[i].positionX -
    demoSprites[i].width/2) <= 0) ||
                        ((demoSprites[i].positionX +
    demoSprites[i].width/2) >= size().width))
                        demoSprites[i].bounceVertical();
                    if (((demoSprites[i].positionY -
    demoSprites[i].height/2) <= 0) ||
                        ((demoSprites[i].positionY +
    demoSprites[i].height/2) >= size().height))
                        demoSprites[i].bounceHorizontal();
                }
            }

            update(getGraphics());
            try {

                Thread.sleep(quantum);
            } catch (InterruptedException e) {
                break;
            }
        }
    }


    public void start() {
        demo = new Thread(this);
        demo.start();
    }
```

```
public void stop() {
    demo.stop();
    demo = null;
}


public final void update(Graphics theG){
    //implements no-flicker graphics
  Dimension dim = size();
  if((offScreenImage==null) || (dim.width !=
      offScreenSize.width) || (dim.height !=
      offScreenSize.height)){
    offScreenImage = createImage(dim.width, dim.height);
    offScreenSize = dim;
    offScreenGraphics = offScreenImage.getGraphics();
    if (showTraces)
  offScreenGraphics.clearRect(0, 0, offScreenSize.width,
      offScreenSize.height);
  }
  if (!showTraces)
  offScreenGraphics.clearRect(0, 0, offScreenSize.width,
      offScreenSize.height);
  paint(offScreenGraphics);
  theG.drawImage(offScreenImage,0,0,null);
}


public void paint(Graphics g) {
    for (int i = 0; i < numSprites; i++) {
        demoSprites[i].paint(g);
    }
}

}
```

If You Want to Do It Yourself...

If you want to move your own pictures about on the screen, the preceding Sprite applet can do the trick for you. You need to change the getImage() call in the applet's init() method to load your own image file.

The showTraces variable controls whether the image leaves behind a trail. (Figure 13-2 show some sprites with trails.) What's happening, of course, is that turning on showTraces prevents the sprite from clearing the screen between each tick (or appearance of on-screen movement).

You may also want to change the variable quantum, which controls the frequency of ticks (you can think of this frequency as a measure of frames-per-second). The heading() method enables you to set the sprite's direction. We build on the Sprite class in the JavaBots sample in Chapter 14.

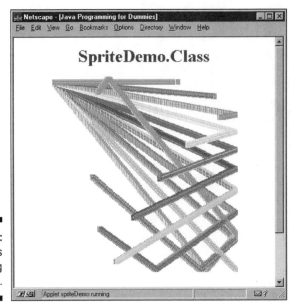

Figure 13-2:
Sprites
leaving
trails.

Chapter 14

JavaBots: Let the Wild Rumpus Begin!

. . . .

In This Chapter

▶ Tracking your objects with vectors

▶ Holding your objects with arrays

▶ Guiding your objects' behavior with a random number generator

▶ Supporting the JavaBots with the Runnable interface

. . . .

This is a meaty chapter. In this chapter, we show you examples of many of the techniques that you've seen so far — and you'll see a few new tricks! A lot is in here, so you may want go over the examples in this chapter more than once.

We use the simple Sprite class that is explained in Chapter 13 to create a virtual world in which colorful little creatures multiply, move about, and devour each other. We use some old friends along the way, including `if`, `for`, `while`, `switch`, threads, exceptions, and double buffering. We think that you'll surprise yourself with how much you've mastered. By this time, you, too, are well on your way to becoming a bona fide Java nerd. If you feel a sudden craving for strong coffee and pizza, don't worry — it's only natural.

The Wild Rumpus

This applet creates a game of life. The world of the applet is populated with sprites like our mutual friends from Chapter 13. But now, we extend the sprites to give them a life of their own.

The behavior of *Creatures* is much more complex than the behavior of simple sprites.

 ✔ These Creature sprites come in a variety of sizes.

 ✔ They come in five colors.

- ✔ There are two sexes.

- ✔ Creature sprites grow as they get older.

- ✔ Eventually, when their age becomes equal to their lifespan, the Creature sprites die.

- ✔ They may get hungry. A larger, hungry Creature sprite that bumps into a smaller sprite will eat it.

- ✔ If two Creature sprites of different sexes above the age of puberty bump into each other, a new sprite may be born (randomly).

- ✔ If both Creature sprites survive an encounter, the speed of the bouncing sprites is related to their relative size.

To give users a chance to participate in the fun, they can add a creature of any given color and size to the rumpus by clicking on the applet in the area of the sprite world.

This is not a fully finished game. We would be very interested to see how you complete and polish this game. If you send us a version that really impresses us, we'll post it on the resource page.

Figure 14-1 shows what our version looks like on-screen.

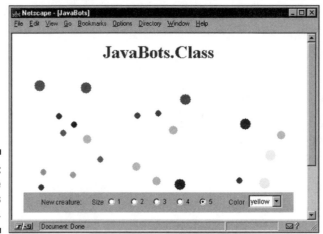

Figure 14-1:
The
JavaBots
have a riot.

The Man behind the Screen

Most of the tricks used to make this applet work were used in earlier chapters. The `Runnable` interface, arrays, and `Math.random` appear in those chapters, but a word or two (or even three) of review is in order. *Vectors* are a programming tool that you may not have heard of before. Vectors enable you to keep track of large and variable collections of objects (such as the creatures of this applet).

Up and running: JavaBots

Like the sprite demo in Chapter 13, the applet that you examine in this chapter, JavaBots, implements the `Runnable` interface to make a class that can perform work in its own thread. Usually, you use a thread when your class is performing some ongoing, noncritical work, such as playing an animation or displaying the current time. In JavaBots, you continuously paint colorful circles that move around the playing area. You don't need to monopolize all the power of the computer to perform this work, so you run it in a thread.

A `Runnable` class must have a `run()` method, which is usually where the action takes place. JavaBots is no exception. We take a look at the JavaBots `run()` method later in this chapter. For now, review the basic structure of a typical implementation:

```
final static int PAUSE_LENGTH = 100;
public void run() {
        while (true) {
                myDoTheWorkMethod(); // do your work here
                try {
                        Thread.sleep(PAUSE_LENGTH);
                } catch (InterruptedException e) {
                        break;
                }
        }
}
```

The system calls `run()` whenever this class's thread can perform its work. `run()` calls `myDoTheWorkMethod()` — an arbitrary method that we made up, which does whatever work you need to do — and pauses for `PAUSE_LENGTH` milliseconds. To pass control to another thread, the system may interrupt the thread, causing an `InterruptedException`, which breaks out of the `while(true)` loop.

Give that programmer arrays!

In Chapter 9, we discuss *arrays*, which are handy data structures for holding a predetermined number of similar objects. Instead of making 100 string variables — myString1, myString2, and so on — arrays let you write the following:

```
final int MAX_STRINGS = 100;
// get space for MAX_STRINGS strings
String[] myStrings = new String[MAX_STRINGS];
// fill the array with MAX_STRINGS strings
for (int i=0; i < MAX_STRINGS; i++) {
        myStrings[i] = new String("string #" + i);
}
// now myStrings[0] is "string #0",

// myStrings[1] is "string #1", and so on.
```

Arrays are so convenient that they are a standard feature of nearly every programming language. Java arrays are a special kind of object (though this is not apparent) and are endowed with more smarts than you might think. Consider what would happen if the user entered 250 in the following code snippet:

```
String[] myStrings = new String[100]; // get space for 100
            strings
int index = getNumberFromUser(); // get a number from the
            user
myNewString = myStrings[index];
```

Because myStrings has 100 elements, the valid values for index are the numbers from 0 to 99. If the user enters 250, a Java array throws an ArrayIndexOutOfBoundsException, which you can catch like any other exception:

```
try {
        myNewString = myStrings[index];
}
catch (ArrayIndexOutOfBoundsException e) {
        // do something about the invalid index
}
```

Arrays also have a single variable, length, which you can inspect but not change:

```
/*  get space for 100 strings */
String[] myStrings = new String[100];
/*  the following line displays: "myStrings can hold up to
        100 strings" */
showStatus("myStrings can hold up to " + myStrings.length +
        "strings");
```

Vectors

Arrays are the ideal tool when you need to store a known number of similar objects. As you tackle complex Java applets, however, you sometimes don't know ahead of time how many objects you have to store.

Suppose that you've written a custom Web browser. Whenever you load a Web page, you want to create a list of all the URLs found on that Web page. A Web page can hold any number of URLs. You can construct an array to hold, say, 100 URLs, but preparing for the maximum case that you rarely, if ever, encounter is inefficient. It's the programming equivalent of cooking dinner for 30 people on the off chance that all your friends drop by for dinner. Inevitably, you run into a Web page with more than 100 URLs, and a number of your friends bring along close companions that you didn't know about.

You need more flexibility. Java provides a close cousin of the array, which gives you more flexibility — this cousin is the *vector*.

The Vector class, found in the java.util package, is a turbo-charged array. Vectors can hold any kind of Java object. (Remember, every class in Java is ultimately descended from the Object class.) Unlike arrays, vectors can grow to accommodate your requirements. This code snippet adds an arbitrary number of strings to a Vector object:

```
// Vector is in the java.util package
import java.util.*;

Vector myStrings = new Vector();
//get some unknown number of strings from the user…
while ((inputString = myGetStringMethod()) != null) {
    // add the string to the vector
    myStrings.addElement(inputString);
}
```

You don't need to worry about the size of the vector. You simply call addElement() for each string that the user enters. Table 14-1 lists some important methods of the Vector class:

Table 14-1	Vector Methods
Method	*Purpose*
`addElement (Object)`	Adds the specified object as the last element of the vector
`setElementAt(Object, int)`	Sets the element at the specified index to be the specified object
`elementAt(int)`	Returns the element at the specified index
`indexOf(Object)`	Searches for the specified object, starting from the first position, and returns an index to it
`contains(Object)`	Returns `true` if the specified object is a value of the collection
`removeAllElements()`	Removes all elements of the vector
`size()`	Returns the number of elements that you have stored in the vector
`elements()`	Returns an Enumeration of the elements; use the `Enumeration` methods on the returned object to fetch the elements sequentially

The `elements()` method is worth looking at closely. Whenever you need to do something with every element in the class, you should use the `elements()` method. The `elements()` method returns an Enumeration, whose sole purpose is to simplify working with items in a collection of objects such as Vector. The `Enumeration` interface has just two methods: `hasMoreElements()`, which returns `TRUE` or `FALSE`, and `nextElement()`, which returns a generic `Object`. The Enumeration is a very useful tool, but the code to use it requires some unfamiliar forms.

The following code to print out all the strings in a vector is a model to follow when you use Enumeration.

```
for (Enumeration e = myStrings.elements() ;
e.hasMoreElements() ;) {
    s = (String) e.nextElement();
    g.drawString(s);
}
```

Notice two special features about the preceding code snippet: the expression `(String) e.nextElement()`, which is called a *cast,* and the `for` loop, which has a non-standard form.

✔ **The cast:** A structure that identifies the class of an object or converts it to a new type. A vector can contain objects of more than one class. Java doesn't know what subclass of Object `nextElement()` is, unless *you* tell Java. By putting the class name in parentheses in front of the call to `nextElement()`, you tell Java what kind of object it is dealing with (see the second line of the code snippet).

✔ **The non-standard** `for` **loop:** In the preceding code snippet, the non-standard `for` loop has these characteristics.

- The initialization statement `Enumeration e = myStrings.elements` is not a counter, it just instantiates the Enumeration.

- The loop contains a test — `e.hasMoreElements()`.

- No increment statement at all is present inside the parentheses of the `for` statement.

What assures that the applet eventually exits from the loop is the `nextElement()` statement inside the loop. You see examples of this non-standard `for` loop for Enumerations in a variety of applets, in this book and elsewhere.

You can use arrays to store primitive types — `int`, `float`, `boolean`, and so on — or any kind of object. Vectors, on the other hand, can hold only Java Objects. If you want to store primitive types in a Vector, you must first wrap them in the appropriate Object, like this:

```
Integer myInt = new Integer (n)
```

Random behavior: generating a color

In the beginning of this chapter, we said that you can create a virtual world in which colorful little creatures multiply, move about, and devour each other. How does that world look without a little random behavior? Chances are, it looks pretty dull. When programmers say *random,* they mean *unpredictable.* And a completely predictable world holds no surprises.

To add a little spice to things, the creatures in your virtual world have a random initial speed, a random initial color, and a random initial sex. If two compatible creatures meet, they may spawn children — or they may not; it's unpredictable.

The technique for producing each of these unpredictable behaviors is the same: you start with a random number. Coming up with good ways to generate random numbers is a fascinating and important area of computer science, you may be surprised to learn. It's a lot trickier than you may think. Fortunately, we are standing on the shoulders of giants. Java provides two ways to generate random numbers: the class `Random` in the `java.util` package, and the static method random() in the java.lang.Math package. In JavaBots, you use the static method random(), which is simple to use. The random() method returns a random number between 0.0 and 1.0.

To generate a random color, you can use the following code snippet:

```
Color(    (int)(Math.random() * 255),
          (int)(Math.random() * 255),
          (int)(Math.random() * 255))
```

The preceding Color constructor takes three parameters: the amount of red, the amount of green, and the amount of blue. By multiplying the random number by 255, you ensure that your values are between 0 and 255, which is what the Color constructor requires. (By the way, 255 is the highest number that can fit in 8 bits. That's why you often see 255 as an upper limit for a parameter.)

The Complete and Unexpurgated Code

Here is the complete code for the applet class and each of the other classes it uses that are not part of the standard Java Class Library. (By the way, you can find a copy of this applet on the CD ROM at the back of the book. If you want to see it run or experiment with modifying it, you don't need to type all the code yourself. If you decide to write your own HTML page, use the tag <APPLET CODE="JavaBots.class" WIDTH=500 HEIGHT=300></APPLET> to start with.)

The first chunk of code declares a number of variables. If you look closely, you see three arrays: sizes[], stringColors[], and colorColors[]. You also see two vectors: creatureList and sysEventList.

```
import java.awt.*;
import java.applet.*;
import java.lang.*;
import java.util.*;

/** Use sprites to create a virtual world
 *    @version 0.2, 5/2/96
 *    @author <A HREF="mailto:anatoly@iscinc.com">Anatoly
 *            Goroshnik</A>
 */
public class JavaBots extends Applet implements Runnable {
    // millisecs to pause between ticks
    final int PAUSE_LENGTH = 10;
    // initial number of creatures
    final int INIT_CREATURES = 10;
```

```
// do sprites show trail?
 final boolean SHOW_TRAIL = false;
 //variables for double-buffered painting...
 Image offScreenImage = null;
Graphics offScreenGraphics = null;
 Dimension offScreenSize = null;
 //user interface objects
 Panel controlPanel = new Panel();
 Panel ecoSystem = new Panel();
 CheckboxGroup creatureSize = new CheckboxGroup();
 Checkbox sizes[] = new Checkbox[Creature.MAXSIZE];
 Choice creatureColor = new Choice();
 //array of color choices
 String stringColors[] = {"red", "green", "blue", "yel-
        low", "black"};
 Color colorColors[] = {Color.red, Color.green,
        Color.blue, Color.yellow, Color.black};
 //a dynamic array of creatures
 Vector creatureList = new Vector();
 //a dynamic array of future events
 Vector sysEventList = new Vector();
 //main thread
 Thread mainThread;
```

In the `init` method, you create the user interface controls and fill the
`ecoSystem` with an initial population of creatures. Note how the creatures are
tracked in the vector `creatureList`.

```
public void init() {
 //create user interface
        setLayout(new BorderLayout());
        controlPanel.add(new Label("New Creature:"));
        controlPanel.add(new Label("Size"));
        for (int i = 0; i < Creature.MAXSIZE; i++) {
            if (i == 0) {
                controlPanel.add(new Checkbox ((i+1) + "",
        creatureSize, true));
            }
            else {
                controlPanel.add(new Checkbox ((i+1) + "",
        creatureSize, false));
            }
        }
        for (int i = 0; i < stringColors.length; i++) {
```

(continued)

(continued)

```
            creatureColor.addItem(stringColors[i]);
          }
          controlPanel.add(new Label("Color"));
          controlPanel.add(creatureColor);
          add("South", controlPanel);
          add("Center", ecoSystem);
          //populate our ecoSystem
          for (int i = 0; i < INIT_CREATURES; i++) {
              creatureList.addElement
                  (new Creature(ecoSystem, 1,
                      // a random color
                      new Color((int)(Math.random() * 255),
                      (int)(Math.random() * 255),
                      (int)(Math.random() * 255)),
                      // a random size
                      (int)(Math.random() * 100),
                      (int)(Math.random() * 100),
                       sysEventList));
          }
        }
```

The run method is where you check regularly for collisions and their consequences in the form of sysEvents. It is also where you update the display.

In this code, we use an Enumeration. You see (Creature) in front of references to the Enumeration. This *cast*, as programmers refer to the naming structure, notifies the computer that the objects in this particular Enumeration must be handled with the methods of the Creature class. Without the additional information provided by the cast, the computer would have available only generic Object class methods.

```
public void run() {
      while (true) {
          for (Enumeration e = creatureList.elements();
          e.hasMoreElements() ;) {
              ((Creature)(e.nextElement())).tick();
                  //let creature know that clock had ticked
          }
          update(ecoSystem.getGraphics()); //update screen
          for (int i = 0; i < creatureList.size() ; i++) {
              for (int j = i + 1; j < creatureList.size() ;
          j++) {
                  Creature firstCreature = (Creature)
          creatureList.elementAt(i);
                  Creature secondCreature = (Creature)
```

```
                creatureList.elementAt(j);
                    firstCreature.checkCollision(secondCreature);
                        //check for collisions
                    }
                }
                handleSysEvents(); //process all events
                try {
                    Thread.sleep(PAUSE_LENGTH); //wait for the
                next clock tick
                } catch (InterruptedException e) {
                    break;
                }
            }
        }
    }

    public void start() {
        mainThread = new Thread(this);
        mainThread.start();
    }

    public void stop() {
        mainThread.stop();
        mainThread = null;
    }
```

The update method implements double buffering, which we talk about in
Chapter 13.

```
public final void update(Graphics g){
    //implements no-flicker graphis
    Dimension dim = size();
    if((offScreenImage == null) ||
        (dim.width != offScreenSize.width) ||
        (dim.height != offScreenSize.height)) {
            offScreenImage = createImage(dim.width,
        dim.height);
            offScreenSize = dim;
            offScreenGraphics =
                    offScreenImage.getGraphics();
            if (SHOW_TRAIL) {
                offScreenGraphics.clearRect(0, 0,
                    offScreenSize.width,
        offScreenSize.height);
            }
        }
```

(continued)

(continued)

```
        if (!SHOW_TRAIL) {
            offScreenGraphics.clearRect(0, 0,
                offScreenSize.width,
            offScreenSize.height);
        }
        paint(offScreenGraphics);
        g.drawImage(offScreenImage, 0, 0, null);
}
```

Here is an example of using the Enumeration interface to go through all the elements of a vector:

```
public void paint(Graphics g) {
    for (Enumeration e = creatureList.elements();
        e.hasMoreElements() ;) {
        ((Creature)(e.nextElement())).paint(g);
        //ask creature to paint itself on screen
    }
}
```

A handleEvent method exists to handle the regular Java events:

```
public boolean handleEvent(Event event) {
    //handle java events
    switch(event.id) {
        case Event.MOUSE_DOWN:
            if (ecoSystem.inside(event.x, event.y)) {
                int size =
        Integer.parseInt(creatureSize.getCurrent().getLabel(),
        10);
                Color col =
        colorColors[creatureColor.getSelectedIndex()];
                sysEventList.addElement(new
        sysEvent(new Creature(ecoSystem, size, col,
        event.x, event.y, sysEventList),
        sysEvent.BIRTH));
                return true;
            }
    }
    return false;
}
```

The handleSysEvents method is the place where you manage the life cycle of the creatures. This is very heavy stuff, fraught with philosophical implications, as you can see from even a brief glance at the code!

```
void handleSysEvents() {
    // handle ecoSystem events
    sysEvent evt = null;
    for (Enumeration e = sysEventList.elements();
        e.hasMoreElements() ;) {
        evt = (sysEvent) e.nextElement();
        switch (evt.action) {
            case sysEvent.KILL:
                //remove creature from the list
                creatureList.removeElement(evt.subject);
                break;
            case sysEvent.BIRTH:
                //add creature to the list
                creatureList.addElement(evt.subject);
                break;
            case sysEvent.GROW:
                //increase creature size
                evt.subject.grow();
                break;
            /* add handlers for other actions here */
        }
    }
    sysEventList.removeAllElements();
}
```

The sprite class is an old friend of yours (we hope). The code is the same as in Chapter 13. We repeat it here to save some page-flipping, if you want to refer to it.

```
/** Sprite class allows to create moving objects on the
            screen. */
class Sprite extends Panel {
    //constants that can be used outside the class
    final static int NORTH = 180;
    final static int SOUTH = 0;
    final static int WEST = 270;
    final static int EAST = 90;
    final static int MAXSPEED = 12;
    //constants accessible only to children of the class
    protected final static int DELTA = 4;
    protected final static int DEFAULTSIZE = 10;

    //some geometrical information
    float positionX = DEFAULTSIZE;
```

(continued)

(continued)

```
        float positionY = DEFAULTSIZE;
        float width = 0;
        float height = 0;
        protected double speed = 0;
        protected float radius = 0;
        protected int direction = SOUTH; //in degrees from SOUTH
        protected boolean isMoving = false;
        protected Image myImage = null;

        /** A protected contructor only accessible to derived
               classes.
            A derived class is expected to set myImage and dimen-
               sions. */
        protected Sprite() {}

        /** Constructor which creates a default graphical repre-
               sentation */
        Sprite (Component c) {
            myImage = c.createImage(DEFAULTSIZE, DEFAULTSIZE);
            Graphics gr;
            gr = myImage.getGraphics();
            gr.setColor(Color.red);
            gr.fillRect(0, 0, DEFAULTSIZE, DEFAULTSIZE);
            setDimensions();
        }

        /** Constructor which accepts an image to be used for
               drawing
            the sprite on screen */
        Sprite (Image img) {
            myImage = img;
            setDimensions();
        }

        /** Constructor which accepts an image to be used for
               drawing
            the sprite on screen, plus starting coordinates */
        Sprite (Image img, int posX, int posY) {
            myImage = img;
            positionX = posX;
            positionY = posY;
            setDimensions();
        }
```

```java
/** Sets the direction of sprite */
public void heading (int dir) {
    direction = dir;
}


/** Sets the speed between 1 and MAXSPEED */
public void setSpeed (double sp) {
    if ((sp >= 1) && (sp <= MAXSPEED))
        speed = sp;
}

/** Causes the sprite to move */
public void startMovement () {
    isMoving = true;
}


/** Causes the sprite to stop moving */
public void stopMovement () {
    isMoving = false;
}


/** The tick method is called by our parent on every time
        tick.
    Here's where we it moves the sprite along its direc-
        tion if necessary. */
public void tick () {
    if ((isMoving) && (speed > 0)){
        positionX += ((float)speed / MAXSPEED) * DELTA *
        Math.sin((2 * Math.PI * direction) / 360);
        positionY += ((float)speed / MAXSPEED) * DELTA *
        Math.cos((2 * Math.PI * direction) / 360);
    }
}

/** Causes the sprite to bounce off the vertical wall */
public void bounceVertical() {
    direction = (0 - direction) % 360;
}
/** Causes the sprite to bounce off the horizontal wall
        */
public void bounceHorizontal() {
    direction = (180 - direction) % 360;
}

public void paint(Graphics g) {
```

(continued)

(continued)

```
            g.drawImage(myImage, (int)(positionX - width/2),
            (int)(positionY - height/2), null);
    }


    protected void setDimensions() {
        while (myImage.getHeight(this) == -1) { /* wait for
            the image to load */ }
        width = myImage.getWidth(this);
        height = myImage.getHeight(this);
        radius = (float) (Math.sqrt(Math.pow(height, 2) +
            Math.pow(width, 2)) / 2);
    }
}
```

This next code builds on `Sprite` to add the new behaviors of creatures. Experimenting with changing the constant values of `BIRTH_RATE`, `PUBERTY_AGE`, `GROWTH_PERIOD`, `HAPPY_PERIOD`, and `LIFESPAN` might be interesting. Or consider how you could set up several different species of creatures with different values for these constants.

```
/** Creature class adds living organism properties to sprite.
        */
class Creature extends Sprite {
    final static int MAXSIZE = 5;
    private final static int DEAD = 0;
    private final static int ALIVE = 1;
    private final static int MALE = 2;
    private final static int FEMALE = 3;
    private final static int DEFAULTDIAMETER = 10;
    private final static double BIRTH_RATE = 0.2;
    private final static int PUBERTY_AGE = 900;
    private final static int GROWTH_PERIOD = 2000;
    // won't eat other creatures if happy
    private final static int HAPPY_PERIOD = 550;
    private final static int LIFESPAN = 9999;
    static Vector sysEventList = null;
    int size = 0;
    Color color = null;
    Graphics gr = null;
    Component cmp = null;
    int status = ALIVE;
    int gender = (Math.random() > 0.5) ? FEMALE : MALE;
    int age = 0;
    int last_happy = 0;
```

Constructing a creature is a fairly complex job.

```
Creature(Component c, int sz, Color col, int posX, int
        posY, Vector evtList) {
    Image img;

    if ((sz >= 1) && (sz <= 5)) {
        size = sz;
        img = c.createImage(DEFAULTDIAMETER + sz*2,
        DEFAULTDIAMETER + sz*2);
        gr = img.getGraphics();
        gr.setColor(col);
        gr.fillOval(0, 0, DEFAULTDIAMETER + sz*2,
        DEFAULTDIAMETER + sz*2);
    }
      else {
        size = MAXSIZE;
        img = c.createImage(DEFAULTDIAMETER + MAXSIZE*2,
        DEFAULTDIAMETER + MAXSIZE*2);
        gr = img.getGraphics();
        gr.setColor(col);
        gr.fillOval(0, 0, DEFAULTDIAMETER + MAXSIZE*2,
        DEFAULTDIAMETER + MAXSIZE*2);
    }
    if (sysEventList == null) //static property, set only
        once
        sysEventList = evtList;
    cmp = c;
    color = col;
    myImage = img;
    positionX = posX;
    positionY = posY;
    setDimensions();
    heading((int)(Math.random() * 90 + 1));
    setSpeed(Math.random() * (MAXSPEED - 1) + 1);
    startMovement();
}
```

Each time the clock ticks, the creatures grow older.

```
public void tick() {
    age++;
    //let sprite do whatever it finds useful first
    super.tick();
    // check for boundary bounce conditions
```

(continued)

(continued)

```
        if ((positionX - width/2) <= 0) {
            bounceVertical();
            positionX = radius;
        }

        if ((positionX + width/2) >= cmp.size().width) {
            bounceVertical();
            positionX = cmp.size().width - width/2;
        }
        if ((positionY - height/2) <= 0) {
            bounceHorizontal();
            positionY = radius;
        }
        if ((positionY + height/2) >= cmp.size().height) {
            bounceHorizontal();
            positionY = cmp.size().height - height/2;
        }
        //old creatures have to expire
        if (age > LIFESPAN) {
            status = DEAD;
            sysEventList.addElement(new sysEvent(this,
            sysEvent.KILL));
        }
        //is it time to grow?
        if ((age % GROWTH_PERIOD) == 0)
            sysEventList.addElement(new sysEvent(this,
            sysEvent.GROW));
    }
```

When two creatures meet, a little drama ensues. Does one creature perish? Is a new creature born, or does each creature just bounce away in its separate direction? Here is your opportunity to change the laws of nature.

```
    public void checkCollision(Creature firstCreature) {
        double d = dist(positionX, firstCreature.positionX,
            positionY, firstCreature.positionY);

        if (d <= (radius + firstCreature.radius)) {
            if (radius == firstCreature.radius) {
                bounce(firstCreature, d);
            }
            else { //is anybody hungry?
                if (radius > firstCreature.radius) {
                    //this wins
                    if (firstCreature.status == ALIVE) {
```

```
                    if ((age - last_happy) >
                        HAPPY_PERIOD) {
                        eat(firstCreature);
                    }
                    else {
                        bounce(firstCreature, d);
                    }
                }
            }
        else { //firstCreature wins
            if (status == ALIVE) {
                if ((firstCreature.age -
firstCreature.last_happy) > HAPPY_PERIOD) {
                    firstCreature.eat(this);
                }
                else {
                    bounce(firstCreature, d);
                }
            }
        }
    }

    //give birth?
    if ((gender != firstCreature.gender) &&
        (Math.random() < BIRTH_RATE) &&
        (age >= PUBERTY_AGE) &&
        (firstCreature.age >= PUBERTY_AGE) &&
        (status == ALIVE) &&
        (firstCreature.status == ALIVE)) {
            Color col = new Color(
                (int)((color.getRed() +
firstCreature.color.getRed()) / 2),
                (int)((color.getGreen() +
firstCreature.color.getGreen()) / 2),
                (int)((color.getBlue() +
firstCreature.color.getBlue()) / 2));
            sysEventList.addElement(new sysEvent
                (new Creature(cmp, 1, col,
(int)(positionX + radius),
                (int)(positionY + radius),
sysEventList), sysEvent.BIRTH));
            last_happy = age; //giving birth is good
            firstCreature.last_happy =
firstCreature.age; //giving birth is good
        }
    }
}
```

This housekeeping stuff should be self-evident.

```
public void paint(Graphics g) {
    super.paint(g);
}

public void grow() {
    Image img;

    if (size < MAXSIZE) {
        size++;
        img = cmp.createImage(DEFAULTDIAMETER + size*2,
        DEFAULTDIAMETER + size*2);
        gr = img.getGraphics();
        gr.setColor(color);
        gr.fillOval(0, 0, DEFAULTDIAMETER + size*2,
        DEFAULTDIAMETER + size*2);
        myImage = img;
        setDimensions();
    }
    last_happy = age; //growing is good
}
```

When creatures bounce, they obey Newton's laws of the conservation of mass and energy.

```
void bounce(Creature firstCreature, double dist) {
    double massThis = radius * radius;
    double massFirst = firstCreature.radius *
        firstCreature.radius;
    double speedThis = (2 * massFirst *
        firstCreature.speed + (massThis - massFirst) *
        speed) / (massThis + massFirst);
    double speedFirst = (2 * massThis * speed +
        (massFirst - massThis) * firstCreature.speed) /
        (massThis + massFirst);
    int combDir = (direction + firstCreature.direction) /
        2;;

    speed = speedThis;
    firstCreature.speed = speedFirst;
    direction = (combDir - (direction - combDir)) % 360;
    firstCreature.direction = (combDir -
        (firstCreature.direction - combDir)) % 360;
    //remove firstCreature from zone of interference
    firstCreature.positionX = (float)(positionX + ((ra-
```

```
                dius + firstCreature.radius) *
                (firstCreature.positionX - positionX) / dist));
        firstCreature.positionY = (float)(positionY + ((ra-
            dius + firstCreature.radius) *
                (firstCreature.positionY - positionY) / dist));
    }
```

If you find violence disturbing, you may want to cover your eyes as you read this method.

```
    void eat(Creature victim) {
        color = new Color((int)((color.getRed() +
            victim.color.getRed()) / 2),
                        (int)((color.getGreen() +
            victim.color.getGreen()) / 2),
                        (int)((color.getBlue() +
            victim.color.getBlue()) / 2));
        gr.setColor(color);
        gr.fillOval(0, 0, (int)width, (int)height);
        sysEventList.addElement(new sysEvent(victim,
            sysEvent.KILL));
        last_happy = age; //food is good
        victim.status = DEAD;
    }

    double dist(float x1, float x2, float y1, float y2) {
        return Math.sqrt(Math.pow((x1 - x2), 2) + Math.pow((y1
            - y2), 2));
    }
}
```

The following class is a good example of the way Java programmers package related bits of data into an object for safekeeping.

```
/** sysEvent class, just a package to hold any creature-
            relevant event */
class sysEvent {
    final static int NOACTION = 0;
    final static int KILL = 1;
    final static int BIRTH = 2;
    final static int GROW = 3;
    /* add more actions here */

    Creature subject = null;
    int action = 0;
```

(continued)

(continued)

```
sysEvent(Creature firstCreature, int a) {
    subject = firstCreature;
    action = a;
}
}
```

Chapter 15
An Applet for Teacher

As every teacher knows, grading homework is a drag. The Java applet we explore in this chapter shows a way to let an applet do some of the work of providing constructive feedback to a self-directed learner. Our example is drawn from the world of business, but teachers and other academics reading this book can easily transpose this model to educational settings.

Learning from a Reference Document

Putting up some reference documentation on a Web site is easy. You can use a variety of tools to help convert word-processing text to HTML. With a little added effort and a modicum of graphic good taste, you can convert those tech manuals to a useful online reference, with an index and hypertext links to help the user navigate the document.

Imagine that you have such a document on your WWW site. For example, suppose that you have a reference guide to HTML tags. As one component of a course to teach HTML, you want to make sure that the learners are familiar with the full range of HTML tags, including some of the less common ones. You want to administer a brief quiz to verify that they actually read and understand the documentation for all the tags. To keep things simple, you make the quiz multiple choice.

1. Which tag should you use to embed a Java applet in an HTML document?

   a. `<APP>`

   b. `<APPLET>`

   c. `<AREA>`

   d. `<UL>`

2. Which HTML tag may be disabled by the user?

   a. `<BLINK>`

   b. `<BGSOUND>`

   c. Both

   d. Neither

3. Which of these items is NOT displayed on-screen?

   a. `HEAD`

   b. `H1`

   c. `H6`

   d. `MARQUEE`

(Answers at the end of the chapter.)

Giving learners instant feedback is nice. That way, if someone already knows some of the information, they can check their knowledge with the quiz and skip reading the documentation. On the other hand, if they need to check the other documentation for an answer, they can simply navigate the documentation with the browser and not lose their place in the quiz.

Oops! To make all this work, we need a way to keep our quiz applet on-screen even when the place where it's anchored in the HTML text moves off-screen. As you may suspect, you can put an applet in its own window so that it doesn't stop running when the user scrolls around in the document. See Figure 15-1 for a picture of the applet we have in mind.

The Secrets of Successful Quizzing

The main features of interest in this applet are all extremely useful extensions of techniques we've already introduced:

✔ How to put an applet in a frame

✔ How to read and parse a file

✔ How to calculate a score

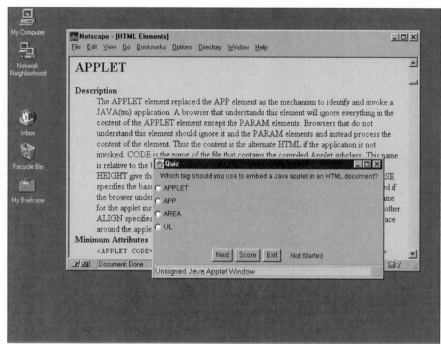

Figure 15-1:
The Quizem
applet.

I've Been Framed

All the applets we've worked with so far have had a fixed location on the HTML page. Like an embedded image, their position remained fixed next to a given bit of text. The Quizem applet requires putting an applet into a `Frame`, which is an object that can be moved around the screen and resized. An applet in a frame can be closed by user choice, just like any other GUI window. A framed applet leads a pretty independent life, but it remains dependent on the browser. When the browser closes, so must the applet.

The catch to putting an applet in a frame is that a frame remains open until it is closed. And you must write the code to handle the closing. Otherwise, the frame just sits around cluttering up the screen until the user exits the browser — not a pretty sight! (And not endearing to users.)

Framing happens in two places — in your selection of parents and in the event handler. To make a `Frame`, you must define a class that extends `Frame`. In the case of Quizem, that class is `QuizFrame`.

```
class QuizFrame extends Frame {
    ...
    the user interface is in the frame
    ...
}
```

By the way, because the applet's work is now done in the Frame, the applet itself should take up very little browser real estate. When you put the applet into your Web page, you are required to give the frame some WIDTH and HEIGHT. But give it a minimum so that the frame doesn't introduce awkward blank space. The following HTML code shows you how to set up the frame space.

```
<APPLET CODE="Quizem.class" WIDTH=5 HEIGHT=5>
<PARAM NAME=QUIZFILE VALUE=htmquiz.data>
</APPLET>
```

After you have put the frame on-screen, you must arrange for a way to take it off-screen when the user clicks the Close button of the window or selects the Close option from the window control menu. The events you need to watch for are WINDOW_DESTROY or an "Exit" ACTION_EVENT. In the following sample code, notice how the event is passed on to the handleEvent method of super if it's not handled in the window.

```
public boolean handleEvent(Event event) {
    switch (event.id)
    {
        case Event.WINDOW_DESTROY:
            dispose();
            System.exit(0);
            return true;

        case Event.ACTION_EVENT:
            if (event.arg.equals("Exit")) {
                dispose();
                System.exit(0);
                return true;
            }
            else {
                return super.handleEvent(event);
            }

        default:
            return super.handleEvent(event);
    }
}
```

Teach me how to read

Being forced to edit the HTML page to insert all questions and answers for a quiz as `<PARAM>` tags would be a big nuisance. So the Quizem applet gets its list of questions and answers from a separate file. That way, you can install a Quizem in the HTML page, but write and update question lists separately. The only thing you need to code into the HTML page is the name of the file containing the quiz contents.

In order to supply your quiz with questions and answers from a file, you must teach the computer how to *parse* the file it reads. Parsing means dividing a file into its individual components and analyzing the components so that you can understand their meaning. In our example, we need to help the computer recognize the beginning of each new question, answer option, and so on.

In Chapter 12, we covered reading a data stream. In Chapter 14, we described how to use a vector to keep track of a variable length collection of objects. These two techniques go together to help read and analyze the file of questions. The `QuizEngine` class reads an input stream and puts it into a vector. But to understand the `QuizEngine`, you first need to find out about a new player — `StringTokenizer`. `StringTokenizer` is the object that breaks up the data input stream into individual items made up of questions and answers.

A `StringTokenizer` breaks up a string into substrings by looking for special characters that are used as breaks. When we read English, we break sentences into words by looking for spaces. For the Quizem applet, we need to break the stream into chunks that are questions and chunks that are answer options. We arbitrarily decided to use $ as the symbol to indicate the breaks between chunks of a quiz item and \n (new line) to indicate the breaks between quiz items. So the layout of the file containing the quiz items looks like this:

```
Question$option 1$ option 2$ option 3$ option 4$answer\n
Question$option 1$ option 2$ option 3$ option 4$answer\n
Question$option 1$ option 2$ option 3$ option 4$answer\n
```

(You can use whatever symbols you want for indicating the breaks in your data.)

The `QuizItem` class is the object that embodies a single quiz item. Its constructor sets up a `StringTokenizer` object that breaks up the input from the file into chunks and passes the chunks on to the `QuizItem` object to organize them. Note the parameter of the constructor that says which characters are used to break up the item — $\n.

When you use a String Tokenizer, you may select whatever character or group of characters is convenient as the break symbols. For example, $ may not be a good symbol to use as a divider if we expect to write questions and answers about financial matters.

```
class QuizItem {
    final static int ANSWERCOUNT = 4;
    String question = null;
    String[] answerList = new String[ANSWERCOUNT];
    URL[] urlList = new URL[ANSWERCOUNT];
    float score = 0;
    int correctAnswer;

    /** Construct a QuizItem from a '$ 'delimitted input
            line.
     *   No error checking.  Expects exactly ANSWERCOUNT can-
            didate answers.
     */
    public QuizItem(String s, URL url) {
        StringTokenizer t = new StringTokenizer(s,"$\n");
        question = t.nextToken();
        String urlString = null;
        for (int i=0; i<answerList.length; i++) {
            answerList[i] = t.nextToken();
            try {
            urlString = t.nextToken();
            urlList[i] =  new URL(url,urlString);
            }
            catch (MalformedURLException e) {
                // catch bad URL's
                System.out.println("Invalid URL in data
            file: " + urlString );
            }
        }
        correctAnswer = Integer.parseInt(t.nextToken());
    }

    public String toString() {
        return question;
    }
}
```

Now that you understand how the individual quiz items are constructed, you can follow this next code to see how the input stream is broken up into quiz-ItemVector, a vector structure containing a variable number of quiz items.

```
class QuizEngine {
    Vector quizItemVector = new Vector();
    Enumeration enum = null;
    int currentItem = 0;
```

```
/** Construct a QuizEngine, loading quiz items (questions
        and answers) from
 *   the specified URL.
 */
public QuizEngine(URL quizFileURL) {
    try {
        // open a stream to read the quiz file
        InputStream inStream = quizFileURL.openStream();
        DataInputStream dataStream =
            new DataInputStream(new
        BufferedInputStream(inStream));
        // load the quiz file into our quizItemVector
        String inLine = null;
        while ((inLine = dataStream.readLine()) != null)
        {
            quizItemVector.addElement(new
        QuizItem(inLine,quizFileURL));
        }
        enum = quizItemVector.elements();
    }
    catch(IOException e) {
        // handle IO errors here
    }

}

public QuizItem getNextQuizItem() {
    if ( enum.hasMoreElements() ) {
        QuizItem q = (QuizItem)enum.nextElement();
        currentItem++;
        return q;
    }
    else {
        return null;
    }
}
```

What's the score?

Quizem is going to give a score for self-evaluation. Of course, you could also arrange for the applet to send scores back to an administrative file to help evaluate the materials or the trainees, or just to keep records of participation. You see an example of how you can set up different data collection and distribution methods in Chapter 16.

You can do the actual score keeping in various ways. The applet keeps track of possibleScore (the number of questions) and actualScore (the number of correct answers). In the following code, you see a programmer's quick and dirty approach to scoring. We divide 100 by the number of possible answers (percentage points per item), multiply by the number of correct items (total points) and convert the result to an integer — (int) in front of the calculation tells Java to convert to an integer.

Before you install this applet in your Web page, give some thought to what kind of feedback you would like to give and modify this section of the code to do what you want. For example, you might want to issue a report like "6 right out of 10." Or you might want to compare scores against some set of standards — if (actualScore > 23) {statusLabel.setText ("Top performer!")}

```
void displayScore() {
statusLabel.setText
("Score: " + ((int)((100/possibleScore)*actualScore)) + "%");
    }
}
```

In Plain Javanese

We give you the complete code for Quizem.

As you see, we make good use of the Java Class Library! Aside from checking out the URL of the quiz file, the Quizem applet class does very little.

```
/** Quizem */
*/
import java.awt.*;
import java.applet.*;
import java.io.*;
import java.util.*;
import java.net.*;
//import java.lang.Math;
public class Quizem extends Applet {
    QuizFrame quizFrame = null;

    public void init() {
        try {
            // construct the URL of the quiz file String
            URL quizURL = new
```

```
            URL(getCodeBase(),getParameter("QUIZFILE"));
            // construct a quizframe with a quizengine
            quizFrame = new QuizFrame(new
            QuizEngine(quizURL),this);
            // pop up the window
            quizFrame.show();
            quizFrame.displayNextQuizItem();
        }
        catch(MalformedURLException e) {
            showStatus("Invalid Quiz URL: " +
            getParameter("QUIZFILE"));
            // catch bad URL's
        }
    }


    public void start() {
        super.start();
        quizFrame.show();
    }


    public void stop() {
        quizFrame.hide();
    }

}
```

`QuizEngine` reads the input file and puts the `QuizItems` into the `quizItemVector`. You can refer to Chapter 14 for more about this process.

```
class QuizEngine {
    Vector quizItemVector = new Vector();
    Enumeration enum = null;
    int currentItem = 0;

    /** Construct a QuizEngine, loading quiz items (questions
            and answers) from
     *    the specified URL.
     */
    public QuizEngine(URL quizFileURL) {
        try {
            // open a stream to read the quiz file
            InputStream inStream = quizFileURL.openStream();
            DataInputStream dataStream =
                new DataInputStream(new
```

(continued)

(continued)

```
        BufferedInputStream(inStream))  // load the quiz
        file into our quizItemVector
        String inLine = null;
        while ((inLine = dataStream.readLine()) != null)
        {
            quizItemVector.addElement(new
        QuizItem(inLine,quizFileURL));
        }
        enum = quizItemVector.elements();
    }
    catch(IOException e) {
        // handle IO errors here
    }
}

//this method returns a QuizItem
public QuizItem getNextQuizItem() {
    if ( enum.hasMoreElements() ) {
        QuizItem q = (QuizItem)enum.nextElement();
        currentItem++;
        return q;
    }
    else {
        return null;
    }
}

public String getStatusString() {
        return ("Question " + currentItem + " of " +
        quizItemVector.size());
}

public String getFinalScoreString() {
    // sum the score
    float possibleScore = quizItemVector.size();
    float actualScore = 0;
    for (Enumeration es = quizItemVector.elements() ;
        es.hasMoreElements() ;) {
        QuizItem q = (QuizItem)es.nextElement();
        actualScore = actualScore + q.score;
    }

    return new String("Score: ");
    }
}
```

QuizItem is in charge of structuring individual items. Note the use of StringTokenizer to break up each input line into a question, answer options, and a correct answer reference.

```
class QuizItem {
    final static int ANSWERCOUNT = 4;
    String question = null;
    String[] answerList = new String[ANSWERCOUNT];
    String[] refList = new String[ANSWERCOUNT];
    float score = 0;
    int correctAnswer;
    /** Construct a QuizItem from a '$ 'delimitted input
            line.
     *  No error checking.  Expects exactly ANSWERCOUNT can-
            didate answers.
     */
    public QuizItem(String s) {
        StringTokenizer t = new StringTokenizer(s,"$\n");
        question = t.nextToken();
        for (int i=0; i<answerList.length; i++) {
            answerList[i] = t.nextToken();
            refList[i] =  t.nextToken();
        }
        correctAnswer = Integer.parseInt(t.nextToken());
    }

    public String toString() {
        return question;
    }
}
```

QuizFrame is the object that lives as a free window and is in charge of the GUI. By the way, if this window gets covered up by the browser window, as may happen in some circumstances, don't be alarmed. You can bring the QuizFrame back to the top in the same way you would any open but temporarily covered window. For example, in an MS Windows environment, press Alt + Tab.

```
class QuizFrame extends Frame {
    QuizEngine quiz;
    Label questionLabel = new Label();
    Label statusLabel = new Label("Pick your answer now.");
    CheckboxGroup answers = new CheckboxGroup();
    Checkbox answerA;
    Checkbox answerB;
    Checkbox answerC;
```

(continued)

(continued)

```
    Checkbox answerD;

    float possibleScore = 0;
    float actualScore = 0;

    Panel ap = new Panel();
    QuizItem item = null;
    Applet applet;

    QuizFrame(QuizEngine quiz, Applet a) {
        super("Quiz");
        this.quiz = quiz;
        reshape(0,0,450,300);
        applet = a;

setBackground(new Color(220,220,255));

        ap.setLayout(new GridLayout(5,1));
        ap.add(questionLabel);
        ap.add(answerA = new Checkbox("A",answers,false));
        ap.add(answerB = new Checkbox("B",answers,false));
        ap.add(answerC = new Checkbox("C",answers,false));
        ap.add(answerD = new Checkbox("D",answers,false));

        Panel cp = new Panel();
        cp.add(new Button("Next"));
        cp.add(new Button("Score"));
        cp.add(new Button("Exit"));
        cp.add(statusLabel);

        add("North",ap);
        add("South",cp);

    }

    /** Handle the WINDOW_DESTROY event so our user can exit.
        */
    public boolean handleEvent(Event event) {
        switch (event.id)
        {
            case Event.WINDOW_DESTROY:
                dispose();
                System.exit(0);
                return true;
```

```
            case Event.ACTION_EVENT:
                if (event.arg.equals("Exit")) {
                    dispose();
                    System.exit(0);
                    return true;
                }
                else if (event.arg.equals("Next")) {
                    updateScore();
                    displayNextQuizItem();
                    return true;
                }
                else if (event.arg.equals("Score")) {
                    displayScore();
                    return true;
                }
                else {
                    return super.handleEvent(event);
                }

            default:
                return super.handleEvent(event);
        }
    }

    void displayNextQuizItem() {
        if( (item = quiz.getNextQuizItem()) != null ) {
            questionLabel.setText(item.question);
            answerA.setLabel(item.answerList[0]);
            answerB.setLabel(item.answerList[1]);
            answerC.setLabel(item.answerList[2]);
            answerD.setLabel(item.answerList[3]);
        }
    }
```

The following updateScore() method compares the response for each item with the correct response and updates the score data. The displayScore() method gives a report to the user.

```
    void updateScore() {
        possibleScore++;

        switch (item.correctAnswer) {
            case 1:
```

(continued)

(continued)

```
                    if (answers.getCurrent() == answerA) {
                        item.score = 1;
                    }
                    else {
                        item.score = 0;
                    }
                if (answers.getCurrent() == answerA) {
                    actualScore++;
                }
                break;
            case 2:
                if (answers.getCurrent() == answerB) {
                    item.score = 1;
                }
                else {
                    item.score = 0;
                }
                if (answers.getCurrent() == answerB) {
                    actualScore++;
                }
                break;
            case 3:
                if (answers.getCurrent() == answerC) {
                    item.score = 1;
                }
                else {
                    item.score = 0;
                }
                if (answers.getCurrent() == answerC) {
                    actualScore++;
                }
                break;
            case 4:
                if (answers.getCurrent() == answerD) {
                    item.score = 1;
                }
                else {
                    item.score = 0;
                }
                if (answers.getCurrent() == answerD) {
                    actualScore++;
                }
                break;
            default:
```

```
                item.score = 0;
                break;
        }
        statusLabel.setText(quiz.getStatusString());
    }

    void displayScore() {
        statusLabel.setText
            ("Score: " +
            ((int)((100/possibleScore)*actualScore)) +
            "%");
    }
}
```

And the Answers

Answers to quiz items from the first section of the chapter: b, a, a.

Chapter 16
Shopping Up a Storm

- -

In This Chapter

▶ An online shopping cart

▶ Setting up list displays

▶ Getting the prices right

▶ Using hyperlinks in your applet

▶ Sending messages to browsers and servers

- -

Several big retail operations in our home town make a business of buying up any kind of surplus merchandise they can find at a good buy. Then they pass along the savings to their customers. From one day to the next, you never know what they'll have in stock. Today, you may find power tools; tomorrow, apricot preserves. Or more likely, you find both on the same day and artificial ivory shirt buttons the next day.

Now, suppose they want to offer online shopping. . . .

Designing a Shopping Cart

To offer online shopping, we must first consider what an online store should contain. An online store must contain an inventory list; we can put together an HTML page with clever descriptions and maybe some photos of the items we have for sale. (Even though some prices are ridiculously low, this *is* merchandising.) Of course, we have to design our page so that we can update it easily as merchandise and prices change.

But how does the customer find his or her way around the store? Traditional, organized departments are not what this online type of store is all about. Our idea is for the customer to pick up a *shopping cart* upon entering the WWW site. The shopping cart is actually a Java applet that moves around the WWW site with the shopper.

The applet is equipped with a complete inventory list. If you, the shopper, are looking for something specific, you can consult the inventory list that is part of the applet and use a hypertext link to retrieve the full description on the WWW site. Or if you like, you can just browse around on the page until you find something you want.

The applet is also equipped with a list of purchases — that's the shopping cart part of the applet. When you decide to buy something, you click on a button to move it from the inventory list to your list of purchases (your cart). You can also change your mind and remove any item from your shopping cart by clicking on another button. See Figure 16-1 for an example of the user interface.

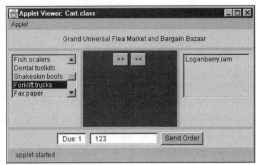

Figure 16-1:
A Shopping
Cart.

In the sample applet, we ask for just a shopper ID number. In a real business application, you may need to implement more elaborate security provisions. In order to save work for our WWW server, I make the applet check that the shopper entered an ID number and that the shopping cart is not empty before sending the purchase list back to the server.

Specials of the Day

The Shopping Cart applet has some similarities to the Quizem applet explained in Chapter 15. Like Quizem, the Shopping Cart applet intends for users to browse various parts of the applet's host document while keeping the applet in view also. Unlike Quizem, we implement this applet in a browser frame (because Netscape offers this option) instead of a Java `Frame`. Using the browser frame makes providing hypertext links between the applet and the rest of the document simpler.

Also like Quizem, Shopping Cart reads a file and puts information into an object that is a collection of other objects. In the case of Shopping Cart, the list the applet reads is a list of items for sale and their prices, and the collection is not a `Vector`, but something similar — a `Hashtable`.

However, we do have some new wrinkles with this applet:

- ✔ Shopping Cart uses the Hashtable of items for sale to fill a List object on-screen so that the user can pick items from the list. Also, Shopping Cart must send a list of selected items back to the server.

- ✔ Shopping Cart is designed to let the applet control hypertext jumps by the browser. Clicking on a link in the applet shifts the text in the browser.

Notice that many of the features of Shopping Cart might be useful in a revised and expanded Quizem. For example, you may want to send answer data back to the server, or you may want to implement hypertext links from the applet to the browser.

I've got a little list

When you keep your data in a vector structure, you identify individual objects in the vector by index number — item 1, item 7, and so on. When all you need to do is work your way from one end of the list to the other, identifying individual objects by number works very well. But our shopper may pick items out of the middle of the list in random order. In this case, keeping track of objects by name is easier. And that is what a Hashtable does.

Like a Vector, a Hashtable is a variable-length collection of objects. Unlike a Vector, a Hashtable gives each object a name string.

In the applet's code, we identify ShoppingItems to put into a hashable structure.

```
ShoppingItem (String n, URL u, long p) {
    itemName = n;
    itemURL = u;
    itemPrice = p;
}
```

When the program reads the input file of items for sale, it uses a StringTokenizer object to parse the input into ShoppingItems and then puts the ShoppingItems into the offer Hashtable with name as the identifying key. The following code is part of the loadOffer method.

```
void loadOffer(URL u) {
    ...
        while ((inLine = dataStream.readLine()) != null) {
        StringTokenizer t  = new
```

(continued)

(continued)

```
        StringTokenizer(inLine,"$\n");
    String     name = t.nextToken();
    URL          url = new URL(u,t.nextToken());
    long       price = (new
        Long(t.nextToken())).longValue();
    ShoppingItem item = new ShoppingItem(name,
        url, price);
    offer.put(name, item);
  }
  ...
}
```

In the preceding code, `offer` is the name of the `Hashtable`. The key used to locate objects in the `Hashtable` is `name`. By using this hashtable structure, you can add, remove, or retrieve items by `name`. When you use a `Vector`, you keep track of items by number, a process which can become quite complicated as you add and remove items.

This next code puts the offered items into the list on the left side of the screen. `Enumeration` is used with `Hashtables` in exactly the same way as with `Vectors`. See Chapter 14 for other information about using these structures.

```
Panel ep = new Panel();
    for (Enumeration e = offer.keys();
        e.hasMoreElements(); ) {
        ShoppingItem s =
        (ShoppingItem)(offer.get(e.nextElement()));
        leftList.addItem(s.itemName);
    }
```

And I'm sending it to you

Sending information back to the server is very similar to receiving it from the server. Java takes care of a great many painful details with objects from the class libraries.

This next list tells you what happens when you send data out to the Web server:

- **Connect:** Use the Web server's URL to establish a connection to the Web server over the Internet.

- **Send header:** Send a string of magical incantations to the Web server to alert the server about what is coming.

▌ ✔ **Send data:** Send the data as a string.

We wrote this example with the assumption that you use a communications method called *CGI* (for Common Gateway Interface). At present, CGI is the most common standard for communicating from Web pages back to servers. Other methods are under development that give greater flexibility and security, but the sequence of events in the communication is similar.

The Socket class is the type of object that establishes a connection. Socket is a library class found in Java.net. The following code sets up a number of strings with the various bits of information to go into the communication from the Web page to the server. Then it instantiates a Socket and a DataOutputStream and uses the writeBytes method of the DataOutputStream to send the information off to the Web server.

```java
public boolean handleEvent(Event e) {
        if (e.target == sendButton) {
            try {

            // your webserver goes here
            String webServer = "www.My-Web-Server.com";

            // the relative path, on your webserver, to the
            CGI script
            String cgiScript = "/cgi-bin/MyScript.cgi";

            // For info on the CGI specification
            see: http://www.w3.org/pub/WWW/CGI/

            // build the argument string
            String dataString = "";
            for (Enumeration elems = take.elements();
                    elems.hasMoreElements(); ) {
                dataString += elems.nextElement();
                dataString += "&"; // provide a delimiter
            }
            dataString += (total + "&");
            dataString += idField.toString();

            Socket sock = new Socket(webServer, 80);
            DataOutputStream outStream = new
                    DataOutputStream(sock.getOutputStream());
```

(continued)

(continued)

```
        // send header
        outStream.writeBytes("POST " + cgiScript + "\n" +
            "Content-type: plain/text\n");

        // tell the server how much data to expect
        outStream.writeBytes("Content-length: " +
            dataString.length() + "\n\n");
        // send the data
        outStream.writeBytes(dataString);
        }

        catch (Exception exception) {
            System.out.println(e);
        }

        return true;
    }
    return false;
}
```

There's more than one way to frame an applet

The Netscape browser provides a feature called *Frames* that allows you to view more than one document at the same time in an organized, tiled window display. See Figure 16-2.

This display organization is formatted in a separate HTML document that uses the <FRAMESET> tag to set up a layout of columns and rows. Then the <FRAME> tag is used to name the separate documents that can be displayed in the areas defined by <FRAMESET>. With the <FRAME> tag, you can also use several attributes to set some rules about the way you want the document displayed. For example, you may set a margin height and width (MARGINHEIGHT and MARGINWIDTH), turn SCROLLING on or off, and permit or prevent resizing (like NORESIZE).

Our Shopping Cart applet is in a <FRAMESET> structure that divides the browser screen into two equal columns. The left column contains the page that holds the applet. The right column contains the catalogue descriptions and other promotional material that make up our online warehouse. This next HTML code is for the main Web page that sets up the frames.

Figure 16-2:
A Netscape
FRAMESET
structure.

```
<HTML>
<HEAD>
<TITLE>Shopping Mall With Cart </TITLE>
</HEAD>
<FRAMESET COLS="50%,50%">
<FRAME NAME=cart SRC=Cart4.html MARGINHEIGHT=2 MARGINWIDTH=2
        SCROLLING="no" NORESIZE>
<FRAME NAME=store SRC=Store.html MARGINHEIGHT=2 MARGINWIDTH=2
        SCROLLING="yes" NORESIZE>
</FRAMESET>
</HTML>
```

In the preceding code, Store.html is the catalogue document and Cart4.html is the page that contains the Shopping Cart applet.

When I say "Jump"

A Java applet can send messages to the browser that is currently displaying its Web page. An Interface called AppletContext implements methods showDocument() and showStatus(), among others. These methods allow the applet programmer to give instructions to the browser.

First you must establish a connection to the AppletContext (also known as the browser) by using a method of the Applet class — getAppletContext(). Then you can send a message to the AppletContext, or browser, to show a document or to show a message in the status line.

The Shopping Cart applet follows this procedure. We want to use a double-click on one of the list items to trigger a hypertext jump to a new location in the document. The lists are part of an object called a DoubleList. The Shopping Cart applet gets the AppletContext and passes it on to the DoubleList object in its constructor:

```
//Constructor for DoubleList
    DoubleList(Cart c, Hashtable o, AppletContext ac) {
        offer = o;
        browser = ac;
        parent = c;
//Instantiation of dl as a DoubleList by the applet Cart
dl = new DoubleList(this, offer, getAppletContext());
```

Double-clicking on a list item generates an event that is handled by dl, the DoubleList object.

```
public boolean handleEvent(Event e) {
    switch(e.id) {
        case Event.ACTION_EVENT:
            ...
            else if (e.target == rightList) {
                    getURL(rightList.getSelectedItem());
            }
            else if (e.target == leftList) {
                    getURL(leftList.getSelectedItem());
            }
            break;

        default:
            return false;
        }
        return true;
    }
```

The getURL() method is the one that speaks to the browser. Courage, a translation follows immediately!

```
void getURL(String item) {
   browser.showDocument(((((ShoppingItem)(offer.get(item))).itemURL),"store");
      }
```

The following list is a breakdown of all the stuff in the preceding parentheses. (Just in case you lost track.)

- `offer.get(item)`
  A message to the `offer` hashtable requesting the item identified by the string you clicked on.
- `(ShoppingItem)`
  Puts the result of `offer.get` into the form of a `ShoppingItem`.
- `(a ShoppingItem).itemURL`
  A message to the particular `ShoppingItem` selected, requesting it to tell us its URL.

So when the computer finishes digesting the parentheses, it ends up with a message to the browser that says `showDocument(`*URL of the selected item*`, "store")`. The first parameter, *URL of the selected item*, tells the browser where to go; the second parameter, `"store"`, tells it the name of the browser frame for displaying the document.

This communication technique works for Netscape browsers. The standards and software support for letting applets speak to the browser is still evolving. Test anything you do in this area. Don't count on its working for all browsers. And don't blame yourself if it doesn't work as expected. The possibilities are too exciting for us to ignore, but the methods are too new for us to give rock solid instructions.

The price is right

Our Shopping Cart applet has a small problem that you may not expect. How do you track and add the prices? If you stop to think about it, dollars and cents are integers. We are in the habit of expecting prices accurate to the penny. For this reason, the correct way to handle the prices is to make them integer numbers of cents. (If you expect to be making extraordinarily large sales, you might want to use a `long` instead of an `int` type of number. See Chapter 10 for more on number types.)

As a practical matter, you wouldn't expect using `floats` (the number type, that is) for your dollar values to make a difference. But in fact, because of some arcane details in the way the computer translates between its internal binary number system and our decimal system, using `floats` can sometimes lead to a cumulation of small rounding errors. As a result, adding to and then removing from the shopping cart a large number of items in random order may leave the shopper buying nothing, but owing $0.01.

How, then, do you make a display that shows dollars and cents with a decimal point? You can use this next trick that takes advantage of the remainder operator (also known as the *modulus*, %) that we told you about in Chapter 10:

1. **Use** `toString(num/100)` **to give you the dollars portion of a price in string form.**

   For example, when using integer math, 1295/100 = 12. Remember, you discard the remainder when you divide integers. The `toString` method then gives you the number 12 as a string you can display.

2. **Use** `toString(num%100)` **to give you the cents portion of the price.**

   The % operator gives you the remainder after a division of integers. So 1295%100 = 95, and `toString` then gives you the number 95 as a string.

3. **Put in the decimal point by combining strings.**

   ```
   ResultString = (toString(num/100)) + "." +
   (toString(num%100)) or 12.95
   ```

Another name for the remainder operator is *modulus* or just *mod* for short.

A Shopping Cart Full of Code

So, here is a complete listing of the applet code. The major components of this applet are the applet class, `Cart`, and a class called `DoubleList` that handles the two lists — the offered items and the taken items. We start the complete code for this applet by making all the necessary library classes available.

```
import java.awt.*;
import java.applet.*;
import java.util.*;
import java.net.*;
import java.io.*;
```

This next code is the applet class.

```
/**
 * This is our MODEL object
 *   an applet dedicated to Aron Koosis, our merchandising
 *            guru
 */
public class Cart extends Applet {
```

```
Label titleLabel  = new Label("Grand Universal Flea
        Market and Bargain Bazaar");
TextField   idField    = new TextField("Your ID Number:
        xxx");
Button      sendButton = new Button("Send Order");
long        total      = 0;
String      amtString  = "Due: ";
TextField   amtField   = new TextField("No Purchases");
DoubleList  dl         = null;
Hashtable   offer      = new Hashtable();
Vector      take       = new Vector();
```

The following code for the `init` method sets up a `BorderLayout` with fields for amount owed and user ID number at the bottom of the screen, and a button to send in the order. The code also checks the URL (`try`).

Notice that this code includes some troubleshooting printout like `System.out.println(e); //this data will help to troubleshoot problems`. These statements appear in the browser's Java console display and may help you to figure out what is going on if trouble strikes. (Check your browser's help file or documentation for how to access the Java console.) Writing and keeping some test prints like these is a good idea, especially when dealing with communications that might go wrong for reasons unrelated to your code.

```
public void init() {
    setLayout(new BorderLayout(5,5));

    Panel np = new Panel();
    np.add(titleLabel);
    add("North",np);
    np.setBackground(Color.cyan);
    np.resize(300,50);

    Panel sp = new Panel();
    add("South",sp);
    sp.add(amtField);
    sp.add(idField);
    sp.add(sendButton);
    sp.resize(300,50);
    sp.setBackground(Color.cyan);
```

(continued)

(continued)

```
        try {
            // construct the URL of the data file String
            URL listURL = new URL(getCodeBase(),
                getParameter("DATAFILE"));
            loadOffer(listURL);
        }
        catch(MalformedURLException e) {
            System.out.println(e); //this data will help t
                troubleshoot problems
            showStatus(e.toString()); // catch bad URL's
        }
        dl = new DoubleList(this, offer, getAppletContext());
        add("Center", dl);
    }
```

In the next code is where we call the method that does the trick to print dollars and cents. AddToCart and removeFromCart are similar packaged routines; you can spell them out fully in the body of the code. By putting the routines into their own separate methods, we make the code easier to read and easier to revise.

```
    public void paint(Graphics g) {
        amtField.setText(amtString +
            MoneyUtil.centsToDollars(total));
        dl.paint(g);
    }

    public void addToCart(String item) {
        take.addElement(item);
        total += ((ShoppingItem)(offer.get(item))).itemPrice;
        repaint();
    }

    public void removeFromCart(String item) {
        take.removeElement(item);
        total -= ((ShoppingItem)(offer.get(item))).itemPrice;
        repaint();
    }
```

The following code contains the loadOffer method that reads the input stream and puts it into the offer Hashtable.

When you write code to read from an input stream, keep the two exception tests you see at the end of this block of code in the order that you see them here.

```
void loadOffer(URL u) {
    try {
        // open a stream to read the data file
        InputStream inStream = u.openStream();
        DataInputStream dataStream =
            new DataInputStream(new
        BufferedInputStream(inStream));
        String          inLine      = null;
        // load the data file into our shopping items
        while ((inLine = dataStream.readLine()) != null) {
            StringTokenizer t       = new
                               StringTokenizer(inLine,"$\n");
            String          name    = t.nextToken();
            URL             url     = new
                               URL(u,t.nextToken());
            long price   = (new
                        Long(t.nextToken())).longValue();
            ShoppingItem    item    = new
                          ShoppingItem(name, url, price);
                offer.put(name, item);
        }
    }
    catch(MalformedURLException e) {
        System.out.println(e);
    }
    catch(IOException e) {
        System.out.println(e);
    }
}
```

Next is the `handleEvent` method of the applet. The `DoubleList` object has its own `handleEvent` method. The applet is responsible for sending data back to the server when the user clicks the Send button.

```
public boolean handleEvent(Event e) {
    if (e.target == sendButton) {
        try {
            // post the data to a cgi script on the web
            server...
            // your webserver name goes here
            String webServer = "www.My-Web-Server.com";
            // the relative path, on your webserver, to the
            CGI script
```

(continued)

(continued)

```
String cgiScript = "/cgi-bin/MyScript.cgi";
// For info on the CGI specification see: http://
www.w3.org/pub/WWW/CGI/

// build the argument string
String dataString = "";
for (Enumeration elems = take.elements();
        elems.hasMoreElements(); ) {
    dataString += elems.nextElement();
    dataString += "&"; // provide a delimiter
}
dataString += (total + "&");
dataString += idField.toString();
 //Instantiate a socket
Socket sock = new Socket(webServer, 80);
DataOutputStream outStream = new
        DataOutputStream(sock.getOutputStream());
// send header
outStream.writeBytes("POST " + cgiScript + "\n" +
                    "Content-type: plain/text\n");
// tell the server how much data to expect
outStream.writeBytes("Content-length: " +
                    dataString.length() + "\n\n");


// send the data
outStream.writeBytes(dataString);
}
catch (Exception exception) {
    System.out.println(e);
}

return true;
}
return false;
}

}
```

The DoubleList class is a container for the two lists objects. You may find this class useful in other situations where you want to be able to move information back and forth between two lists.

```
/** A DoubleList (for lack of a better name) is two lists
          with buttons to
 *  transfer stuff between them.
 * This is our VIEW object
 */
class DoubleList extends Panel {
    Button        toRightButton = new Button(">>");
    Button        toLeftButton  = new Button("<<");
    List          leftList      = new List(5, false);
    List          rightList     = new List(5, false);
    Cart          parent        = null;
    Hashtable     offer         = null;
    AppletContext browser       = null;

    //Constructor
    DoubleList(Cart c, Hashtable o, AppletContext ac) {
        offer = o;
        browser = ac;
        parent = c;

        setLayout(new BorderLayout(5,5));

        Panel ep = new Panel();
        for (Enumeration e = offer.keys();
            e.hasMoreElements(); ) {
            ShoppingItem s =
            (ShoppingItem)(offer.get(e.nextElement()));
            leftList.addItem(s.itemName);
        }
        ep.add(rightList);
        add("East",ep);
        ep.resize(125,200);
        ep.setBackground(Color.cyan);

        Panel wp = new Panel();
        wp.add(leftList);
        add("West",wp);
        wp.resize(125,200);
        wp.setBackground(Color.cyan);

        Panel cp = new Panel();
        add("Center",cp);
        cp.setBackground(Color.blue);
        cp.resize(50,200);
```

(continued)

(continued)

```
        cp.setLayout(new FlowLayout());
        cp.add(toRightButton);
        cp.add(toLeftButton);
    }
```

Next we show code for the `handleEvent` method for `DoublePanel`. This code handles shifting items from the offered list to the taken list, and back. Also in this code, `DoublePanel` responds to double-clicks on the lists by sending a message to the browser.

```
public boolean handleEvent(Event e) {
    switch(e.id) {
        case Event.ACTION_EVENT:
            if (e.target == toRightButton) {
              parent.addToCart(leftList.getSelectedItem());
              rightList.addItem(leftList.getSelectedItem());
              leftList.delItem(leftList.getSelectedIndex());
              }
            else if (e.target == toLeftButton) {
        parent.removeFromCart(rightList.getSelectedItem());
              leftList.addItem(rightList.getSelectedItem());
          rightList.delItem(rightList.getSelectedIndex());


              }
            else if (e.target == rightList) {
                    getURL(rightList.getSelectedItem());
            }
            else if (e.target == leftList) {
                    getURL(leftList.getSelectedItem());
            }
            break;

        default:
            return false;
        }
    return true;
    }

  void getURL(String item) {
  browser.showDocument((((ShoppingItem)(offer.get(item))).itemURL),"store");
    }
}
```

ShoppingItem is a convenience class that wraps a few items of data into a class.

```
class ShoppingItem {
    String   itemName;
    URL      itemURL;
    long     itemPrice;

    ShoppingItem (String n, URL u, long p) {
        itemName = n;
        itemURL = u;
        itemPrice = p;
    }
}
```

MoneyUtil is a convenience class that allows us to convert cents to dollars. You ought to find this class useful in lots of places!

```
class MoneyUtil {
    static public String centsToDollars(long cents) {
        return ((cents/100) + "." + (cents%100));
    }
}
```

Chapter 17

Fun with Fractals

• •

In This Chapter

▶ Fishing for fractals

▶ Comparing methods of animation

• •

A fractal is a geometric shape that is self-similar and has fractional dimensions. *Self-similar* means that if you magnify a fractal, no matter how much, you end up with something that looks very much like that with which you started. Fractals can describe the shape of clouds, mountains, coastlines, and other naturally occurring forms. More important, for our purposes, fractals are interesting to look at and explore. (We provide some good starting points for exploring fractals at the end of this chapter.) Figure 17-1 is one snapshot of a particularly famous fractal, called the Julia set, after its discoverer, Gaston Julia.

Figure 17-1:
A view of the world-famous Julia set.

Give a Friend a Fractal...

Here already? Well, I don't expect one snapshot of a Julia fractal to hold your attention very long. Give a friend a fractal, and you entertain that friend for a day; teach a friend to make fractals, and you entertain your friend for a lifetime. With the fractal applet in this chapter and the power of your computer, you can generate an infinite number of fractal images. You can view these images in full color, play with the source code, and alter and improve this applet to your heart's content. (If you tell us about your experiments, we'll be happy to include a link to your work on the resource Web page for this book!)

An Explanation of Animation

The fractal applet isn't exactly an animation — it's more like a "picture generator." Although we make this distinction, you should understand some useful points about Java applets and animations.

If you're an experienced Web developer, you may know the technique of building small animations using GIF89 images. (If you haven't heard of these techniques and are interested, we refer you to Netscape's website — `http://www.netscape.com` — where you can search for the word "animation." We also provide references on the resource page for this book: `http://www.iscinc.com/JPFD`)

Comparing Java animation to GIF

We are often asked how Java animation compares to these other techniques. A quick comparison follows:

Most image files on the Web are stored in Graphics Interchange Format (sm) — *GIF* — a standard published by CompuServe and last revised in 1989.

Optimize your applet

It's only fair to warn you: generating a complete fractal may take many minutes on an average computer. You will probably want to tell the Java compiler to *optimize* your applet by using the *-O* flag, like so:

```
javac -O Fractal.java
```
It takes longer to compile with optimization, but you will notice that your resulting Class files are smaller and your applets run faster.

Though you have seen hundreds of GIF pictures in Web pages, you may not have realized that GIF images can display a series of pictures sequentially, like a film strip. That's right — the GIF 1989 standard provides a way to include many images within a single file and to loop through these images.

Because browsers from Netscape and others support the GIF 1989 standard, you can create an animation using a multi-image GIF file.

One basic approach for using Java to do simple frame-by-frame animation is to download a series of images as well as a Java applet to "play" the images. This technique is used in the Animator demo, which is part of the Java Development Kit included on the CD accompanying this book.

The fact is, the current release of Java does not give you a lot of benefits for the kind of animation we've just described. The main problem is that the current release of Java is pretty slow when it comes to downloading multiple files. If your applet requires, say, three class files and seven GIFs (animation frames), Java opens a network connection, fetches a file, and closes the connection *ten times!* This is the programming equivalent of hanging up the phone and redialing at the end of every paragraph. It's a performance problem that Java's designers intend to remedy, as they say in the business, RSN (Real Soon Now).

Using Java animation intelligently

On the other hand, if your animation is one in which a single image moves across a background — perhaps a fish moving through the water — Java may be just right for you. The fish moving through water is, of course, the perfect job for a `Sprite` class like the one we work with in Chapters 13 and 14. A Java Sprite animation takes advantage of your computer's power to "generate" all of the snapshots of your fish moving from Point A to Point B.

The Fractal applet in this chapter is a similar example. Instead of downloading thousands of images to illustrate the beauty of fractals, you download a small applet that knows how to generate an infinite number of images.

Yet another compelling use of Java would be, for example, as a viewer for CAD (computer-aided design) files. CAD drawings are line drawings of the sort typically used by architects and engineers to display building plans, circuit diagrams, and similar pictures. With a CAD-viewing applet, users could download a single CAD picture and then view it at any angle or magnification they wish. Again, the applet uses the power of the applet user's computer to generate thousands of possible images from a single description.

A Java animation also differs from a GIF animation in that it can have a lot more smarts. It can start playing or change images or jump to a URL or pop up a dialog box in response to a mouse click or the time of day or some other external input.

The Code

```
import java.awt.*;
import java.applet.*;
import java.net.*;

/**
 * Fractal applet allows you to interractively explore
 * the infinite beauty of fractal world
 * @author Anatoly Goroshnik
 */
public class Fractal extends Applet {
    //constants
    final static double INIT_ZOOM_X_MANDELBROT = -50;
    final static double INIT_ZOOM_Y_MANDELBROT = 0;
    final static double INIT_ZOOM_X_JULIA = 0;
    final static double INIT_ZOOM_Y_JULIA = 0;
    // user interface objects
    Panel staticPanel1 = new Panel();
    Panel staticPanel2 = new Panel();
    Panel drawPanel = new Panel();
    CheckboxGroup zoomGroup;
    Checkbox zoomIn;
    Checkbox zoomOut;
```

Using numColors

One of the more interesting parameters for you to experiment with is numColors. The numColors parameter indicates the maximum number of different colors. If you set numColors very small, you will quickly generate a relatively dull fractal image. If you set numColors to the maximum — 255 — you slowly generate a relatively interesting fractal image.

```
// image generation parameters
int numRows = 100;
int numCols = 200;
int numColors = 200;
int colors[] = new int[256];
// initial image parameters
double zoom = 1;
double zoomPointx = 0;
double zoomPointy = 0;
double priorZoomPointx = 0;
double priorZoomPointy = 0;
GenFractal genObject = null;
int currentFractal;
//image to draw on to keep memory of generated image
Image    oImg = null;
Graphics oGr = null;
private void setRGBpalette(int c, int r, int g, int b) {
    colors[c] = r * 256 * 256 * 4 + g * 256 * 4 + b * 4;
}
```

Using initColors

You can also have some fun with this section. initColors loads our crayon box with colors. You must experiment some to come up with color combinations that are pleasing. In general, as you zoom in to the fractal, you end up favoring the high end of the array. If all the colors in the top half of your array are very similar, your fractal won't be very interesting. For this reason, the following code puts a greater variety of colors at the higher end of the array.

```
private void initColors() {
    int j;
    int c = 0;
    for (j = 0; j < 1; j++, c++)
        setRGBpalette(c, 0, 0, 0);
    for (j = 0; j < 14; j++, c++)
        setRGBpalette(c, (14-j)*4, j*4, 0);
    for (j = 0; j < 14; j++, c++)
        setRGBpalette(c, 0, (14-j)*4, j*4);
    for (j = 0; j < 14; j++, c++)
        setRGBpalette(c, (14-j)*4, 0, j*4);
```

(continued)

(continued)

```
        for (j = 0; j < 14; j++, c++)
            setRGBpalette(c, (14-j)*4, j*4, j*4);
        for (j = 0; j < 60; j++, c++)
            setRGBpalette(c, 0, 60-j, j);
        for (j = 0; j < 60; j++, c++)
            setRGBpalette(c, j, 0, 60-j);
        for (j = 0; j < 60; j++, c++)
            setRGBpalette(c, 60-j, j, 0);
        setRGBpalette(255, 60, 60, 60);
    }

    private void generateFractal(int fractalType) {
        if (genObject!= null) {
            genObject.stop();
            genObject = null;
            System.gc();
        }
        genObject = new GenFractal(this, numRows, numCols,
                numColors, colors, zoom, zoomPointx, zoomPointy,
                drawPanel, oGr, currentFractal);
        genObject.start();
    }

    public void update(Graphics g) {
        Graphics drawPanelGraphics = drawPanel.getGraphics();
        drawPanelGraphics.drawImage(oImg, 0, 0, this);
    }
```

Setting up the interface

In the code that follows, we set up the interface. A radio button is at the top, a panel on which the fractal is painted is in the middle, and three buttons are at the bottom.

```
public void init() {
    setBackground(Color.white);
    setLayout(new BorderLayout());
    add("Center", drawPanel);
    staticPanel1.setBackground(Color.gray);
    staticPanel1.setLayout(new FlowLayout());
    staticPanel1.add(new Button("Repaint"));
    staticPanel1.add(new Button("Mandelbrot"));
    staticPanel1.add(new Button("Julia"));
    add("South", staticPanel1);
```

```
    zoomGroup = new CheckboxGroup();
    zoomIn = new Checkbox("zoom in", zoomGroup, true);
    zoomOut = new Checkbox("zoom out", zoomGroup, false);
    staticPanel2.setBackground(Color.gray);
    staticPanel2.setLayout(new FlowLayout());
    staticPanel2.add(new Label("On Mouse Click:"));
    staticPanel2.add(zoomIn);
    staticPanel2.add(zoomOut);
    add("North", staticPanel2);
    //create off screen image
    oImg = drawPanel.createImage(numCols*2, numRows*2);
        oGr = oImg.getGraphics();
    //initialize graphics
    initColors();
    repaint();
}
```

Zooming around with mouseDown

The mouseDown() handler in the following code is the only interactive part of this applet. If you click on the current fractal image, you *zoom in* or *zoom out,* depending on which radio button is currently selected. To *zoom,* in this case, simply means to perform the same calculations we started with, using the current state and the position of the mouse click in order to generate a new state.

```
public boolean mouseDown(Event ev, int x, int y) {
    // calculate zoom point in rows, columns coordinates
    x = x - drawPanel.location().x;
    y = y - drawPanel.location().y;
    zoomPointx = (double)(x - numCols) / zoom;
    zoomPointy = (double)(numRows - y) / zoom;
    zoomPointx = zoomPointx + priorZoomPointx;
    zoomPointy = zoomPointy + priorZoomPointy;
    priorZoomPointx = zoomPointx;
    priorZoomPointy = zoomPointy;
    if (zoomGroup.getCurrent() == zoomIn)
        zoom = zoom * 10;
    else
        zoom = zoom / 10;
    generateFractal(currentFractal);
    return true;
}
```

(continued)

(continued)

```java
public boolean action(Event evt, Object arg) {
  if ("Repaint".equals(arg)) {
    repaint();
    return true;
  }
  else if ("Mandelbrot".equals(arg)) {
    currentFractal = GenFractal.MANDELBROT;
    zoom = 1;
    zoomPointx = INIT_ZOOM_X_MANDELBROT;
    zoomPointy = INIT_ZOOM_Y_MANDELBROT;
    priorZoomPointx = INIT_ZOOM_X_MANDELBROT;
    priorZoomPointy = INIT_ZOOM_Y_MANDELBROT;
      generateFractal(GenFractal.MANDELBROT);
      return true;
  }
  else if ("Julia".equals(arg)) {
    currentFractal = GenFractal.JULIA;
    zoom = 1;
    zoomPointx = INIT_ZOOM_X_JULIA;
    zoomPointy = INIT_ZOOM_Y_JULIA;
    priorZoomPointx = INIT_ZOOM_X_JULIA;
    priorZoomPointy = INIT_ZOOM_Y_JULIA;
      generateFractal(GenFractal.JULIA);
      return true;
  }
  return false;
}
}
```

Mandelbrot sets

The GenFractal class knows how to generate two kinds of fractals: Julia sets, as in Figure 17-1 at the beginning of this chapter, and Mandelbrot sets, as in Figure 17-2.

```java
class GenFractal implements Runnable {
  final static int MANDELBROT = 0;
  final static int JULIA = 1;

  private Applet parent;
```

```
int numRows;
int numCols;
int numColors;
int colors[];
double zoom;
double zoomPointx;
double zoomPointy;
Graphics oGr;
Graphics gr;
int fractalType;
Thread me = null;

public GenFractal(Applet p, int rows, int cols, int
        ncolors, int acolors[], double z, double zpx,
        double zpy, Panel dp, Graphics g, int fType) {
   parent = p;
   numRows = rows;
   numCols = cols;
   numColors = ncolors;
   colors = acolors;
   zoom = z;
   zoomPointx = zpx;
   zoomPointy = zpy;
   oGr = g;
   gr = dp.getGraphics();
   fractalType = fType;
}
```

Figure 17-2:
A view of Benoit Mandelbrot's favorite fractal, the Mandelbrot set.

Using run ( )

The run( ) method calculates colors and sets screen pixels accordingly. As you may expect, run( ) is where the action takes place.

```java
public void run() {
    int thresh = 4;
    double cx;
    double cy;
    double x;
    double y;
    double tmp;
    double fsq;
    int count;
    Color curColor;

    for (int path = 0; path < 4; path++) {
        for (int i = -numCols; i <= numCols; i += 4-path) {
            for (int j = -numRows; j <= numRows; j += 4-path) {
                //the magic part
    x = cx = (zoomPointx*zoom+(double)i)/
        ((double)numCols*zoom);
    y = cy = (zoomPointy*zoom+(double)j)/
        ((double)numRows*zoom);
    fsq = x * x + y * y;
    for (count = 1; (count <= numColors) && (fsq <=
        thresh); count++) {
        tmp = x;
    if (fractalType == MANDELBROT) {
        x = x * x - y * y + cx;
        y = 2.0 * tmp * y + cy;
    }
    else { // JULIA
        x = x * x - y * y + 0.025;
        y = 2.0 * tmp * y - 0.65;
    }
    fsq = x * x + y * y;
        }
        curColor = new Color(colors[count]);
        // draw on screen as we go
        gr.setColor(curColor);
        gr.fillRect(i + numCols, numRows - j, 4-path, 4-
            path);
```

```
           // keep memory of image
           oGr.setColor(curColor);
           oGr.fillRect(i + numCols, numRows - j, 4-path, 4-
           path);
           try { Thread.sleep(0); }
           catch (InterruptedException e) { return; }
       }
   }
}
parent.showStatus("Current zoom: "+(new
           Double(zoom)).toString() +
    " Zoom center: "+(new Double(zoomPointx)).toString()+",
           "+ (new Double(zoomPointy)).toString()+" Done!");
}

   public void start() {
      me = new Thread(this);
      me.start();
   }

   public void stop() {
      if (me != null) {
         me.stop();
         me = null;
      }
   }
}
```

Part IV
Only Java

The 5th Wave   By Rich Tennant

dy·nam'ic al'ter·nate rout·ing

In this part . . .

What can we say about Part IV? It's only Java, and Java stands alone. We introduce you to the potential of Java programming for creating more than just applets for use on World Wide Web pages. Java is a programming language that can make secure, portable, platform-independent, multithreaded, and stand-alone applications. And we show you how to make the transition from applet to application.

In Part IV, we compare and contrast the relative merits of Java with other object-oriented programming languages. We point out how Java has become a rising star in the Internet community as every major vendor in the Internet-related world seeks to integrate support for Java into their own applications.

Chapter 18

Java Stands Alone

*Y*ou can use Java to write applications that run without the support of a browser. That is, you can create Java applications that run on their own (stand alone). A *stand-alone* Java application does not depend on a browser for its existence and is not subject to the applet's security restrictions.

For example, although an applet is not permitted to touch the contents of the user's hard drive, a stand-alone Java application may create a new translation of *War and Peace* and store it on the user's hard drive. Similarly, an applet may connect to data only in the same Internet location as the HTML page it lives on, but a stand-alone Java application may access any address on the Internet.

In this chapter, we investigate the main differences between Java applets and applications, and we show you some code for making a stand-alone application. We also look at a bigger picture by comparing Java to C++ (another object-oriented programming language) and giving you a glimpse of the gathering support for Java.

Java without a Browser

When you run a Java applet in a browser, the applet depends on the browser for its existence. The browser provides for communications between the applet and the user's computer hardware and software. If you close the browser, the applet closes also.

Security is one of the special advantages of Java for creating applets that run over the Internet. By running the applet in a restricted *virtual machine* with limited capabilities, the browser enforces security restrictions on what an applet is permitted to do — especially restrictions on moving information in and out of the user's system. However, when you want to store information for future use or to communicate with more than one Internet address, the security advantage turns into a disadvantage.

The *theoretical* design of the Java language enables users to make exceptions to the security rules to give an applet some access to the local system or the Internet. However, at the time of this writing, only HotJava, from Sun Microsystems, Inc., supports that capability.

Moreover, you may simply want an application that runs in its own space without the overhead of running a browser. You're in luck! You can overcome these applet restrictions by making stand-alone Java applications.

The main *difference in standing alone*

We already presented all the hard stuff for figuring out how to write a Java applet. The difference between the code of an applet and the code of a stand-alone application is a class. That is, a stand-alone application must have one class that takes the place of the browser and HTML page. This *master class* is the starting point for the Java bytecode interpreter and must include a method called main. The stand-alone application may take input parameters in exactly the same way that the applet takes parameters from the HTML page (see Chapter 3).

The following code is an example of the simplest of Java stand-alone applications:

```
public class StandAloneApp {
    public static void main (String args[]){
        System.out.println("This is an application.");
    }
}
```

As you no doubt suspect, running the application represented by the preceding code puts the words *This is an application.* on your screen. Not much different from our "Hello, World" applet from Chapter 2, is it? See Figure 17-1.

When you run a stand-alone Java program, you run the Java interpreter by typing a command-line instruction like the following one, where java calls out the interpreter and StandAloneApp is the name of your stand-alone program:

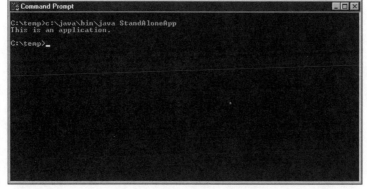

Figure 18-1:
This is a
stand-alone
Java
application.

```
java StandAloneApp
```

Careful! Don't include .class in your command, as you would run the compiler.

Some code to play with

You can save this code in a file named MyApplet.java and compile it as usual. If you invoke Java from the command line by keying **java MyApplet,** the program will run as a stand-alone program. If you put an applet tag for MyApplet in an HTML page, the code will run as an applet.

The code adds a main method to the applet. When you use the java command to run the applet class, the computer executes the main method. The main method constructs a frame for the applet to run in (in place of the browser) and constructs a new instance of the applet class that then does its thing inside the frame. When you run the applet from a browser, the browser never calls the main method. Instead, it calls the init and start methods of the applet, and the applet performs inside the browser.

When you copy this code, pay particular attention to the handleEvent method of MyAppletFrame. This method is required so that you can gracefully exit the application by clicking on the close option of the window.

The dispose() instruction gives up control of any system resources that the application has established a claim to, and System.exit(0) is the instruction that stops running the Java interpreter. If you make an error in this code or put it in the wrong place, you may be unable to close the applet frame in a normal way.

```java
import java.awt.*;
import java.applet.*;

/** This Java program can run as an applet or an application.
        Wow! */
public class MyApplet extends Applet {
    //the code for the applet goes here
    Button button = new Button("Press Me");
    Label label = new Label("Go ahead, press the button!");

    public void init() {
        add(button);
        add(label);
    }

    public boolean handleEvent(Event event) {
        if (event.target == button) {
                    label.setText("Button pressed!");
                    return true;
        }
        else {
                    return false;
        }
    }

    //  main() is only called when you run this program as a
            stand-alone application
    public static void main(String args[]) {
            MyAppletFrame appletFrame= new MyAppletFrame ("My
            Applet");
            //The following makes a new instance of MyApplet
            MyApplet myNewApplet = new MyApplet();
            myNewApplet.init();
            myNewApplet.start();
            appletFrame.add("Center",myNewApplet);
            appletFrame.resize(500,500);
            appletFrame.show();
    }
}

/** Appletframe takes the place of the browser when you run
            this program as
    a stand-alone application */
class MyAppletFrame extends Frame {
```

```
    public MyAppletFrame(String s) {
        super(s);
    }
    public boolean handleEvent(Event event) {
        if (event.id == Event.WINDOW_DESTROY) {
            dispose();
            System.exit(0);
            return true;
        }
        else {
            return super.handleEvent(event);
        }
    }
}
```

Why Write in Java When I Could Learn C++?

Because you are reading this book, we assume that you are not fluent in C++. You are probably not interested in a deep technical discussion on the differences between C++ and Java. Nevertheless, a brief overview can help you recognize when you need a second opinion from your brother-in-law or some other trusted technical guru.

Java is easy to understand

One goal of the Java developers was to build on the C and C++ programming languages, but to fix what they saw as gaps and inconsistencies. The literature about Java devotes much attention to how it resembles and differs from C++. One key difference relates to the use of pointers.

C++ relies heavily on pointers, bits of code that let you directly manipulate your computer's memory. These pointers are hard to understand and hard to keep track of, even when you do understand them. As a result, many programming errors relate to the use of pointers.

In the C and C++ languages, responsibility for preventing errors related to the use of pointers rests almost exclusively with the programmer. Behind the scenes, Java organizes the connections between classes and their objects in a way similar to that of C++. But the Java compiler takes care of the complex clerical task of using pointers and leaves only the overall direction to the programmer. (Taking care of complex tasks is what computers are for, isn't it?)

Java developers addressed a variety of other small and large issues. Speaking from personal experience, believe me: Java is easier to learn than C++!

Java helps to bug proof and virus proof

Just as the Java compiler takes care of pointers without bothering the programmer about the messy details, Java also handles a number of similar tiresome and trouble-prone housekeeping tasks.

- ✔ The programmer can rely on the Java system to make sure that the program does not keep reading past the end of a string of data and accidentally wander off into some other program's data or instructions. This accounting process shuts off one of the common entry points for bugs and viruses.

- ✔ As a program instantiates objects, it sets aside computer memory to keep track of the objects' data and methods.

- ✔ When the object is no longer needed by the program, the computer must somehow be notified that the related block of memory may be reused for something else. If the computer is not notified and more objects are instantiated, you eventually encounter the dread `Out of Memory` message. Java has automatic *garbage collection* to help avoid this dreadful situation. That is, Java helps the computer to clean up after the program, without the need for the programmer to write specific clean-up code.

- ✔ Java also checks all code to make sure that instructions are legitimate program codes that perform legal steps. By doing this code checking, the Java interpreter can stop a virus that tries to revise the computer's operating system by sneaking in as bytecode.

Java supports new standards

The computing community relies on standards of various kinds to keep everyone's different software products and projects working together. Java comes fully equipped to recognize and work with the most recently adopted standards. These include not only the Internet standards for communication, file transfer, and so on, but also the CORBA standard for trading bundles of data and methods among programs and operating environments. ("Bundles of data and methods..." sounds like an object — and it is!)

Also, the use of *threads*, which is inherent in Java (see Chapter 12), enables the Java programmer to more easily work with modern hardware and operating system software to coax more productivity out of systems. That is, Java threads enable computer systems to be more productive by running multiple tasks at the same time.

Although various operating systems and languages support threads, Java makes them easy for programmers to use.

Why Write in C++ When I Know Java?

The preceding heading voices a good question! For now, one good answer is that you may need the support tools available to a mature development environment (like C++). Although support for Java is developing with surprising speed, a commercial software product relies on a long list of support items — like device drivers for printers and other peripherals and platform-specific code that allows programs to intercommunicate.

And even the Java AWT (Abstract Windowing Toolkit), which is a good start, does not yet provide the wide range of controls available from a mature GUI (graphical user interface) such as on the Macintosh, Microsoft Windows, or Motif. If you develop applets or applications in Java, you'll probably have to do-it-yourself from time to time.

Another consideration for Java programming is that Java is not designed to provide low-level control of hardware. Unless the computerchip you are cooking up in your kitchen is designed to run Java bytecode, you need to write its operating system in some other language. Several vendors (Borland, Asymetrix, Symantec) have announced plans to produce a chip that does run Java bytecode.

For the same reason (lack of low-level control), don't plan to use Java to squeeze the maximum possible performance out of an application. If you are designing a graphics-based game that requires lightning fast response in processing gigabytes of data, you need a programming language that stays very close to the hardware, like C++. With such a language, you can use every little trick to save a tick of processor time.

Is Java Real?

Is Java real? At the time we are writing this book, we have several reasons to believe so. The following list points out these reasons for you:

✔ At the time we are writing, every major operating system and computer vendor has announced support for the Java language. Microsoft Corporation has announced plans to incorporate Java into the Windows operating system. Novell has announced plans to incorporate Java into the Netware operating system. And even a Java interpreter for IBM mainframes has been announced!

✔ Several vendors announced development work on support tools, called *precompilers* or *just-in-time compilers,* that do the work of translating from Java bytecode to machine code in advance. These tools make the Java applet or Java program run faster than it can under the basic Java interpreter.

✔ Sun Microsystems, Inc., and other Java vendors and users have agreed on a standard to let Java applets and applications interact with remote databases without compromising security. The first software tools to implement this standard are coming on the market now.

✔ Many developer toolkits are in the works, and some of them are already commercially available.

Yes, Java is real!

Part V
The Part of Tens

"I HEARD THEY WANTED TO FILL OUT THE SHOW A LITTLE THIS YEAR."

In this part . . .

Part V includes some top-ten lists for you. To help you troubleshoot, you find the top ten (or so) common mistakes. We include two chapters of URLs for Web sites that contain further Java lore or hot Java applets. Another top-ten list helps you out with programming in style. And, so as not to ignore the *other* Java, we've included ten interesting facts about that nation and its culture as well.

Chapter 19
Ten Common Mistakes

Missing ( ){}

A missing parenthesis or brace causes the Java compiler to lose track of where one thing begins and another ends. Occasionally, the compiler is smart enough to know what's going on, but often it only knows that nothing seems to make sense anymore (it's a lot like people that way). When that happens, the compiler gives you a long series of error messages. Look for a missing grouping character somewhere on or shortly before the line that produced the first error message.

A good way to avoid missing grouping characters is to make a habit of putting both the open and the close character first, before you fill in the information that goes between parentheses or braces.

Lost or Forgotten Imports

You can easily forget to include an import statement at the top of your code file.

When writing applets, you must always import `java.applet.*`. Usually, you will want to import `java.awt.*` and `java.lang.*`. You may also have a package of your own classes, or you may want to use a class from another part of the Java Class Library.

Remember to import everything to which your code refers.

Mistaking a Class for an Object

A class is just the blueprint for an object.

Even when the object is one of a kind, you must both define the class and then construct an instance of the class. Afterward, in methods that refer to the object, be sure to use the object name and not the class name.

You will be on the right track if you get in the habit of declaring and instantiating each object at the start of the class definition:

```
Thing myThing = new Thing (parameter1, parameter2);
```

Spellng Rong

Each Java Class Library is full of variable and class names that are extremely similar. Sometimes, only the capitalization distinguishes one thing from another.

Be careful not to create errors through misspelling or inattention to case.

Incorrect Signatures

Each constructor and method have specific signatures — the group or parameters that go within the parentheses. If the number and type of parameters do not match the signature of the specific constructor or method you have in mind, you may get an error message from the compiler. Worse yet, you may compile your code successfully and get behavior that is not what you intended.

Make it a habit to check the documentation to make sure you have the right signature for each AWT method you use.

A Method That Gives Nothing in Return

Every method (except a constructor) must return something. If it has nothing else to return, it returns *void*.

The Wrong Kind of Equality

To test if two objects are "equal" — for example, to test if two strings contain the same series of characters — use the `Object.equals` method. You may compare two numbers using = = (double equal sign). If you want to assign a value to an object but *not* make a comparison, use = (just one equal sign). These usages are not interchangeable.

`a=b;` means "change *a* so that it becomes equal to *b*."

`(a==b)` is an expression (that may or may not be true) that says "*a* and *b* are in fact equal."

Use == in if, for, and while statements.

Tight Loops

You want to be sure iteration statements always reach an exit from the loop, no matter what data is entered. If your program does not provide an exit, the computer will happily continue looping as long as you leave the power on.

Step through your loop mentally to make sure it will always reach an exit.

Going Public

Only one class in a file may be public — the class the file is named after. If a method or class is going to be used by classes from another file, you must decare that method or class public.

When you are working on a code file and want to save a copy of the old version, rename the old version so that the new, revised version keeps the name of the class you are working on.

Trusting Yourself Too Much

Suppose that you find only three small, obvious things wrong with your applet. You fix the errors, compile the code, and turn the applet over to be installed on your Web page. No need to check the thing for the umpteenth time. Right? Wrong!

Trivial revisions have a way of introducing unexpected consequences. Always test the last change you make.

Chapter 20

Ten Hot Pages to Peek At

In This Chapter

▶ Examples of what Java can do

▶ Sites that may have hot news

▶ Creations that we think are neat

*T*hings are changing rapidly in the world of Java programming. Sometimes WWW sites are abandoned because the WebMaster got too busy doing other things. Sometimes they're abandoned because they became too successful and, hence, demanded too much work to support. Sometimes they're restructured and become just plain dull.

Of the sites listed in this chapter, some may go the way of those that looked promising and then faded away. But others are sure to still be there when you read this book. We listed these Java-related sites in no particular order.

Caffeine Connection

A Java-related Web site:

```
http://www.online-magazine.com/cafeconn.htm
```

Shareware

A Java-enhanced search engine for shareware:

```
http://www.shareware.com
```

Virtual Boston

An example of what Java can do with maps:

```
http://www.pmg.lcs.mit.edu/~ng/Map/
```

Blue Skies for Java

Live weather data:

```
http://cirrus.sprl.umich.edu/javaweather/
```

The Wall

A place to write graffiti online:

```
http://militzer.me.tuns.ca/cgi-bin/wall.cgi
```

WallStreetWeb

Financial applications by BulletProof.com:

```
http://www.bulletproof.com/WallStreetWeb/
```

Search for a Cambridge Title

Use a Java applet to speed search the Cambridge University Press catalogue:

```
http://www.cup.cam.ac.uk/Titles/Search.html
```

HotWired

A journal of Internet cultural frontiers:

```
http://www.hotwired.com
```

Cafe Del Sol

From a new development group within Sun Microsystems, Inc.:

```
http://www.xm.com/cafe/
```

Java Central

Hearst New Media Center — one publisher's toe in the water:

```
http://hearstnewmedia.com/javacentral.html
```

Pepsi World

Like it says, *Pepsi* . . . with Java:

```
http://www.pepsi.com/
```

Chapter 21
Ten Web Sites for Java Lore

In This Chapter

▶ Places to find out more about Java

▶ Reference resources

▶ Places for moral support

 *B*ecause we know that you're really intrigued and delighted by this Java programming stuff, we're using this chapter to give you an idea of where to look on the Web for more details.

JavaSoft

```
http://www.javasoft.com
```

The preceding is the home page of the JavaSoft business group within Sun Microsystems. This site contains links to Sun online documentation, among other useful things.

Gamelan

```
http://www.gamelan.com
```

Gamelan is an Internet directory and registry of Java-based programs and resources for developers and users of the Java programming language.

Java World

```
http://www.javaworld.com
```

The preceding is the home page of *Java World* magazine. On this page, you get product announcements and other business news, tips and tricks, and articles from the magazine.

Java Report

```
http://www.sigs.com
```

This URL address takes you to the home page of *Java Report,* a technical journal for serious Java programmers.

Java Applet Rating Service

```
http://www.jars.com
```

The preceding represents the Academy Awards of applets. At this site, you find a collection of Java applets selected by a rating system with links to lots of good applets. Some are published with source code.

Java Newsgroup

```
comp.lang.java
```

This URL is for an Internet newsgroup for Java programmers featuring technical questions and answers and trade talk of all kinds related to Java programming.

W3 Organization

```
http://www.w3.org
```

This URL takes you to the home page of the W3 organization, the standards group for the World Wide Web. Here, you find technical specifications for WWW documents and so on.

A Handy HTML Reference

```
http://www.sandia.gov/sci_compute/html_ref.html
```

Visit the preceding site for a good, brief online reference to HTML.

Java Users Groups

Java users groups are locally-based groups of people interested in Java who meet periodically to exchange information and sometimes even socialize. Because users groups change officers and addresses from time to time, the best thing is to check the WWW for listings of groups in your area. One place to check is the Sun users group at

```
http://www.sug.org.
```

Java Programming For Dummies Resource Page

```
http://www.iscinc.com/JPFD
```

The authors have posted sample code from this book, update information, and links to other useful Internet resources on this resource page that is designed *especially* for you.

Chapter 22

Ten Tenets of Style

We live in an uncertain and changing world, and so do our programs. Because of this, people as well as computers must read programs.

Good style makes a program easier for people to read. So far as we know, computers are not particularly sensitive to matters of style. That is, an ugly program can run just as well as a beautiful program. But a beautiful program is easier for a person to read and understand. When time comes to revise or debug or adapt a piece of code, code that was written with attention to matters of style is easier to work with.

Logically Group the Elements of Your Code

Group the elements of your code so that things that go together logically are near each other on your editing screen or the printed page. When unrelated methods are mixed randomly, the computer has no trouble finding the code it wants, but a human programmer may have trouble seeing the logic of the program.

If you find that making a small modification to a class requires you to jump to many different places in the code, something may be wrong with the way your code is organized.

Use Indentation and Alignment to Chunk Code

Braces (like these) mark off chunks of code. For humans to understand what is going on, quickly spotting the beginning and end of each code chunk is important. Use a format that enables the eye to scan the code and identify the chunks of code without having to read every line.

For example, try putting the closing brace at the same distance from the margin as the keyword it closes for and indenting the contents of the code block.

```
for (n=1; n<= 10, n++){
    someCode();
    for (m=1; m<=25; m++){
        moreCode();
        yetMoreCode();
    }
    someMoreCode();
}
```

The following is an example of another style that we like:

```
for (n=1; n<= 10, n++)
    {
    someCode();
    for (m=1; m<=25; m++)
        {
        moreCode();
        yetMoreCode();
        }
    someMoreCode();
    }
```

Use White Space and Blank Lines to Group Code

White space is just what it sounds like, spaces, tabs, anything that puts empty space between two characters on the screen. The computer ignores white space and blank lines. But to human readers, white space is an important part of the information on a printed page.

Use spaces to make your expressions more readable. Use blank lines to flag breaks between chunks of code.

Use Short Comments to Clarify the Code

Use short comments to provide titles to sections of the code or to explain steps that may not be obvious to a reader of the code. For example:

```
//Center the bar chart
c += Math.max((size().width - (columns*(barWidth + (2 *
            barSpace))))/2, 0);
```

Write Comments for Javadoc

Write comments that result in a useful Javadoc map of the code you have written. This is especially important if you are writing classes that may be reused in more than one applet and by more than one programmer. (See Chapter 11 for more information on Javadoc comments.)

Give Methods and Variables Meaningful Names

Giving meaningful names to variables makes your code much easier to read — and to write. Consider the difference between

```
for (n = 1; n <= 10; n ++){ ...
```

and

```
for (row = 1; row <= 10; row ++){ ...
```

Similarly, `intToString` is a more helpful method name than is `iTS`.

Capitalize Constants

Constants are values that the program never changes. Occasionally, constants are numbers like PI. Often, they are choices that are arbitrarily coded as integers, for example, `LEFT`, `RIGHT`, `CENTER`. The custom among programmers is to give constants names in all caps.

Use Capitalization to Add Meaning to Names

Capitalization within a method name or class name can make the name more meaningful. For example, `setFrameNum()` is a more useful name than is `frmnum()`.

Commit No Violence Over Matters of Style

Layout and style of programming are tools that make it easier for programmers to communicate with each other. When collaborating programmers use a consistent style, each programmer saves time when reading the others' work. Conversely, being forced to decode a new style or — worse yet — coming to grips with the code of a programmer who has no consistent style is very irritating.

Some programmers defend to the death their style of indentation or their variable naming conventions. Let them live.

Write Code Like a Novel

The best code reads like a novel. It has well-defined characters, a clear plot line, and themes that can be appreciated at several levels of abstraction — all expressed in clear, yet elegant, language.

Chapter 23

Ten Facts about the Other Java

*J*ava, the programming language, is named for the invigorating brew that programmers use on occasion to keep themselves alert and creative when the demo is scheduled for tomorrow. Of course, another Java exists — it is the place where the coffee comes from.

As marketers searched for product names that carry associations with Java, some followed the coffee connection with names like *Latte* and *Cafe* and *Joe*. Others have honored the geographic connection.

Java Is a Large Island

Java is one of the thousands of islands that make up the nation of Indonesia, which is the fifth most populous country in the world. In addition to coffee, Java is known for batik fabrics, electronics, and the remains of "Java man," a human ancestor that is one of the earliest specimens of *homo erectus*.

Jakarta Is a City

Jakarta is the largest city in Java and the capital of Indonesia. It is also the prerelease code name for a suite of Java development tools (now under development by Microsoft).

Wayang Kulit Are Shadow Puppets

Wayang kulit are among the more famous cultural artifacts of Indonesia. Beautifully intricate shadow puppets, they are cut from buffalo hide and painted in additional detail that is never seen by the audience; the audience sees only the shadow of the flat puppet projected through a translucent screen.

Hmm . . . let me see how I can code that class:

```
public class WayangKulit extends class BuffaloHide
    private Color faceColor . . .
```

As far as I know, no one has as yet developed this theme, but be prepared.

Gamelan Is an Orchestra

Gamelan is the percussion orchestra that accompanies Wayang Kulit performances and other Javanese theatrical events. The orchestra consists of gongs, bells, and chimes — a description doesn't do it justice. You have to hear it.

Gamelan is also a WWW site that contains postings of Java applets and other Java-related data.

The Dalang Is the Puppet Master

The Dalang is the puppet master who performs the Wayang Kulit shadow puppet plays. Similarly, the Dalang is also the Web Master of the Gamelan WWW site.

Garuda Is a God

Garuda is a god who takes the form of a bird and whose statues appear quite ferocious. Garuda is also the name of the Indonesian national airline. (This fact has no connection with programming; I just thought you might like to know.)

The Kris Is a Weapon

The kris is an Indonesian dagger — a thrusting weapon held not like a sword but like a pistol. Myth and mysticism accompany tales of this instrument. Some say that certain kris can fly; others say that once removed from its case, a kris will not return until it has drawn blood. The most popularly held belief is that a kris's blade holds the soul of its first or most courageous owner. The earliest known kris dates to 1342.

Although I have no inside information, I am ready to bet that we'll see Kris as a Java development tool real soon now.

Batik Is an Art Form

Batik is the process of printing a length of cloth with a wax-and-dye procedure. Beeswax is applied to both sides of the cloth in the areas that do not require color. The cloth is then dipped in dye until the correct color is achieved; then the wax is removed. A new pattern of wax is then applied, and a second color is applied. This process is repeated with as many as five different colors to build up an intricate pattern. Batik is usually printed on fine cotton or linen (sometimes silk is used). Traditional batik is still done by hand, but modernity has brought machinery to do much of the work. Look for the new fractal batik patterns in the next edition of this book.

Kuda Kepang Is a Folk Dance

Kuda kepang translates to the horse trance dance. Dancers ride bamboo hobby horses and dance themselves into a trance. In the trance stage, they dismount their horses and eat anything that is offered to them, including unhulled rice and glass.

Java Is a Land of Volcanoes

More than a hundred volcanic cones and craters dot Java's mountainous borders. Thirty-five of the volcanoes are active, and seven of them are under constant watch.

Part VI
Appendixes

The 5th Wave   By Rich Tennant

" 'MORNING MR. DREXEL. I HEARD YOU SAY YOUR COMPUTERS ALL
HAD BUGS; WELL, I FIGURE THEY'RE CRAWLING IN THROUGH THOSE
SLOTS THEY HAVE, SO I JAMMED A COUPLE OF ROACH-DISKS IN
EACH ONE. LET ME KNOW IF YOU HAVE ANY MORE PROBLEMS."

In this part . . .

Part VI contains some helpful appendixes that tell you what systems currently run Java (the number is changing even as we write), how to download the most current version of the Java Development Kit from the Internet, and information about the CD that comes with this book. We've enjoyed introducing you to the wonderful world of Java, and hope that your journeys onward in this remarkable program are both fun and fruitful.

Appendix A

Which Systems Run Java?

This appendix contains our most current list of sites with downloadable Java implementations or information about ports to new systems. If you are looking for a Java implementation on a system that isn't listed in the following table, don't despair. New implementations are announced frequently. Check out the WWW site for the hardware manufacturer or operating system vendor that you're interested in. You can also look for information at users' group sites.

Web Resources on Java Implementations for Different Systems

System	URL or How to Get Information
Windows NT 3.5 (Intel x86)	`http://www.javasoft.com/`
Windows 95	`http://www.javasoft.com/`
Solaris 2.3 - 2.5 (SPARC)	`http://www.javasoft.com/`
Solaris 2.5 (Intel)	`http://www.javasoft.com/`
Macintosh System 7.5	`http://www.javasoft.com/`
OS/2 Warp	`http://ncc.hursley.ibm.com/javainfo/`
AIX	`http://ncc.hursley.ibm.com/javainfo/`
OSF/1	`http://www.NetJunkies.Com/Java/osf1-port.html`
Linux	`http://www.blackdown.org/java-linux.html`
HP-UX	`http://hpcc998.external.hp.com:80/gsyinternet/technology/java/JDK.html`

(continued)

System	URL or How to Get Information

Amiga	send e-mail to:
	`amiga-hotjava-announce@mail.iMNet.de`
	`majordomo@mail.iMNet.de`
	subscribe amiga-hotjava-announce

NEXTSTEP	send e-mail to:
	`next-java@friday.com`
	`next-java-request@friday.com`
	subscribe

Appendix B

Installing and Configuring the Java Developer's Kit for Windows NT and Windows 95

● ●

In This Appendix

▶ Where to find the Java Developer's Kit

▶ Preparing your computer for Java

▶ Downloading the self-extracting archive file

▶ Running the self-extracting archive file

▶ Editing AUTOEXEC.BAT

▶ Testing the compiler

● ●

*I*n this appendix, we tell you what you need to know to set up the Java Developer's Kit (JDK) for use with Window NT or Windows 95 systems. To use the JDK on these systens you need at least 8meg RAM (12 is better) and 9meg free disk space.

Downloading

The CD that comes with this book contains everything you need to get started with Java programming for the following systems:

- ✔ Windows 95
- ✔ Windows NT (Intel)
- ✔ Solaris (SPARC)
- ✔ Macintosh System 7.5

See Appendix E, "About the CD" for more information. If your system is not in the preceding list, you may still be in luck. Reportedly, efforts are underway to move (or *port,* as programmers say) the Java Developer's Kit to many different computer systems including OS/2 Warp and Windows NT for DEC Alpha machines. See Appendix A, "Which Systems Run Java?" for further information.

If Sun releases an updated version of Java, or if you don't have easy access to a CD-ROM drive, you may prefer to download the Java Developer's Kit from the Internet. You download from the Internet as described in the following sections.

What to download

If you are running Windows 95 or Windows NT on an Intel-based or compatible computer, Sun has a version of the Java Developer's Kit just for you!

Download the file that goes by the affectionate name `JDK-1_0_1-win32-x86.exe.`

The characters *1_0_1* identify the version of the Java Developer's Kit in the file, in this case version 1.0.1. The *win32* part of the name refers to the Windows 32-bit operating systems, namely Windows NT and Windows 95 (but **not** Windows 3.1). And the *x86* refers to the Intel computer chip family of 386, 486, and Pentium processors.

Implementations of Java are reportedly under development for Windows 3.1 and Windows NT for DEC Alpha machines, but they have not been released as of this writing. When these implementations are released, the procedure for downloading and installation is likely to be very similar to what is described in this chapter, but the name of the file you download will certainly be different.

How to download

Assuming you have a full-featured Web browser such as Netscape 2.0, the downloading procedure is very simple. You download a compressed file. Then you allow the file to expand itself into a complete Java Developer's Kit installation, untouched by human hands.

Clean house first

Before you download, do some housekeeping. The compressed file for the Java Developer's Kit is designed to put its files in a directory called *Java.* Furthermore, it creates the Java directory automatically as part of the downloading process. If you already have a directory named Java in the root directory of your computer, rename it or delete it before you start the downloading process.

If you are not sure how to delete or rename a directory, or if your psychological well-being depends on having two Java directories in different places, refer to *Windows 95 For Dummies* by Andy Rathbone, published by IDG Books Worldwide, Inc., or to your system documentation for instructions. Technically, you can arrange things so that you have several directories named Java located in different subdirectories. For most of us, one Java directory is enough.

All right. Housekeeping done?

Download the JDK archive file

The complete Java Developer's Kit contains over a hundred files organized in several subdirectories. These files are combined into a single *self-extracting* file to make downloading the entire kit easy. You download the one combined file and then *run* it to create a complete Java Developer's Kit. Because we can't guarantee that a URL maintained by Sun and other companies can remain unchanged, we keep an up-to-date list of links at the resource Web page for this book:

```
http://www.iscinc.com/JPFD/
```

Use the following steps to download the JDK self-extracting archive:

1. **Use your WWW browser to connect to the Java Web site of Sun Microsystems.**

   At the time of this writing, the Web page for downloading the Windows 95/ Windows NT version of the Java Developer's Kit is at:

   ```
   http://www.javasoft.com/JDK-1.0/installation-win32-x86.html
   ```

2. **Locate the links to ftp sites.**

   That is the phrase you should look for on screen: ftp.

   ```
   ftp://ftp.javasoft.com/pub/JDK-1_0_1-win32-x86.exe
   ```

   Read carefully to be sure the file name in the link includes win32 and x86. Be sure the file name ends with .exe.

3. **Click on the link to download the file.**

   When the Save dialog appears, be sure you instruct the program to save the downloaded file in the root of your main directory — which is probably C:\.

Patience! If you are using a modem, downloading the file may take 15 minutes or more. When you have finished this process, you should find on your hard drive a file named `C:\JDK-Beta2-win32-x86.exe`. If you find the downloaded file in a subdirectory, move it to the root before you do anything else.

Run the self-extracting file

Run, or expand, the file that you have just downloaded. This, too, takes some time.

Steps for expanding the self-extracting archive under Windows 95:

1. **Choose Start⇨Run.**

2. **In the resulting dialog box, type in the name of the file:**

   ```
   JDK-Beta2-win32-x86.exe
   ```

3. **Click OK.**

Steps for expanding the self-extracting archive under Windows NT:

1. **In Program Manager, choose File⇨Run**

2. **In the resulting dialog box, type in the name of the file:**

   ```
   JDK-Beta2-win32-x86.exe
   ```

3. **Select OK.**

When the program completes its work, you find on your hard drive a directory named C:\Java. Within the Java directory, you find a number of subdirectories and files.

Don't rearrange or rename the subdirectories and/or files. Don't try to *unzip* the file named `classes.zip`! This file is designed to remain in zipped form in the Java development environment.

Tell your computer where to find the Java files

Before you can use the Java Developer's Kit, you must tell your computer where to find the Java files. You do this by editing your AUTOEXEC.BAT file. You need to add `\JAVA\BIN` to the path and to set an environment variable named `CLASSPATH`. Use the following steps under Windows 95:

1. **Use Notepad to open C:\AUTOEXEC.BAT.**

2. **Locate the line that reads** `SET PATH=` . . .

3. **As an addition to this line type** `C:\JAVA\BIN;`

4. Add a new line by typing in the following.

```
SET CLASSPATH=C:\JAVA\LIB\CLASSES\CLASSES.ZIP
```

5. Save the revised AUTOEXEC.BAT file.

When you are done, your AUTOEXEC.BAT file contains lines that read something like the following.

```
SET
PATH=C:\WINDOWS;C:\WINDOWS\COMMAND;C:\;C:\DOS;C:\JAVA\BIN;
SET CLASSPATH=C:\JAVA\LIB\CLASSES\CLASSES.ZIP
```

6. Reboot your computer so that the changed AUTOEXEC.BAT information takes effect.

To set the environment variable under Windows NT, follow these steps:

1. Open the System windows applet in Control Panel.

2. In the field labeled Variable, type in CLASSPATH.

3. In the field labeled Value, type in the following line.

```
C:\JAVA\LIB\CLASSES\CLASSES.ZIP
```

4. Click the Set button to save your entries.

5. Press OK.

Log off and log on to your computer so that the changed environment variables take effect.

Try It Out

We assume you have already installed a Web browser that supports Java applets. See if your browser can run the applets in the demo directory. Examine the contents of the Java\demo subdirectory. Under Java\demo, you find a number of subdirectories with suggestive names such as Animator, Barchart, Blink, and Bouncing Heads. Within each of these directories, you find .Java files, .class files, and .html files.

To see the Java applets with your Web browser, you must open the corresponding html pages. For example, use your Web browser to open the file C:\Java\demo\TicTacToe\example1.html.

Test the Programming Software

To be sure the Developer's Kit components are properly installed, you can perform the following test steps.

Make a small, but visible, change in an applet

Open `C:\Java\demo\blink\Blink.java` and make the following changes.

1. Locate the line near the beginning of the code that reads

```
public class Blink extends java.applet.Applet implements
      Runnable {
```

2. Edit the line to read

```
public class Foo extends java.applet.Applet implements
      Runnable {
```

3. Locate the line towards the end that reads

```
g.drawString(word, x, y);
```

4. Edit this line to read

```
g.drawString("Foo", x, y);
```

Save the changed file as `C:\Java\demo\Blink\Foo.java`.

And set up an HTML example page to display the applet

Open `C:\Java\demo\Blink\example1.html`. (Use Notepad to open it so that you can edit the HTML source code.)

1. Locate the applet tag at the top of the document that reads

```
<applet code="Blink.class" width=300 height=100>
```

2. **Edit the line to read**

```
<applet code="Foo.class" width=300 height=100>
```

Save the edited file as `C:\Java\demo\Blink\example2.html`

Use the Java compiler to create a new class file

Follow these next steps to compile your Java applet:

1. **Open a Command window (for example, a DOS Window) and change the directory to** `C:\Java\demo\Blink`.

2. **Type the following command to the Java compiler.**

```
javac Foo.java
```

In a moment you see some messages from the java compiler.

3. **In the directory** `C:\Java\demo\Blink`, **look for the following new file.**

```
C:\Java\demo\Blink\Foo.class
```

Congratulations! You have written and compiled a Java applet! Now see if it works.

Run the revised applet

Use your browser to open `C:\Java\demo\Blink\example1`. Pay attention to the words that bounce around the screen. Concentrate closely. Your eyes are feeling heavy . . . Okay.

Close `example1` and open the revised HTML page that you created `C:\Java\demo\Blink\example2`. Again, pay attention to the words that appear on-screen. The applet should now display the most potent of all programming invocations — Foo! Proof that the change you made took effect and that your compiled applet runs, however uselessly. Proof, also, that you have successfully installed the Java Developer's Kit.

Appendix C

Installing and Configuring the Java Developer's Kit for Macintosh

• •

In This Chapter

▶ Where to find the Java Developer's Kit for the Macintosh

▶ Preparing your computer for Java

▶ Downloading the installer

▶ Running the installer

▶ Testing the compiler

• •

*T*he CD that comes with this book contains everything you need to get started with Java programming for the following systems:

✔ Windows 95

✔ Windows NT (Intel)

✔ Solaris (SPARC)

✔ Macintosh System 7.5

See Appendix E, "About the CD" for more information. If Sun releases an updated version of Java, or if you don't have easy access to a CD-ROM drive, you may prefer to download the Java Developer's Kit from the Internet. The following sections tell you how.

For Macintosh . . .

If you are running System 7.5 on a Power Macintosh or Macintosh computer with a 68030 processor or better, the Java Developer's Kit has a version just for you! You need at least 8 meg RAM and at least 7 meg free disk space for this to work.

What to download

The file you need to download for this version goes by the affectionate name `JDK-1_0_2-MacOS.sea.bin` (for MacBinary format) or `JDK-1_0_2-MacOS.sea.hqx` (for HQX format)

1_0_2 identifies the version of the Java Developer's Kit in the file.

The *MacOS* part of the name, of course, refers to the Macintosh.

If a fresh version of the JDK is released by the time you read this, the file name may change slightly.

How to download

Assuming you have a full-featured Web browser such as Netscape 2.0, the downloading procedure is very simple. You will download the installer file and run it.

Clean house first

Before you download, do some housekeeping. The Java Developer's Kit for Macintosh requires about seven megabytes of disk space. By default, the installer creates a folder called *JDK-1.0.2-mac.* (You can rename it later, if you wish.) Make sure that you have sufficient disk space.

All right. Housekeeping done?

Download the JDK archive file

The complete Java Developer's Kit contains more than a hundred files. These files have been combined into a single installer file to make it easy to download the entire kit. You will download the one file and then run it to create a complete Java Developer's Kit.

Because we can't guarantee that URLs maintained by Sun and other companies remain unchanged, we maintain an up-to-date list of links at the resource Web page for this book at `http://www.iscinc.com/JPFD/`.

We recommend that you use Fetch or Anarchie to download the JDK because these utilities download and decompress the file at the same time.

If you use an FTP utility, you must decompress the downloaded file as a separate step.

> ✔ To decompress the MacBinary version (`JDK-1_0_2-MacOS.sea.bin`), use StuffIt.
>
> ✔ To decompress the HQX version (`JDK-1_0_2-MacOS.sea.hqx`), use BinHex4.

After downloading, run the installer program, which will create a folder called *JDK-1.0.2-mac.* Congratulations! You are ready to test drive Java.

You can run the Applet Viewer by doing the following:

1. **Open the folder Sample Applets.**
2. **Open the folder WireFrame.**
3. **Drop the file** `example1.html` **on the application Applet Viewer.**

Try It Out

We assume you have already installed a Web browser that supports Java applets. See if your browser can run the applets in the *Sample Applets* folder. Examine the contents of the *Sample Applets* folder. You will find a number of folders with suggestive names such as *Animator, Barchart, Blink,* and *Bouncing Heads.* Within each of these folders are Java files, class files, and HTML files.

To see the Java applets with your Web browser, drop the corresponding HTML pages on the icon for your Java-powered browser.

Test the Programming Software

To be sure the Developer's Kit components are properly installed, you can perform the following test steps.

Make a small but visible change in an applet

Open `Blink.java` in an editor and make these changes.

1. **Locate the line near the beginning of the code that reads**

```
public class Blink extends java.applet.Applet implements
       Runnable {
```

2. Edit the line to read

```
public class Foo extends java.applet.Applet implements
        Runnable {
```

3. Locate the line towards the end that reads

```
g.drawString(word, x, y);
```

4. Edit this line to read instead

```
g.drawString("Foo", x, y);
```

5. Save the changed file as Foo.java.

Set up an HTML example page to display the applet

Using a text editor, open example1.html in the Blink folder.

1. Locate the applet tag at the top of the document that reads

```
<applet code="Blink.class" width=300 height=100>
```

2. Edit the line to read

```
<applet code="Foo.class" width=300 height=100>
```

3. Save the edited file as example2.html

Use the Java compiler to create a new class file

1. Type the following command into the Java compiler:

```
Drop Foo.java on the Java Compiler
```

In a moment, you see some messages from the Java compiler.

2. Check the contents of the Blink folder.

You should find a new file: Foo.class

Congratulations! You have written and compiled a Java applet! Now, see if it works.

Run the revised applet

Open `example1.html` in the *Blink* folder in your browser. Pay attention to the words that bounce around the screen. Concentrate closely — your eyes are feeling heavy — okay.

Close `example1.html` and open the revised HTML page you created: `example2.html`. Again, pay attention to the words that appear on-screen. The applet should now display the most potent of all programming invocations — Foo! Proof that the change you made took effect and that your compiled applet runs, however uselessly. Proof also that you have successfully installed the Java Developer's Kit.

Appendix D

Installing and Configuring the Java Developer's Kit for Solaris

● ●

In This Chapter

▶ Where to find the Java Developer's Kit

▶ Preparing your computer for Java

▶ Downloading the self-extracting archive file

▶ Running the self-extracting archive file

▶ Setting the CLASSPATH environment variable

▶ Testing the compiler

● ●

*T*he CD that comes with this book contains everything you need to get started with Java programming for the following systems:

✔ Windows 95

✔ Windows NT (Intel)

✔ Solaris (SPARC)

✔ Macintosh System 7.5

See the section "About the CD" at the back of this book for more information. If your system is not listed above, you may still be in luck. Reportedly, efforts are under way to move (or *port,* as programmers say) the Java Developer's Kit to many different computer systems including OS/2 Warp and Windows NT for DEC Alpha machines. See Appendix A, "Which Systems Run Java?" for further information.

If Sun releases an updated version of Java, or if you don't have easy access to a CD-ROM drive, you may prefer to download the Java Developer's Kit from the Internet. The following sections tell you how.

For Solaris . . .

If you are running Solaris 2.3 or higher on a SPARC-based or compatible computer with 15 meg of free disk space, you can find a version of the Java Developer's Kit just for you!

What to download

The file that you need to download for Solaris 3.2 or higher goes by the affectionate name:

```
JDK-1_0_1-solaris2-sparc.tar.Z
```

The 1_0_1 part of the filename identifies the version of the Java Developer's Kit in the file, in this case Version 1.0.1. The *solaris2* part of the name refers to the Sun's Solaris operating system, and *sparc* refers to the SPARC family of computer processors.

How to download

Assuming that you have a full-featured Web browser such as Netscape 2.0, the downloading procedure is very simple. You download a compressed UNIX archive file. Then you uncompress and extract the file to a complete Java Developer's Kit installation, untouched by human hands.

Clean house first

Before you download, do some housekeeping. That is, create a directory called *Java* in which you would like to install the Java Developer's Kit.

Download the JDK archive file

The complete Java Developer's Kit contains over a hundred files organized in several subdirectories. These files are combined into a single *self-extracting* file to make downloading the entire kit easy. You download the one file and then run it to create a complete Java Developer's Kit. Because we can't guarantee that URLs maintained by Sun and other companies remain unchanged, we maintain an up-to-date list of links at the resource Web page for this book at http://www.iscinc.com/JPFD/.

Use the following steps to download the JDK self-extracting archive:

1. **Use your WWW browser to connect to Sun's Java Web site.**

   At the time of this writing, the Web page for downloading the Solaris version of the Java Developer's Kit is at:

```
http://www.javasoft.com/JDK-1.0/installation-solaris2-
          sparc.html
```

2. **Locate the links to ftp sites. That is, *ftp* is the phrase you look for on-screen:**

```
ftp://www.blackdown.org/pub/Java/pub/JDK-1_0_1-solaris2-
          sparc.tar.Z
```

Read carefully to be sure that the filename in the link includes *solaris* and *sparc* and that the filename ends with *.Z*.

3. **Click on the link to download the file.**

When the Save dialog appears, be sure that you instruct the program to save the downloaded file in the root of your main directory — which is probably C:\

Patience! If you are using a modem, downloading the file may take 15 minutes or more. When you have finished this process, you find, in your Java directory, a file named

```
JDK-1_0_1-solaris2-sparc.tar.Z
```

Run the self-extracting file

Uncompress the file by typing in the following command:

```
zcat JDK-1_0_1-solaris2-sparc.tar.Z | tar xf -
```

When the program completes its work, you find a number of subdirectories and files within the Java directory.

Don't rearrange or rename the files or subdirectories that you find! Don't try to unzip the file named `classes.zip`! The `classes.zip` file is designed to remain in zipped form in the Java development environment.

Tell your computer where to find the Java files

Before you can use the Java Developer's Kit, you must tell your computer where to find the Java files. You do this by setting the CLASSPATH environment variable to the location of your `Java/lib/classes.zip` file with the following command:

```
setenv CLASSPATH .:$HOME/Java/lib/classes.zip
```

You may want to place this line in your shell startup file, whose name depends on your particular environment.

Try It Out

We assume that you have already installed a Web browser that supports Java applets. Now we want you to see whether your browser can run the applets in the demo directory. Examine the contents of the Java\demo subdirectory; in this subdirectory, you can find a number of other subdirectories with suggestive names such as *Animator, Barchart, Blink,* and *Bouncing Heads.* Within each of these subdirectories, you find .Java files, .class files, and .html files.

To see the Java applets with your Web browser, you must open the corresponding HTML pages. For example, use your Web browser to open the file $HOME/Java/demo/TicTacToe/example1.html.

Test the Programming Software

Now you can test that the Developer's Kit components are properly installed by making changes to an applet, setting up an HTML page to view the changed applet, compiling the applet into a new class file, and finally, running the applet.

Make a small but visible change in an applet

Open $HOME/Java/demo/blink/Blink.java and make these small but visible changes to the applet:

1. **Locate the line near the beginning of the code that reads like this next code line.**

```
public class Blink extends java.applet.Applet implements
        Runnable {
```

2. **Edit the code line to read as follows:**

```
public class Foo extends java.applet.Applet implements
        Runnable {
```

3. **Locate the line towards the end that reads like this next code line.**

```
g.drawString(word, x, y);
```

4. **Edit this line to read as follows:**

```
g.drawString("Foo", x, y);
```

5. **Save the changed file as** $HOME/Java/demo/Blink/Foo.java.

And set up an HTML example page to display the applet

Open `$HOME/Java/demo/Blink/example1.html`. You can use any text editor such as EMACS or vi; then follow these steps to set up the HTML example page to display your changed applet:

1. **Locate the applet tag at the top of the document that reads like the following line.**

   ```
   <APPLET CODE="Blink.class" WIDTH=300 HEIGHT=100>
   ```

2. **Edit the HTML coded line to read as follows:**

   ```
   <APPLET CODE="Foo.class" WIDTH=300 HEIGHT=100>
   ```

3. **Save the edited file as** `$HOME/Java/demo/Blink/example2.html`.

Use the Java compiler to create a new class file

Open a Command (that is, an operating system) window and change the directory to `$HOME/Java/demo/Blink`. Then type the following command to the Java compiler:

```
javac Foo.java
```

In a moment, you see some messages from the Java compiler. Check the contents of the `$HOME/Java/demo/Blink` directory. You should find a new file, as follows:

```
$HOME/Java/demo/Blink/Foo.class
```

Congratulations! You have written and compiled a Java applet! Now see if it works.

Run the revised applet

Use your browser to open `$HOME/Java/demo/Blink/example1.html`. Pay attention to the words that bounce around the screen. Concentrate closely — your eyes are feeling heavy . . . Okay.

Close Example1 and open the revised HTML page that you created `$HOME/Java/demo/Blink/example2.html`. Again, pay attention to the words that appear on-screen. The applet should now display the most potent of all programming invocations — Foo! You can see the proof that the change you made took effect and that your compiled applet runs, however uselessly. This test also proves that you successfully installed the Java Developer's Kit.

Appendix E
About the CD

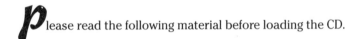

In This Appendix

▶ Copyright information

▶ How to view the CD

▶ What's on the CD

*P*lease read the following material before loading the CD.

Welcome to *Java Programming For Dummies*!

We recommend that you browse the contents of this CD using a Web browser that supports Java applets. Simply start up your Web browser and load the file named `index.html`, which is located in the root directory of the CD.

Some hypertext links you see are links to other files on the CD. Other hypertext links are to Web pages found on the World Wide Web. To follow links to pages on the World Wide Web, you need to have your Internet connection up and running.

What's on the CD

This CD contains the Java Developer's Kit 1.02, the sample applets from this book, and sample applets contributed by the Java Internet programming community.

The Java Developer's Kit 1.02

The Java Developer's Kit (JDK) provides everything you need to compile, test, debug, and document Java applets and applications.

This CD includes JDK 1.02 for the following platforms:

- ✔ Windows 95 (Java is not available for Windows 3.1)
- ✔ Windows NT
- ✔ Sun Solaris [2.3, 2.4, or 2.5] for SPARC
- ✔ Solaris 2.5 for Intel
- ✔ Macintosh (using System 7.5.*x* on a Macintosh with at least a 68030 processor)

The JDK also contains many sample applets that you may find interesting and useful.

The files are stored on the CD in archives appropriate to the platform you're using.

Installing JDK using your Web browser

You can install the appropriate version to your computer by using your Web browser. To do so:

1. **Start your Web browser.**
2. **Open the file** `jdk.html`, **located in the JDK folder on the CD.**
3. **Click on the link of the version you need.**

Your Web browser will dutifully copy the archive to a location on your computer that you choose. To complete installation, skip to item 5 in the next section, "Installing JDK without a Web browser."

Installing JDK without a Web browser

1. **Insert the CD into your computer's CD-ROM drive.**
2. **Open the JDK folder on the CD.**

3. **Open the folder which represents your computer's operating system. That is, if you're using Windows 95, open the Windows folder.**

4. **Copy the archive in this folder to the hard disk drive of your computer.**

5. **Windows users: Open the self-extracting .EXE archive to begin decompressing the JDK. Mac users: Use a decompression utility such as StuffIt Expander from Aladdin Systems (www.aladdinsys.com) to open any of the archives from the disk. Solaris users should use a decompression utility appropriate for their platform.**

Sample applets described in Java Programming For Dummies

To see these applets in action, start your Web browser, then open the file `applets.html`, located in the JPFD folder. You'll find links to each of the applets.

The source code for these applets can be found in the JPFD folder on the CD.

- Calendar — a simple applet for selecting dates
- Ticker Tape — displays a scrolling message from a text file
- Sprite — a building block for animations
- JavaBots — an animated virtual ecosystem
- JavaBots 2 — a bonus! — the souped up version of JavaBots
- Quizem — an interactive quiz engine
- ShoppingCart (located in the Cart folder on the CD) — a simple shopping cart applet
- Fractal — an interactive fractal explorer

Sample applets contributed by the Java Internet programming community

These applets were created by Java developers throughout the world. To see these applets do their thing, start your Web browser and then open the file `applets.html`, located in the JPFD folder. You'll find links to each of the applets.

The source code for these applets can be found in the Applets folder on the CD.

- CrazyText — fancy text effects by Patrick Taylor in the United States
- Cube — a 3-D puzzle by Karl Hörnell in Sweden

- Fifteen — a 15-Square puzzle by Anatoly Goroshnik in the United States (NY)

- Fireworks — animated fireworks by Tzu-Tai Liu in Taiwan

- FishTank — swimming fish by Leyth Kedidi in the United States

- Frog — a hungry frog by Karl Hörnell in Sweden

- Hands — sophisticated finger counting by Lee Oades in England

- Iceblox — a game by Karl Hörnell in Sweden

- Invaders — a game by Michael Girdley in the United States

- Mankala — the ancient game of Mankala by Roger E. Critchlow Jr. in the United States (CA)

- Mortgage — a mortgage calculator by Karl Jeacle in Ireland

- Puzzle — a 15-square puzzle using an image by Rick Field in Australia

- Skip — for experimenting with circuit diagrams by Jean-Claude Dufourd in France

- Tile — by John F. Cottrell in the United States

- Travel — the classic traveling salesman problem by Martin Hagerup in Denmark

For updates, corrections, and additions to the contents of this CD, check out the *Java Programming For Dummies Resource Page* at

`http://www.iscinc.com/JPFD`

If you have a problem during the installation of files or programs from the CD, please call the IDG Books Worldwide Customer Service phone number: 1-800-762-2974. Outside the United States, you may call (317) 596-5261.

Index

• E •

● *L* ●

Notes

Notes

Notes

Notes

The Fun & Easy Way™ to learn about computers and more!

Windows® 3.11 For Dummies® 3rd Edition
by Andy Rathbone

ISBN: 1-56884-370-4
$16.95 USA/
$22.95 Canada

Mutual Funds For Dummies™
by Eric Tyson

ISBN: 1-56884-226-0
$16.99 USA/
$22.99 Canada

DOS For Dummies® 2nd Edition
by Dan Gookin

ISBN: 1-878058-75-4
$16.95 USA/
$22.95 Canada

The Internet For Dummies® 2nd Edition
by John Levine & Carol Baroudi

ISBN: 1-56884-222-8
$19.99 USA/
$26.99 Canada

Personal Finance For Dummies™
by Eric Tyson

ISBN: 1-56884-150-7
$16.95 USA/
$22.95 Canada

PCs For Dummies® 3rd Edition
by Dan Gookin & Andy Rathbone

ISBN: 1-56884-904-4
$16.99 USA/
$22.99 Canada

Macs® For Dummies® 3rd Edition
by David Pogue

ISBN: 1-56884-239-2
$19.99 USA/
$26.99 Canada

The SAT® I For Dummies™
by Suzee Vlk

ISBN: 1-56884-213-9
$14.99 USA/
$20.99 Canada

Here's a complete listing of IDG Books' ...For Dummies® titles

Title	Author	ISBN	Price
DATABASE			
Access 2 For Dummies®	by Scott Palmer	ISBN: 1-56884-090-X	$19.95 USA/$26.95 Canada
Access Programming For Dummies®	by Rob Krumm	ISBN: 1-56884-091-8	$19.95 USA/$26.95 Canada
Approach 3 For Windows® For Dummies®	by Doug Lowe	ISBN: 1-56884-233-3	$19.99 USA/$26.99 Canada
dBASE For DOS For Dummies®	by Scott Palmer & Michael Stabler	ISBN: 1-56884-188-4	$19.95 USA/$26.95 Canada
dBASE For Windows® For Dummies®	by Scott Palmer	ISBN: 1-56884-179-5	$19.95 USA/$26.95 Canada
dBASE 5 For Windows® Programming For Dummies®	by Ted Coombs & Jason Coombs	ISBN: 1-56884-215-5	$19.99 USA/$26.99 Canada
FoxPro 2.6 For Windows® For Dummies®	by John Kaufeld	ISBN: 1-56884-187-6	$19.95 USA/$26.95 Canada
Paradox 5 For Windows® For Dummies®	by John Kaufeld	ISBN: 1-56884-185-X	$19.95 USA/$26.95 Canada
DESKTOP PUBLISHING/ILLUSTRATION/GRAPHICS			
CorelDRAW! 5 For Dummies®	by Deke McClelland	ISBN: 1-56884-157-4	$19.95 USA/$26.95 Canada
CorelDRAW! For Dummies®	by Deke McClelland	ISBN: 1-56884-042-X	$19.95 USA/$26.95 Canada
Desktop Publishing & Design For Dummies®	by Roger C. Parker	ISBN: 1-56884-234-1	$19.99 USA/$26.99 Canada
Harvard Graphics 2 For Windows® For Dummies®	by Roger C. Parker	ISBN: 1-56884-092-6	$19.95 USA/$26.95 Canada
PageMaker 5 For Macs® For Dummies®	by Galen Gruman & Deke McClelland	ISBN: 1-56884-178-7	$19.95 USA/$26.95 Canada
PageMaker 5 For Windows® For Dummies®	by Deke McClelland & Galen Gruman	ISBN: 1-56884-160-4	$19.95 USA/$26.95 Canada
Photoshop 3 For Macs® For Dummies®	by Deke McClelland	ISBN: 1-56884-208-2	$19.99 USA/$26.99 Canada
QuarkXPress 3.3 For Dummies®	by Galen Gruman & Barbara Assadi	ISBN: 1-56884-217-1	$19.99 USA/$26.99 Canada
FINANCE/PERSONAL FINANCE/TEST TAKING REFERENCE			
Everyday Math For Dummies™	by Charles Seiter	ISBN: 1-56884-248-1	$14.99 USA/$22.99 Canada
Personal Finance For Dummies™ For Canadians	by Eric Tyson & Tony Martin	ISBN: 1-56884-378-X	$18.99 USA/$24.99 Canada
QuickBooks 3 For Dummies®	by Stephen L. Nelson	ISBN: 1-56884-227-9	$19.99 USA/$26.99 Canada
Quicken 8 For DOS For Dummies® 2nd Edition	by Stephen L. Nelson	ISBN: 1-56884-210-4	$19.95 USA/$26.95 Canada
Quicken 5 For Macs® For Dummies®	by Stephen L. Nelson	ISBN: 1-56884-211-2	$19.95 USA/$26.95 Canada
Quicken 4 For Windows® For Dummies® 2nd Edition	by Stephen L. Nelson	ISBN: 1-56884-209-0	$19.95 USA/$26.95 Canada
Taxes For Dummies™ 1995 Edition	by Eric Tyson & David J. Silverman	ISBN: 1-56884-220-1	$14.99 USA/$20.99 Canada
The GMAT® For Dummies®	by Suzee Vlk, Series Editor	ISBN: 1-56884-376-3	$14.99 USA/$20.99 Canada
The GRE® For Dummies™	by Suzee Vlk, Series Editor	ISBN: 1-56884-375-5	$14.99 USA/$20.99 Canada
Time Management For Dummies™	by Jeffrey J. Mayer	ISBN: 1-56884-360-7	$16.99 USA/$22.99 Canada
TurboTax For Windows® For Dummies®	by Gail A. Helsel, CPA	ISBN: 1-56884-228-7	$19.99 USA/$26.99 Canada
GROUPWARE/INTEGRATED			
ClarisWorks For Macs® For Dummies®	by Frank Higgins	ISBN: 1-56884-363-1	$19.99 USA/$26.99 Canada
Lotus Notes For Dummies®	by Pat Freeland & Stephen Londergan	ISBN: 1-56884-212-0	$19.95 USA/$26.95 Canada
Microsoft® Office 4 For Windows® For Dummies®	by Roger C. Parker	ISBN: 1-56884-183-3	$19.95 USA/$26.95 Canada
Microsoft® Works 3 For Windows® For Dummies®	by David C. Kay	ISBN: 1-56884-214-7	$19.99 USA/$26.99 Canada
SmartSuite 3 For Dummies®	by Jan Weingarten & John Weingarten	ISBN: 1-56884-367-4	$19.99 USA/$26.99 Canada
INTERNET/COMMUNICATIONS/NETWORKING			
America Online® For Dummies® 2nd Edition	by John Kaufeld	ISBN: 1-56884-933-8	$19.99 USA/$26.99 Canada
CompuServe For Dummies® 2nd Edition	by Wallace Wang	ISBN: 1-56884-937-0	$19.99 USA/$26.99 Canada
Modems For Dummies® 2nd Edition	by Tina Rathbone	ISBN: 1-56884-223-6	$19.99 USA/$26.99 Canada
MORE Internet For Dummies®	by John R. Levine & Margaret Levine Young	ISBN: 1-56884-164-7	$19.95 USA/$26.95 Canada
MORE Modems & On-line Services For Dummies®	by Tina Rathbone	ISBN: 1-56884-365-8	$19.99 USA/$26.99 Canada
Mosaic For Dummies® Windows Edition	by David Angell & Brent Heslop	ISBN: 1-56884-242-2	$19.99 USA/$26.99 Canada
NetWare For Dummies® 2nd Edition	by Ed Tittel, Deni Connor & Earl Follis	ISBN: 1-56884-369-0	$19.99 USA/$26.99 Canada
Networking For Dummies®	by Doug Lowe	ISBN: 1-56884-079-9	$19.95 USA/$26.95 Canada
PROCOMM PLUS 2 For Windows® For Dummies®	by Wallace Wang	ISBN: 1-56884-219-8	$19.99 USA/$26.99 Canada
TCP/IP For Dummies®	by Marshall Wilensky & Candace Leiden	ISBN: 1-56884-241-4	$19.99 USA/$26.99 Canada

For scholastic requests & educational orders please call Educational Sales at 1. 800. 434. 2086

FOR MORE INFO OR TO ORDER, PLEASE CALL ▶ 800 762 2974

For volume discounts & special orders please call Tony Real, Special Sales, at 415. 655. 3048

Title	Author	ISBN	Price
The Internet For Macs® For Dummies® 2nd Edition	by Charles Seiter	ISBN: 1-56884-371-2	$19.99 USA/$26.99 Canada
The Internet For Macs® For Dummies® Starter Kit	by Charles Seiter	ISBN: 1-56884-244-9	$29.99 USA/$39.99 Canada
The Internet For Macs® For Dummies® Starter Kit Bestseller Edition	by Charles Seiter	ISBN: 1-56884-245-7	$39.99 USA/$54.99 Canada
The Internet For Windows® For Dummies® Starter Kit	by John R. Levine & Margaret Levine Young	ISBN: 1-56884-237-6	$34.99 USA/$44.99 Canada
The Internet For Windows® For Dummies® Starter Kit, Bestseller Edition	by John R. Levine & Margaret Levine Young	ISBN: 1-56884-246-5	$39.99 USA/$54.99 Canada

MACINTOSH

Title	Author	ISBN	Price
Mac® Programming For Dummies®	by Dan Parks Sydow	ISBN: 1-56884-173-6	$19.95 USA/$26.95 Canada
Macintosh® System 7.5 For Dummies®	by Bob LeVitus	ISBN: 1-56884-197-3	$19.95 USA/$26.95 Canada
MORE Macs® For Dummies®	by David Pogue	ISBN: 1-56884-087-X	$19.95 USA/$26.95 Canada
PageMaker 5 For Macs® For Dummies®	by Galen Gruman & Deke McClelland	ISBN: 1-56884-178-7	$19.95 USA/$26.95 Canada
QuarkXPress 3.3 For Dummies®	by Galen Gruman & Barbara Assadi	ISBN: 1-56884-217-1	$19.95 USA/$26.99 Canada
Upgrading and Fixing Macs® For Dummies®	by Kearney Rietmann & Frank Higgins	ISBN: 1-56884-189-2	$19.95 USA/$26.95 Canada

MULTIMEDIA

Title	Author	ISBN	Price
Multimedia & CD-ROMs For Dummies® 2nd Edition	by Andy Rathbone	ISBN: 1-56884-907-9	$19.99 USA/$26.99 Canada
Multimedia & CD-ROMs For Dummies® Interactive Multimedia Value Pack, 2nd Edition	by Andy Rathbone	ISBN: 1-56884-909-5	$29.99 USA/$39.99 Canada

OPERATING SYSTEMS:

DOS

Title	Author	ISBN	Price
MORE DOS For Dummies®	by Dan Gookin	ISBN: 1-56884-046-2	$19.95 USA/$26.95 Canada
OS/2® Warp For Dummies® 2nd Edition	by Andy Rathbone	ISBN: 1-56884-205-8	$19.99 USA/$26.99 Canada

UNIX

Title	Author	ISBN	Price
MORE UNIX® For Dummies®	by John R. Levine & Margaret Levine Young	ISBN: 1-56884-361-5	$19.99 USA/$26.99 Canada
UNIX® For Dummies®	by John R. Levine & Margaret Levine Young	ISBN: 1-878058-58-4	$19.95 USA/$26.95 Canada

WINDOWS

Title	Author	ISBN	Price
MORE Windows® For Dummies® 2nd Edition	by Andy Rathbone	ISBN: 1-56884-048-9	$19.95 USA/$26.95 Canada
Windows® 95 For Dummies®	by Andy Rathbone	ISBN: 1-56884-240-6	$19.99 USA/$26.99 Canada

PCS/HARDWARE

Title	Author	ISBN	Price
Illustrated Computer Dictionary For Dummies® 2nd Edition	by Dan Gookin & Wallace Wang	ISBN: 1-56884-218-X	$12.95 USA/$16.95 Canada
Upgrading and Fixing PCs For Dummies® 2nd Edition	by Andy Rathbone	ISBN: 1-56884-903-6	$19.99 USA/$26.99 Canada

PRESENTATION/AUTOCAD

Title	Author	ISBN	Price
AutoCAD For Dummies®	by Bud Smith	ISBN: 1-56884-191-4	$19.95 USA/$26.95 Canada
PowerPoint 4 For Windows® For Dummies®	by Doug Lowe	ISBN: 1-56884-161-2	$16.99 USA/$22.99 Canada

PROGRAMMING

Title	Author	ISBN	Price
Borland C++ For Dummies®	by Michael Hyman	ISBN: 1-56884-162-0	$19.95 USA/$26.95 Canada
C For Dummies® Volume 1	by Dan Gookin	ISBN: 1-878058-78-9	$19.95 USA/$26.95 Canada
C++ For Dummies®	by Stephen R. Davis	ISBN: 1-56884-163-9	$19.95 USA/$26.95 Canada
Delphi Programming For Dummies®	by Neil Rubenking	ISBN: 1-56884-200-7	$19.99 USA/$26.99 Canada
Mac® Programming For Dummies®	by Dan Parks Sydow	ISBN: 1-56884-173-6	$19.95 USA/$26.95 Canada
PowerBuilder 4 Programming For Dummies®	by Ted Coombs & Jason Coombs	ISBN: 1-56884-325-9	$19.99 USA/$26.99 Canada
QBasic Programming For Dummies®	by Douglas Hergert	ISBN: 1-56884-093-4	$19.95 USA/$26.95 Canada
Visual Basic 3 For Dummies®	by Wallace Wang	ISBN: 1-56884-076-4	$19.95 USA/$26.95 Canada
Visual Basic "X" For Dummies®	by Wallace Wang	ISBN: 1-56884-230-9	$19.99 USA/$26.99 Canada
Visual C++ 2 For Dummies®	by Michael Hyman & Bob Arnson	ISBN: 1-56884-328-3	$19.99 USA/$26.99 Canada
Windows® 95 Programming For Dummies®	by S. Randy Davis	ISBN: 1-56884-327-5	$19.99 USA/$26.99 Canada

SPREADSHEET

Title	Author	ISBN	Price
1-2-3 For Dummies®	by Greg Harvey	ISBN: 1-878058-60-6	$16.95 USA/$22.95 Canada
1-2-3 For Windows® 5 For Dummies® 2nd Edition	by John Walkenbach	ISBN: 1-56884-216-3	$16.95 USA/$22.95 Canada
Excel 5 For Macs® For Dummies®	by Greg Harvey	ISBN: 1-56884-186-8	$19.95 USA/$26.95 Canada
Excel For Dummies® 2nd Edition	by Greg Harvey	ISBN: 1-56884-050-0	$16.95 USA/$22.95 Canada
MORE 1-2-3 For DOS For Dummies®	by John Weingarten	ISBN: 1-56884-224-4	$19.99 USA/$26.99 Canada
MORE Excel 5 For Windows® For Dummies®	by Greg Harvey	ISBN: 1-56884-207-4	$19.95 USA/$26.95 Canada
Quattro Pro 6 For Windows® For Dummies®	by John Walkenbach	ISBN: 1-56884-174-4	$19.95 USA/$26.95 Canada
Quattro Pro For DOS For Dummies®	by John Walkenbach	ISBN: 1-56884-023-3	$16.95 USA/$22.95 Canada

UTILITIES

Title	Author	ISBN	Price
Norton Utilities 8 For Dummies®	by Beth Slick	ISBN: 1-56884-166-3	$19.95 USA/$26.95 Canada

VCRS/CAMCORDERS

Title	Author	ISBN	Price
VCRs & Camcorders For Dummies™	by Gordon McComb & Andy Rathbone	ISBN: 1-56884-229-5	$14.99 USA/$20.99 Canada

WORD PROCESSING

Title	Author	ISBN	Price
Ami Pro For Dummies®	by Jim Meade	ISBN: 1-56884-049-7	$19.95 USA/$26.95 Canada
MORE Word For Windows® 6 For Dummies®	by Doug Lowe	ISBN: 1-56884-165-5	$19.95 USA/$26.95 Canada
MORE WordPerfect® 6 For Windows® For Dummies®	by Margaret Levine Young & David C. Kay	ISBN: 1-56884-206-6	$19.95 USA/$26.95 Canada
MORE WordPerfect® 6 For DOS For Dummies®	by Wallace Wang, edited by Dan Gookin	ISBN: 1-56884-047-0	$19.95 USA/$26.95 Canada
Word 6 For Macs® For Dummies®	by Dan Gookin	ISBN: 1-56884-190-6	$19.95 USA/$26.95 Canada
Word For Windows® 6 For Dummies®	by Dan Gookin	ISBN: 1-56884-075-6	$16.95 USA/$22.95 Canada
Word For Windows® For Dummies®	by Dan Gookin & Ray Werner	ISBN: 1-878058-86-X	$16.95 USA/$22.95 Canada
WordPerfect® 6 For DOS For Dummies®	by Dan Gookin	ISBN: 1-878058-77-0	$16.95 USA/$22.95 Canada
WordPerfect® 6.1 For Windows® For Dummies® 2nd Edition	by Margaret Levine Young & David Kay	ISBN: 1-56884-243-0	$16.95 USA/$22.95 Canada
WordPerfect® For Dummies®	by Dan Gookin	ISBN: 1-878058-52-5	$16.95 USA/$22.95 Canada

For scholastic requests & educational orders please call Educational Sales at 1. 800. 434. 2086

FOR MORE INFO OR TO ORDER, PLEASE CALL ▶ 800.762.2974

For volume discounts & special orders please call Tony Real, Special Sales, at 415. 655. 3048

Fun, Fast, & Cheap!™

NEW!

NEW!

SUPER STAR

SUPER STAR

The Internet For Macs® For Dummies® Quick Reference
by Charles Seiter

ISBN:1-56884-967-2
$9.99 USA/$12.99 Canada

Windows® 95 For Dummies® Quick Reference
by Greg Harvey

ISBN: 1-56884-964-8
$9.99 USA/$12.99 Canada

Photoshop 3 For Macs® For Dummies® Quick Reference
by Deke McClelland

ISBN: 1-56884-968-0
$9.99 USA/$12.99 Canada

WordPerfect® For DOS For Dummies® Quick Reference
by Greg Harvey

ISBN: 1-56884-009-8
$8.95 USA/$12.95 Canada

Title	Author	ISBN	Price
DATABASE			
Access 2 For Dummies® Quick Reference	by Stuart J. Stuple	ISBN: 1-56884-167-1	$8.95 USA/$11.95 Canada
dBASE 5 For DOS For Dummies® Quick Reference	by Barrie Sosinsky	ISBN: 1-56884-954-0	$9.99 USA/$12.99 Canada
dBASE 5 For Windows® For Dummies® Quick Reference	by Stuart J. Stuple	ISBN: 1-56884-953-2	$9.99 USA/$12.99 Canada
Paradox 5 For Windows® For Dummies® Quick Reference	by Scott Palmer	ISBN: 1-56884-960-5	$9.99 USA/$12.99 Canada
DESKTOP PUBLISHING/ILLUSTRATION/GRAPHICS			
CorelDRAW! 5 For Dummies® Quick Reference	by Raymond E. Werner	ISBN: 1-56884-952-4	$9.99 USA/$12.99 Canada
Harvard Graphics For Windows® For Dummies® Quick Reference	by Raymond E. Werner	ISBN: 1-56884-962-1	$9.99 USA/$12.99 Canada
Photoshop 3 For Macs® For Dummies® Quick Reference	by Deke McClelland	ISBN: 1-56884-968-0	$9.99 USA/$12.99 Canada
FINANCE/PERSONAL FINANCE			
Quicken 4 For Windows® For Dummies® Quick Reference	by Stephen L. Nelson	ISBN: 1-56884-950-8	$9.95 USA/$12.95 Canada
GROUPWARE/INTEGRATED			
Microsoft® Office 4 For Windows® For Dummies® Quick Reference	by Doug Lowe	ISBN: 1-56884-958-3	$9.99 USA/$12.99 Canada
Microsoft® Works 3 For Windows® For Dummies® Quick Reference	by Michael Partington	ISBN: 1-56884-959-1	$9.99 USA/$12.99 Canada
INTERNET/COMMUNICATIONS/NETWORKING			
The Internet For Dummies® Quick Reference	by John R. Levine & Margaret Levine Young	ISBN: 1-56884-168-X	$8.95 USA/$11.95 Canada
MACINTOSH			
Macintosh® System 7.5 For Dummies® Quick Reference	by Stuart J. Stuple	ISBN: 1-56884-956-7	$9.99 USA/$12.99 Canada
OPERATING SYSTEMS:			
DOS			
DOS For Dummies® Quick Reference	by Greg Harvey	ISBN: 1-56884-007-1	$8.95 USA/$11.95 Canada
UNIX			
UNIX® For Dummies® Quick Reference	by John R. Levine & Margaret Levine Young	ISBN: 1-56884-094-2	$8.95 USA/$11.95 Canada
WINDOWS			
Windows® 3.1 For Dummies® Quick Reference, 2nd Edition	by Greg Harvey	ISBN: 1-56884-951-6	$8.95 USA/$11.95 Canada
PCs/HARDWARE			
Memory Management For Dummies® Quick Reference	by Doug Lowe	ISBN: 1-56884-362-3	$9.99 USA/$12.99 Canada
PRESENTATION/AUTOCAD			
AutoCAD For Dummies® Quick Reference	by Ellen Finkelstein	ISBN: 1-56884-198-1	$9.95 USA/$12.95 Canada
SPREADSHEET			
1-2-3 For Dummies® Quick Reference	by John Walkenbach	ISBN: 1-56884-027-6	$8.95 USA/$11.95 Canada
1-2-3 For Windows® 5 For Dummies® Quick Reference	by John Walkenbach	ISBN: 1-56884-957-5	$9.95 USA/$12.95 Canada
Excel For Windows® For Dummies® Quick Reference, 2nd Edition	by John Walkenbach	ISBN: 1-56884-096-9	$8.95 USA/$11.95 Canada
Quattro Pro 6 For Windows® For Dummies® Quick Reference	by Stuart J. Stuple	ISBN: 1-56884-172-8	$9.95 USA/$12.95 Canada
WORD PROCESSING			
Word For Windows® 6 For Dummies® Quick Reference	by George Lynch	ISBN: 1-56884-095-0	$8.95 USA/$11.95 Canada
Word For Windows® For Dummies® Quick Reference	by George Lynch	ISBN: 1-56884-029-2	$8.95 USA/$11.95 Canada
WordPerfect® 6.1 For Windows® For Dummies® Quick Reference, 2nd Edition	by Greg Harvey	ISBN: 1-56884-966-4	$9.99 USA/$12.99/Canada

"A lot easier to use than the book Excel gives you!"

Lisa Schmeckpeper, New Berlin, WI, on PC World Excel 5 For Windows Handbook

Official Hayes Modem Communications Companion

by Caroline M. Halliday

ISBN: 1-56884-072-1
$29.95 USA/$39.95 Canada
Includes software.

1,001 Komputer Answers from Kim Komando

by Kim Komando

ISBN: 1-56884-460-3
$29.99 USA/$39.99 Canada
Includes software.

PC World DOS 6 Handbook, 2nd Edition

by John Socha, Clint Hicks, & Devra Hall

ISBN: 1-878058-79-7
$34.95 USA/$44.95 Canada
Includes software.

BESTSELLER!

PC World Word For Windows® 6 Handbook

by Brent Heslop & David Angell

ISBN: 1-56884-054-3
$34.95 USA/$44.95 Canada
Includes software.

BESTSELLER!

PC World Microsoft® Access 2 Bible, 2nd Edition

by Cary N. Prague & Michael R. Irwin

ISBN: 1-56884-086-1
$39.95 USA/$52.95 Canada
Includes software.

PC World Excel 5 For Windows® Handbook, 2nd Edition

by John Walkenbach & Dave Maguiness

ISBN: 1-56884-056-X
$34.95 USA/$44.95 Canada
Includes software.

PC World WordPerfect® 6 Handbook

by Greg Harvey

ISBN: 1-878058-80-0
$34.95 USA/$44.95 Canada
Includes software.

QuarkXPress For Windows® Designer Handbook

by Barbara Assadi & Galen Gruman

ISBN: 1-878058-45-2
$29.95 USA/$39.95 Canada

NATIONAL BESTSELLER!

Official XTree Companion, 3rd Edition

by Beth Slick

ISBN: 1-878058-57-6
$19.95 USA/$26.95 Canada

NATIONAL BESTSELLER!

PC World DOS 6 Command Reference and Problem Solver

by John Socha & Devra Hall

ISBN: 1-56884-055-1
$24.95 USA/$32.95 Canada

SUPER STAR

Client/Server Strategies™: A Survival Guide for Corporate Reengineers

by David Vaskevitch

ISBN: 1-56884-064-0
$29.95 USA/$39.95 Canada

"PC World Word For Windows 6 Handbook is very easy to follow with lots of 'hands on' examples. The 'Task at a Glance' is very helpful!"

Jacqueline Martens, Tacoma, WA

"Thanks for publishing this book! It's the best money I've spent this year!"

Robert D. Templeton, Ft. Worth, TX, on MORE Windows 3.1 SECRETS